# Issues in American Christianity

# Issues in American Christianity

## Primary Sources with Introductions

### Keith J. Hardman

Baker Books
A Division of Baker Book House Co
Grand Rapids, Michigan 49516

© 1993 by Keith J. Hardman

Published by Baker Books
a division of Baker Book House Company
P.O. Box 6287, Grand Rapids, Michigan 49516-6287

Printed in the United States of America

### Library of Congress Cataloging-in-Publication Data

Hardman, Keith J.
    Issues in American Christianity : primary sources with introductions / Keith J. Hardman.
        p.    cm.
    Includes bibliographical references and index.
    ISBN 0-8010-4381-6
    1. Christianity—United States—Sources. 2. United States—Church history—Sources. I. Title.
    BR514.H37 1993
    227.3—dc20
                                 93-18021

Cover artwork: John Steuart Curry. *Baptism in Kansas.* 1928. oil on canvas. 40 x 50 inches.
Collection of Whitney Museum of American Art. Gift of Gertrude Vanderbilt Whitney 31.159.

# Contents

# Introduction

Alexis de Tocqueville, a young French aristocrat and magistrate, arrived in the United States in May 1831, accompanied by his friend Gustave de Beaumont. While their ostensible purpose was to examine the American prison system, their chief desire was to examine democracy and its ramifications at first hand. Frequently Tocqueville turned his attention to America's religious beliefs and institutions, and he expressed surprise and admiration at what he found:

> Upon my arrival in the United States, the religious aspect of the country was the first thing that struck my attention; and the longer I stayed there the more did I perceive the great political consequences resulting from this state of things, to which I was unaccustomed. . . . The Americans combine the notions of Christianity and of liberty so intimately in their minds that it is impossible to make them conceive the one without the other. . . . The sects which exist in the United States are innumerable. In the United States the sovereign authority is religious, and consequently hypocrisy must be common; but there is no country in the whole world in which the Christian religion retains a greater influence over the souls of men than in America; and there can be no greater proof of its utility, and of its conformity to human nature, than that its influence is most powerfully felt over the most enlightened and free nation of the earth.[1]

Nine months later, Tocqueville returned to France to write his classic critique *Democracy in America,* first published in 1835 and 1840. In this work he provided an abundance of analysis, description, and prediction concerning almost every aspect of the American scene. With parts of it, as might be expected, reviewers have disagreed. But some of his observations concerning Christianity in America are accurate, not only for that period but for all of American history, for religious faith always has been one of the country's salient characteristics. Having no established national church—as was Tocqueville's European experience—has offered great benefits to all churches in America. Tocqueville declared:

In France I had almost always seen the spirit of religion and the spirit of free-dom pursuing courses diametrically opposed to each other, but in America I found that they were intimately united, and that they reigned in common over the same country. My desire to discover the causes of this phenomenon increased from day to day. . . . I more especially sought the society of the clergy. . . . They mainly attributed the peaceful dominion of religion in their country to the sep-aration of Church and State. I do not hesitate to affirm that during my stay in America I did not meet with a single individual, of the clergy or of the laity, who was not of the same opinion upon this point.[2]

For all of Tocqueville's inadequacies as a social observer and the excessive subjectivity of his approach, his generalizations concerning religion, politics, art, government, and much else in democratic America are amazingly shrewd and perceptive. This has made *Democracy in America* an enduring book. Many of his intuitive insights into the dynamics of nineteenth-century democratic life hold true for our own time. History has borne out a great number of his predictions and observations. Among character traits and social patterns the discerning Frenchman noted was the significant American phenomena of asso-ciations formed for the public good, including churches, and volunteer enter-prises designed to solve whatever problems plagued society. Tocqueville said that "Americans of all ages, all conditions, and all dispositions, constantly form associations . . . religious, moral, serious, futile, extensive or restricted, enor-mous or diminutive . . . to give entertainments, to found establishments for education, to build inns, to construct churches, to diffuse books, to send mis-sionaries to the antipodes."[3]

That is not to say that all of the patterns of the 1830s hold today. Tocqueville could observe American religion as monolithic and almost entirely Protestant. Today an almost bewildering diversity is apparent. But underneath the diver-sity, public polls consistently show that most Americans still believe in God (94 percent in one 1990s survey). The proportion of believers dwarfs that of any other advanced nation. An astounding two-thirds of all Americans belong to a church or synagogue. Diversity has increased with a shifting religious pat-tern. In the late 1900s mainstream Protestant denominations lost millions of members, while evangelical or fundamentalist churches gained greatly. The Roman Catholic Church retains much of its vitality in the United States, but its authority in the lives of its members has greatly diminished. Attendance at mass and enlistment of priests and nuns have slipped badly.

This book is obviously neither a complete history of Christianity in Amer-ica nor a thorough compilation of source documents. Rather, it attempts to identify issues that have proved determinative. The aim has been to concentrate on movements and debates that involved the larger community, rather than matters that occupied one group or denomination. Even readers with little awareness of the past will recognize some of the issues that have galvanized our ancestors:

- patriotism in the newly-founded nation and dazzling visions of future power and glory;
- revivals and awakenings;
- challenges to orthodoxy;
- the shattering debates between the new sciences and religion;
- the break with long-accepted patterns and customs and concern for women's rights, slavery, and "the huddled masses yearning to breathe free."

The list could go on and on. Shock waves that reverberated from these clashes of the past helped to mold the country we live in.

In combing the past the historian hears many voices—jubilant shouts, suffering cries, prophetic utterances, strident demands, and persuasive arguments. This presentation allows some of these voices to be heard again. There are limitations; space demands that these documents be pared down, hopefully not beyond their essentials. Those who wish to read further may consult notes and bibliographic references. In addition, presenting an issue in a confrontational manner may lead the reader to become partisan too soon. Today, after many of these controversial issues have been partially or fully resolved, we know the outcome and what finally was rendered as the decisions of the churches. But when the outcome was not known feelings ran high in these debates. If we are convinced that the democratic process is the best we must admit that even acrimonious and sometimes furious dispute is one of the most suitable means to air differences among humans.

In producing this book, assistance has come from many sources. I am particularly indebted to President Richard P. Richter and Dean William E. Akin of Ursinus College for granting me a sabbatical leave to complete this volume and to the staff of the college's library, especially Joan Rhodes, Judith E. Fryer, and David H. Mill, for invaluable assistance. My wife Jean deserves gratitude for her patience and support during the writing of this book, and my children, Carolyn, Keith, and Colleen, know that their father is less visible and available during such a time.

The staff of Baker Book House, especially Jim Weaver and Paul Ingram, deserve much gratitude for their encouragement and help in bringing this work to completed form, and I thank them all.

# 1

# Hopes for the New World

It is difficult for us to imagine the hopes and dreams of the first settlers in the New World. Surrounded by subcultures of violent crime, drugs, and other addictions, we are no longer shocked by social problems of urban ghettos, waves of illegal immigrants, and corrupt politicians. Hopes and dreams are harder to come by.

Perhaps the dreamers of previous times looked to the future with naïveté; had they glimpsed what would occur, one may say, they would have tempered their visionary optimism with more realism. Yet even the pessimist can conjure up in imagination the excitement and fears that quickened the pulse of early explorers as they contemplated vast uncharted territories and new paths that they might lay out for later generations. Religious people particularly looked to the future with such hope, and they tried to set good precedents. Protestants owned the added conviction that God had withheld knowledge of the New World until the Reformation under Luther and Calvin restored true religion. They saw the rich and unspoiled lands as peculiarly theirs to settle.

One of the first to voice this grand expectation was Alexander Whitaker. Doubts and evidence to the contrary notwithstanding, in 1613 he sketched a vision of glory in *Good Newes from Virginia*. In 1654, Edward Johnson wrote along the same lines in his *Wonder-Working Providence of Sions Saviour*, transferring the hopes to New England. Somewhat later, Cotton Mather's *Magnalia Christi Americana* amplified Johnson's ideas, offering abundant evidence of "Christ's Wonders in America." Still later, as Jonathan Edwards considered God's outpouring in what came to be called the Great Awakening, he advanced the idea that God had special blessings in store for the New World:

'Tis not unlikely that this work of God's Spirit, that is so extraordinary and wonderful, is the dawning, or at least a prelude, of the glorious work of God so often
foretold in Scripture, which in the progress and issue of it shall renew the world
of mankind. . . . And there are many things that make it probable that this work
will begin in America.[1]

## Exploration and settlement

However, during the first hundred years after Columbus's explorations,
England's response to the opportunities of the New World was slow and dis-
organized. Henry VII (1485–1509), the tight-fisted Tutor, outfitted a freelanc-
ing Italian navigator by the name of John Cabot. In 1497 and again in 1498
this bold mariner voyaged along the coast of North America between Newfoundland and Chesapeake Bay, searching for a trans-American route to the
Indies. Upon this rather casual exploration all of England's claims to North
America rested until they were fortified by military power. Henry VII was
happy with Cabot's work but not generous; Cabot received a cash reward of
£10 for all his labor.

English interest in the New World slumbered until Elizabeth I came to the
throne. Then John Hawkins, Francis Drake, and Martin Frobisher all made
voyages to America in the 1560s and 1570s. Sir Humphrey Gilbert attempted
to plant a colony on the bleak coast of Newfoundland but lost his gamble and
his life in 1583 when his ship sank in a storm. Then Sir Walter Raleigh, Gilbert's
brave half-brother, undertook to start a colony farther south (1585–1587), choosing North Carolina's Roanoke Island, but the entire population mysteriously
disappeared.

Finally, after the Spanish Armada had been destroyed in 1588, England found
the way open to mastery of the seas. But it was May 1607 before a settlement,
Jamestown, was begun on the wooded and malarial banks of the James River
in Virginia. For the Virginia Company of London, which backed the expedi-
tion, the chief motivation was hoped-for gold, while secondary plans included
the conversion of the Indians and finding a passage to India. The cost of the
experiment was enormous. The Virginia Company was bankrupt and at least
4400 colonists had lost their lives by 1623. Yet somehow, despite every kind of
adversity, the colony survived. Writing in 1613, Alexander Whitaker took the
most positive view of the situation in *Good Newes from Virginia* (selection 1).

England's efforts at colonization then shifted to New England. Some Puritans who had separated from the Church of England fled to Holland in 1608.
During the ensuing twelve years of poverty and toil they longed to find a haven
where they could live and die as Englishmen. They negotiated the rights to

settle under the jurisdiction of the Virginia Company, but their crowded Mayflower, after sixty-five days at sea, missed its destination and arrived off the rocky coast of Massachusetts in November 1620. Fewer than half of the 102 passengers were Separatists. Prominent among those who were not was Captain Myles Standish, a stocky soldier of fortune who rendered invaluable service as an Indian fighter and negotiator.

## The Puritans at Plymouth

Before the Pilgrims landed at Plymouth they formed a "combination," brought about by "discontented & mutinous speeches" that a few had "let fall." They then drew up the famous *Mayflower Compact*, which begins:

> In the name of God, Amen. We whose names are underwriten, the loyall subjects of our dread soveraigne Lord, King James, by the grace of God, of Great Britaine, Franc, & Ireland king, defender of the faith, &c., having undertaken, for the glorie of God, and advancemente of the Christian faith, and honour of our king & countrie, a voyage to plant the first colonie in the Northerne parts of Virginia, doe by these presents solemnly & mutualy in the presence of God, and one of another, covenant and combine our selves togeather into a civill body politick, for our better ordering & preservation, & furtherance of the ends aforesaid; and by vertue hereof to enacte constitute, and frame such just & equall lawes, ordinances, acts, constitutions, & offices, from time to time, as shall be thought most meete & convenient for the generall good of the Colonie, unto which we promise all due submission and obedience.[2]

Governor William Bradford's *History of Plimoth Plantation* described the Pilgrims' arrival in Cape Cod Bay in November 1620:

> Being thus arived in a good harbor and brought safe to land, they fell upon their knees & blessed the God of heaven, who had brought them over the vast & furious ocean, and delivered them from all the periles & miseries thereof, againe to set their feete on the firme and stable earth, their proper elemente. . . .
>
> But hear I cannot but stay and make a pause, and stand half amased at this poore peoples presente condition; and so I thinke will the reader too, when he well considers the same. . . . [T]hey had now no friends to wellcome them, nor inns to entertaine or refresh their weatherbeaten bodys, no houses or much less townes to repaire too, to seeke for succoure. . . . Besides, what could they see but a hidious and desolate wildernes, full of wild beasts and willd men? . . . What could now sustaine them but the spirite of God and his grace?[3]

The next decade saw only slight colonial activity in New England. The colony at Plymouth grew very slowly, so severe were the conditions there. Then, in 1629, a much larger colonizing effort began when King Charles I chartered the Massachusetts Bay Company. In 1630 Governor John Winthrop (1588–1649) led a group of nonseparatist Puritans to Massachusetts Bay. He composed *A Modell of Christian Charity* (selection 2) aboard the *Arbella* as the ship approached the shore. Here was described the design of the Puritan theocracy, based on the biblical idea of the covenant.

## Select Bibliography

Ahlstrom, Sydney E. *A Religious History of the American People.* New Haven, Conn.: Yale University Press, 1972.

Gaustad, Edwin S., ed. *A Documentary History of Religion in America,* 2 vols. Grand Rapids: Eerdmans, 1982.

Hudson, Winthrop S. *Religion in America: An Historical Account of the Development of American Religious Life,* 3d ed. New York: Scribner's, 1981.

Miller, Perry, and Thomas H. Johnson. *The Puritans: A Sourcebook of Their Writings,* 2 vols. New York: Harper and Row, 1938.

Olmstead, Clifton E. *History of Religion in the United States.* Englewood Cliffs, N.J.: Prentice-Hall, 1960.

Smith, H. Shelton, Robert T. Handy, and Lefferts Loetscher. *American Christianity: An Historical Interpretation with Representative Documents,* 2 vols. New York: Scribner's, 1960–63.

# Good Newes from Virginia

## *Alexander Whitaker (1613)*

[sent to] The Right Worshipful Sir Thomas Smith, Knight, Treasurer of the English Colonie in Virginia

Let me turne your eyes, my brethren of England, to behold the waters of *Virginia:* where you may behold a fit subject for the exercise of your Liberalitie, persons enough on whom you may cast away your Bread, and yet not without hope, after many daies to finde it. Yea, I will not feare to affirme unto you, that those men whom God hath made able any way to be helpefull to this Plantation, and made knowne unto them the necessities of our wants, are bound in conscience by vertue of this precept, to lay their helping hands to it, either with their purse, persons, or prayers, so farre forth as God hath made them fit for it. For it is evident that our wise God hath bestowed no gift upon any man, for their private use, but for the good of other men, whom God shall offer to their Liberalitie.

Wherefore, since God hath opened the doore of *Virginia,* to our countrey of England, wee are to thinke that God hath, as it were, by word of mouth called us in, to bestow our severall Charity on them [the settlers]. And that this may the better appeare, we have many reasons to encourage us to bee Liberall minded and open-handed toward them.

First, if we consider the almost miraculous beginning, and continuance of this plantation, we must needs confesse that God hath opened this passage unto us, and led us by the hand unto this work. For the Marriners that were sent hither first to discover this Bay of Chaesapeac, found it onely by the meere directions of Gods providence: for I heard one of them confesse, that even then, when they were entred within the mouth of the Bay, they deemed the place they sought for to have beene many degrees further. The finding was not so strange, but the continuance and upholding of it hath bin most wonderful. I may fitly compare it to the growth of an Infant, which hath been afflicted from his birth with some grievous sicknes, that many times no hope of life hath

Source: Alexander Whitaker, *Good Newes from Virginia* (London: John Hales, 1613), 21–32, 44, passim.

remained, and yet it liveth still. Againe, if there were nothing else to encourage us, yet this one thing may stirre us up to go on chearefully with it: that the Divell is a capitall enemy against it, and continually seeketh which way to hinder the prosperitie and good proceedings of it. Yea, hath heretofore so farre prevailed, by his Instruments, the covetous hearts of many back-sliding Adventurers at home, and also by his servants here: some striving for superioritie, others by murmurings, mutinies, & plaine treasons; & others by fornication, prophanenes, idlenes, and such monstrous sinnes; that he had almost thrust us out of this kingdome, and had indeed quitted this Land of us, if God had not then (as one awaked out of sleepe) stood up and sent us meanes of great helpe, when we needed most, and expected least reliefe. . . . So this Plantation, which the divell hath so often troden downe, is by the miraculous blessing of God revived, and daily groweth to more happy and more hopefull successe. I have shut up many things in few words, and have alleadged this onely to prove unto us, that the finger of God hath been the onely true worker heere; that God first shewed us the place, God first called us hither, and here God by his speciall providence hath maintained us. Wherefore, by him let us be encouraged to lay our helping hands to this good work (yea Gods work) with all the strength of our abilitie. . . .

But lest I may seeme to exhort you to an unprofitable Liberalitie, or to argue God of forgetfulnes to those that serve him faithfully: heare now what a comfortable promise of reward God hath made unto us in these words: which is, "That after many dayes we shall find." If God should have commanded us to cast away without finding, some discouragement there might have been to our weake nature; but since God hath assuredly promised us, that we shall find in the end, who will not obey the command? who will not be Liberall. God hath been alwayes found true in his word, most faithfull in his promises. If God do promise Abraham that his seed shall inherit the Land of Canaan: Abrahams posteritie shall after many daies in the appointed time be planted peaceably in the land of Canaan. If God promise Salomon wisdome and riches: Salomon shall be wiser and richer than any Prince of the earth. If God promiseth that he will give his only Sonne, that whosoever beleeveth in him shall not perish, but have life everlasting: his Sonne Jesus Christ shal be borne into the world at the appointed time, and undergoe the weight of Gods wrath for redemption of beleevers. Shall God then faithfully performe all his promises in so great matters, and be unfaithfull in lesser matters: oh let no such base conceit of the Almightie enter into our minds, as to thinke that he that spared not his owne Sonne, to performe his promises to us, will be so unmindfull of us in so small a thing. . . .

Wherefore you (right wise and noble Adventurers of Virginia) whose hearts God hath stirred up to build him a Temple, to make him an house, to conquer a Kingdome for him here: be not discouraged with those many lamentable assaults that the divell hath made against us: he now rageth most, because he knoweth his kingdome is to have a short end. Goe forward boldly, and remember that you fight under the banner of Jesus Christ, that you plant his Kingdome, who hath already broken the Serpents head: God may deferre his temporall reward for a season, but be assured that in the end you shall find riches and honour in this world, and blessed immortality in the world to come. And you my brethren my fellow labourers, send up your earnest prayers to God for his Church in Virginia, that since his harvest heere is great, but the labourers few, hee would thrust forth labourers into his harvest; and pray also for mee that the ministration of his Gospell may be powerfull and effectuall by me to the salvation of many, and advancement of the kingdome of Jesus Christ, to whom with the Father and the holy Spirit, bee all honour and glorie for evermore, Amen.

---

## Selection 2

---

# A Modell of Christian Charity

## *John Winthrop (1630)*

Written On Boarde the Arrabella, On the Attlantick Ocean

### Christian charitie

#### *A Modell Hereof*

God Almightie in his most holy and wise providence hath soe disposed of the Condicion of mankinde, as in all times some must be rich, some poore, some highe and eminent in power and dignitie; others meane and in subjeccion.

#### *The Reason Hereof*

I. Reason: *First,* to hold conformity with the rest of his workes, being delighted to shewe forthe the glory of his wisdome in the variety and differ-

Source: John Winthrop, *Winthrop Papers* (Boston: Massachusetts Historical Society, 1931), 2:282–84, 292–95.

ence of the Creatures and the glory of his power, in ordering all these differences for the preservacion and good of the whole; and the glory of his greatnes that as it is the glory of princes to have many officers, soe this great King will have many Stewards, counting himselfe more honoured in dispenceing his guifts to man by man, than if hee did it by his owne immediate hand.

John Winthrop,
first governor of Massachusetts.

2. Reason: *Secondly,* That he might have the more occasion to manifest the worke of his Spirit: first, upon the wicked in moderateing and restraineing them: soe that the riche and mighty should not eate upp the poore, nor the poore and dispised rise upp against their superiours and shake off theire yoake; secondly in the regenerate in exerciseing his graces in them, as in the greate ones, their love, mercy, gentlenes, temperance, etc., in the poore and inferiour sorte, theire faithe, patience, obedience, etc.

3. Reason: *Thirdly,* That every man might have need of other, and from hence they might be all knitt more nearly together in the Bond of brotherly affeccion: from hence it appeares plainely that noe man is made more honourable than another or more wealthy etc., out of any perticuler and singuler respect to himselfe but for the glory of his Creator and the Common good of the Creature, Man. . . .

For the worke wee have in hand, it is by a mutuall consent through a speciall overruleing providence, and a more than an ordinary approbation of the Churches of Christ to seeke out a place of Cohabitation and Consorteshipp under a due forme of Government both civill and ecclesiasticall. In such cases as this the care of the publique must oversway all private respects, by which not onely conscience, but meare Civill pollicy doth binde us; for it is a true rule that perticuler estates cannott subsist in the ruine of the publique.

The end is to improve our lives, to doe more service to the Lord, the comforte and encrease of the body of Christe whereof wee are members, that our selves and posterity may be the better preserved from the Common corrupcions of this evill world, to serve the Lord and worke out our Salvacion under the power and purity of his holy Ordinances.

For the meanes whereby this must bee effected, they are twofold, a Conformity with the worke and end wee aime at; these wee see are extraordinary, therefore wee must not content our selves with usuall ordinary meanes. Whatsoever wee did or ought to have done when wee lived in England, the same must wee doe and more allsoe where wee goe: That which the most in theire Churches mainteine as a truthe in profession onely, wee must bring into familiar and constant practice, as in this duty of love wee must love brotherly without dissimulation, wee must love one another with a pure hearte fervently, wee must beare one anothers burthens, wee must not looke onely on our owne things but allsoe on the things of our brethren, neither must wee think that the lord will beare with such faileings at our hands as hee dothe from those among whome wee have lived. . . .

Thus stands the cause betweene God and us. Wee are entered into Covenant with him for this worke, wee have taken out a Commission, the Lord hath given us leave to draw our owne Articles, wee have professed to enterprise these Accions upon these and these ends, wee have hereupon besought him of favour and blessing: Now if the Lord shall please to heare us, and bring us in peace to the place wee desire, then hath hee ratified this Covenant and sealed our Commission [and] will expect a strickt performance of the Articles contained in it, but if wee shall neglect the observacion of these Articles which are the ends wee have propounded, and dissembling with our God, shall fall to embrace this present world and prosecute our carnall intencions seekeing great things for our selves and our posterity, the Lord will surely breake out in wrathe against us, be revenged of such a perjured people and make us knowe the price of the breache of such a Covenant.

Now the onely way to avoyde this shipwracke and to provide for our posterity is to followe the Counsell of Micah, to doe Justly, to love mercy, to walke humbly with our God. For this end, wee must be knitt together in this worke as one man, wee must entertaine each other in brotherly Affeccion, wee must be willing to abridge our selves of our superfluities, for the supply of others necessities, wee must uphold a familiar Commerce together in all meeknes, gentlenes, patience and liberallity, wee must delight in each other, make others Condicions our owne, rejoyce together, mourne together, labour and suffer together, allwayes haveing before our eyes our Commission and Community in the worke, our Community as members of the same body, soe shall wee keepe the unitie of the spirit in the bond of peace, the Lord will be our God and delight to dwell among us as his owne people and will commaund a blessing upon us in all our wayes, soe that wee shall see much more of his wisdome, power, goodnes and truthe than formerly wee have beene acquainted with. Wee shall finde that the God of Israell is among us, when tenn of us shall be able to resist a thousand of our enemies, when hee shall make us a prayse and glory, that men shall say of succeeding plantacions: the Lord make it like that of New England: for wee must Consider that wee shall be as a Citty upon a Hill, the eies of all people are uppon us; soe that if wee shall deale falsely with our God in this worke wee have undertaken and soe cause him to withdrawe his present help from us, wee shall shame the faces of many of gods worthy servants, and cause theire prayers to be turned into Cursses upon us till wee be consumed out of the good land whither wee are goeing: And to shutt upp this discourse with that exhortacion of Moses, that faithfull servant of the Lord in his last farewell to Israell, Deut. 30. Beloved there is now sett before us life, and good, deathe and evill in that wee are Commaunded this day to love the Lord our God, and to love one another, to walke in his wayes and to keepe his Commaundements and his Ordinance, and his lawes, and the Articles of our Covenant with him that wee may live and be multiplied, and that the Lord our God may blesse us in the land whither we goe to possesse it: But if our heartes shall turne away soe that wee will not obey, but shall be seduced and worship other Gods, our pleasures, and proffitts, and serve them; it is propounded unto us this day, wee shall surely perishe out of the good Land whither wee passe over this vast Sea to possesse it;

Therefore lett us choose life,
that wee, and our Seede,
may live; by obeyeing his
voyce, and cleaveing to him,
for hee is our life, and
our prosperity.

# Problems within American Puritanism

Puritanism began as an English Protestant reform movement during the reign of Queen Elizabeth I (1558–1603). Its leader was Thomas Cartwright (1535–1603), a professor at Cambridge, who demanded that England's episcopal system of church government be replaced with presbyterian polity. By 1582 when Robert Browne wrote his separatist polemic *A Treatise of Reformation Without Tarying for Anie* there were sizable numbers who agreed with his radical stand against "tarying" in episcopalianism. During the reign of James I (1603–1625) the Puritans grew in power and numbers, and the majority was content to stay within the Church of England. John Foxe and others had convinced them that England was an "elect nation" with a divine mission to save the Reformation. Also, the archbishopric of Canterbury was occupied by Calvinists who were largely sympathetic to Puritanism.

The coming of Charles I to the English throne, from 1625 to 1649, dimmed Puritan hopes for reforming the church from within. William Laud, an implacable enemy of the Puritans, was made archbishop of Canterbury in 1633. By then some of them had already departed from England, having been "hunted & persecuted on every side." The congregation at Scrooby had decided in 1607 to separate from the Anglican Church and flee to Leyden, Holland, remaining there until July 1620, when they returned to England on the *Speedwell.* There they joined other Puritans, and the entire group sailed from Plymouth harbor in September aboard the *Mayflower.* These "Pilgrims" arrived in Cape Cod Bay in November 1620.

During the 1630s the great Puritan migration to America continued, taking along notable scholars, leaders, and clergy to set up a new order in the wilderness. If England could not be made God's "elect nation," they reasoned, perhaps a New World theocracy, a Zion, could establish a more righteous, truly Christian society. In October 1629 a Suffolk landowner, John Winthrop, was elected the first governor of Massachusetts Bay Colony, and the next spring a fleet of eleven ships assembled at Southampton to take Puritans to the New World. On March 29, 1630, the first four ships departed with four hundred aboard. By the end of that year six hundred more followed. By 1643 more than 20,000 people had come to Massachusetts. All seemed to bode well for the wilderness Zion.

## People of the covenants

Most of these people came to the New World because they were Puritans, and one cannot understand the Puritans without comprehending the *covenants* under which they operated. Especially is it important to understand the preeminent *covenant of grace*, from which followed church and social/political covenants.[1] The foremost student of the Puritans, Perry Miller, has written,

> By the word "covenant" federal theologians understood just such a contract as was used among men of business, a bond or a mortgage, an agreement between two parties, signed and sworn to, and binding upon both. . . . Hence the terms of the first covenant, the Covenant of Works, are what we know as the law of nature, and by failing to keep them, Adam, and we as his posterity, incurred the just penalty. But God did not rest there. Beginning with Abraham, He commenced a new covenant, the Covenant of Grace, which is a true contract of mutual obligation, but this time the condition for the mortal partner is not a deed but a faith. . . . Because fallen man is unable any longer to fulfill the moral law, God in the person of Christ takes the task upon Himself.[2]

This covenant of grace was initiated with Abraham, in Genesis 17, and the condition for him and all people since has been faith in the atoning death of Jesus Christ. Since the Puritans had determined to leave England because they regarded the churches there as insufficiently reformed, in New England they had to be far more certain of a regenerate church membership. John Cotton, the eminent scholar and pastor of the church in Boston, preached that new members had to demonstrate "certain and infallible signs of their regeneration."[3] The other eminent scholar of New England, Thomas Hooker, declared that "people may be said to be *within the covenant* two waies. Either, *Externally* in the judgment of *charity: Internally* and spiritually, according to the judgment of *verity* and truth."[4]

The external or outward covenant of grace was established between God and a people in a larger, more nearly national sense and might include hypocrites or people who hoped eventually to be saved but were still without saving grace. The internal or inward covenant of grace was held between the individual souls of the elect and God; it was this covenant which created the invisible church of the saints. The visible church admitted members upon a reasonable assumption of their possession of true saving faith in Christ. When there were a number of the elect, Hooker maintained that "mutuall covenanting and confoederation of the Saints in the fellowship of the faith according to the order of the Gospel, is that which gives constitution and being to a visible church."[5]

## Orthodoxy in turmoil

But a pure and compatible church in the Massachusetts Bay Colony was hardly to be. From the first there was contention. This was to be expected, inasmuch as many Separatists who came to New England held divergent views from one another on a number of theological points. The most thoroughgoing and troublesome exemplar of this tendency was Roger Williams (1603?–1683), who arrived in the Bay Colony in 1631 from England. An expert at stepping on toes, he refused to become the teacher of the Boston church because it had not clearly separated from the Church of England. For maintaining a number of disputed points (such as that civil magistrates have no right to enforce the first five Commandments, and that the king had no title to Indian lands and therefore no right to issue royal charters giving these lands away), Williams was tried and banished from the Bay Colony in 1635. Fleeing into the wilderness he founded Providence on land he purchased from the Indians. This new plantation quickly became a refuge for the persecuted or those of radical and unorthodox views, and Williams himself successively was a Separatist, a Baptist, and finally a Seeker.[6]

Although Williams had purchased Rhode Island, other colonies eyed this land, and it quickly became apparent that he needed one of the royal charters he had earlier condemned. He sailed for London, arriving in the summer of 1643. England was then engaged in its Civil War, and Williams had to wait patiently. Finally in March 1644 a patent for "Providence Plantations" was granted to Providence, Portsmouth, and Newport. While waiting for the patent, Williams made good use of his time, writing his classic defense of religious freedom, one of the greatest Puritan books, *The Bloudy Tenent of Persecution* (selection 3). Hastily written, *The Bloudy Tenent* is sometimes repetitive and crude in style, yet it was nonetheless bold and ahead of its time in demanding full religious liberty. He insisted on a strict separation between church and state, arguing that civil magistrates may never rule in religious matters and that

# The Eighteenth Century

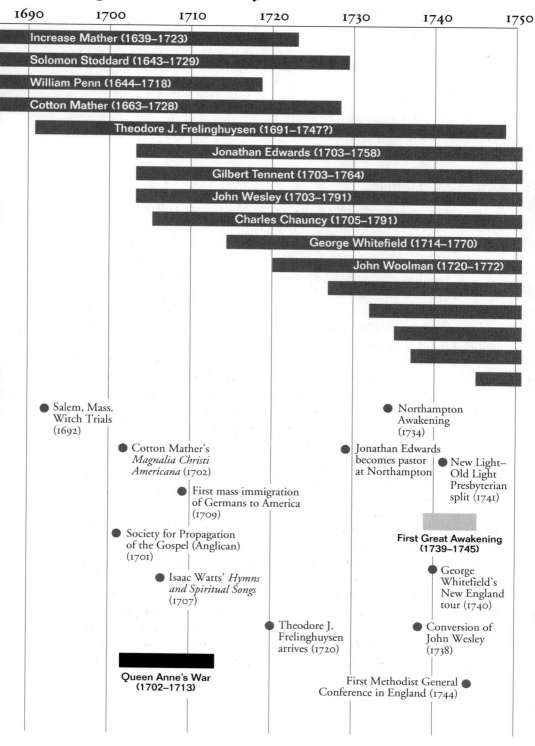

| 1690 | 1700 | 1710 | 1720 | 1730 | 1740 | 1750 |
|------|------|------|------|------|------|------|

Increase Mather (1639–1723)

Solomon Stoddard (1643–1729)

William Penn (1644–1718)

Cotton Mather (1663–1728)

Theodore J. Frelinghuysen (1691–1747?)

Jonathan Edwards (1703–1758)

Gilbert Tennent (1703–1764)

John Wesley (1703–1791)

Charles Chauncy (1705–1791)

George Whitefield (1714–1770)

John Woolman (1720–1772)

● Salem, Mass.
Witch Trials
(1692)

● Cotton Mather's
*Magnalia Christi
Americana* (1702)

● First mass immigration
of Germans to America
(1709)

● Society for Propagation
of the Gospel (Anglican)
(1701)

● Isaac Watts' *Hymns
and Spiritual Songs*
(1707)

● Theodore J.
Frelinghuysen
arrives (1720)

**Queen Anne's War
(1702–1713)**

● Northampton
Awakening
(1734)

● Jonathan Edwards
becomes pastor
at Northampton

● New Light–
Old Light
Presbyterian
split (1741)

**First Great Awakening
(1739–1745)**

● George
Whitefield's
New England
tour (1740)

● Conversion of
John Wesley
(1738)

First Methodist General ●
Conference in England (1744)

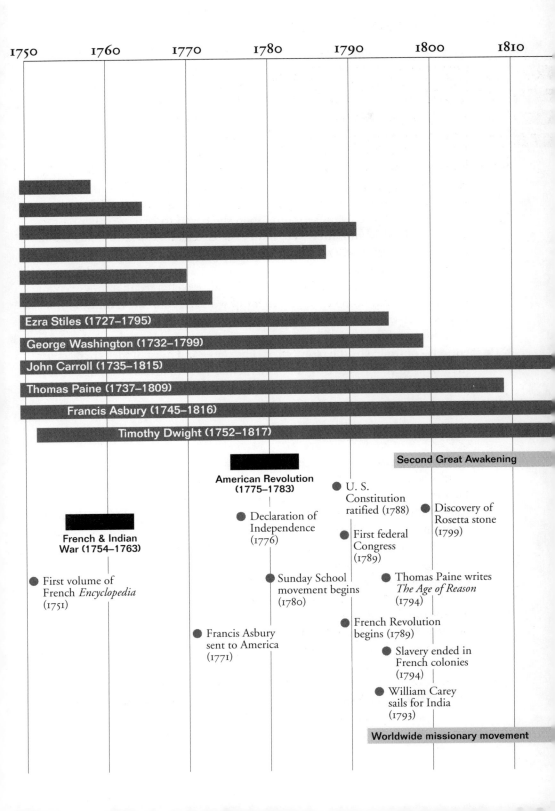

1750    1760    1770    1780    1790    1800    1810

Ezra Stiles (1727–1795)

George Washington (1732–1799)

John Carroll (1735–1815)

Thomas Paine (1737–1809)

Francis Asbury (1745–1816)

Timothy Dwight (1752–1817)

Second Great Awakening

American Revolution
(1775–1783)

U. S.
Constitution
ratified (1788)

Discovery of
Rosetta stone
(1799)

Declaration of
Independence
(1776)

First federal
Congress
(1789)

French & Indian
War (1754–1763)

First volume of
French *Encyclopedia*
(1751)

Sunday School
movement begins
(1780)

Thomas Paine writes
*The Age of Reason*
(1794)

Francis Asbury
sent to America
(1771)

French Revolution
begins (1789)

Slavery ended in
French colonies
(1794)

William Carey
sails for India
(1793)

Worldwide missionary movement

religious persecution is totally contrary to the doctrines of Christ. Whereas the Puritan ideal was to pattern the New England churches on the model of the Old Testament Israel—a regenerate people operating under a theocracy—that plan collided squarely with Williams's schismatic propensities.

Even before *The Bloudy Tenent* was written, another turmoil beset the Bay Colony, one that was so widespread it threatened to shatter the colony. Anne Hutchinson, called by John Winthrop "that American Jezabel,"[7] a remarkable lay theologian and prophetess, arrived in 1634 from the original Boston, Lincolnshire, England, where she had been a follower of John Cotton. Hutchinson emigrated with Cotton's group and began holding well-attended meetings in her home to discuss his sermons. Soon she began to criticize other pastors as unconverted, saying they were under the covenant of works. Thus began the so-called *Antinomian Crisis*, the opening chapter in American intellectual history. *Antinomianism* (lit. "against the law") teaches that the moral law is of no use under the dispensation of grace. Hutchinson charged that the covenant of grace rendered obsolete the covenant of works, so that no amount of holiness is evidence of salvation. Since the Holy Spirit personally indwells a saved soul, human laws no longer apply to such a person. His or her behavior is entirely controlled by the Holy Spirit. The clergy and most of the general court members were outraged by her statements. Eventually, after much furor, Hutchinson and her brother-in-law, John Wheelwright, were banished from the colony in November 1637.

## The "half-way" children

With the passing of the years a new generation came upon the scene— youths who had not undergone agonizing persecution in an unfriendly land. New generations heard why their parents and grandparents had come to America, but the spirit of self-sacrifice and devotion to high spiritual ideals that persecution had engendered was not transmitted unimpaired. In New England no agents of the king tried to silence Puritan preachers and harass dissenting congregations. Instead, different problems were uppermost: Indian wars, maintaining the food supply, and materialistic concerns.

Church membership, zeal, and conversions all declined. Particularly acute was the problem of grown and baptized children of church members who could not give evidence of conversion and a changed life. They were termed *half-way covenanters* and presented a great challenge when they demanded baptism for their own children.

After much wrangling over this most sensitive and distressing issue of the time, the *Boston Synod of 1662* passed the *Half-Way Covenant*, allowing baptism to these children. Despite its good intentions, this measure did nothing to arrest the drift away from the churches. In great fear the General Court of Massachusetts in 1679 called what became known as the *Reforming Synod* to consider: (1) what evils had provoked the Lord to bring judgment on New England, and (2) what could be done to reform these evils. Thirteen causes were specified for the spiritual laxity, among them a decay of godliness on the part of Christians, pride and extravagance in dress, absence of Sabbath observance, covetousness and love of the world, and a refusal to repent.

## Witch hysteria at Salem

Still the slide continued. Samuel Torrey, pastor of the church in Weymouth, declared in 1683, "There is already a great death upon religion. . . . Consider we then how much it is dying respecting the very being of it, by the general failure of the work of conversion; whereby only it is that religion is propagated, continued, and upheld in being among any people."

Then came the most shameful, and notorious, episode in Massachusetts history, the Salem witch trials. In that day almost everyone believed in witches, and witchcraft was a capital crime in England, France, Germany, and other civilized countries. While this in no way exonerates the participants at Salem, the fear and execution of witches in Europe far exceeded anything done in the New World. During 1645–1646, for example, the notorious judge Matthew Hopkins sent 200 witches to the gallows in England, and similar cases were common in Germany. The people in Salem were no more superstitious than elsewhere.

The mania began when two West Indian slaves stirred up fears through their tales of voodooism. The daughter and niece of Salem Village's pastor, Samuel Parris, experienced sickness in the winter of 1691–1692. Physicians could find no physical cause and speculated that witchcraft might be to blame. When some other girls complained of similar distress—pains as from being jabbed with sharp pins—and accused their neighbors of Satanic powers, the witch hunt began. The jail was filled with suspects, most of good reputation. No confessions were extracted, but "spectral evidence" was allowed, which assumed that a bewitched subject could recognize in the specter, or apparition, the likeness of the person who was bewitching him or her. It further assumed that a specter could not assume the likeness of an innocent person.

Sir William Phips, the newly appointed royal governor, appointed a special court to hear the cases, and it convened on June 2. One of the judges was the revered Samuel Sewall. By September 22 the court had executed twenty persons, all of whom declared their innocence to the final moment.

Cotton Mather (1663–1728) is chiefly remembered as the persecutor of witches, although, as Perry Miller writes, "all he had to do with the miserable proceedings at Salem in 1692 was—and this is reprehensible enough—urge the Court on and then write a defense of its actions after everybody, including Cotton Mather, realized that it had been caught in a panic and had proceeded on fallacious legal principles."[8] Born in Boston, the eldest son of Increase Mather (1639–1723), he was educated at Harvard College. Entering the ministry, he served Second Church of Boston, first as his father's colleague and then as senior pastor. Miller notes that his accomplishment in erudition was a "staggering success," for he published in his lifetime over 400 titles. The most massive is *Magnalia Christi Americana,* published in London in 1702. His *Memorable Providences* (Boston, 1689) may have helped feed the witchcraft panic.

If the ministers were somewhat responsible for the fear of witches—and they were, along with the frenzy and mass madness that confused even the wisest—some of the leading clergymen were the first to caution the court to show greater prudence in trying the accused, and other clergy were the ones who stopped it. As soon as the enormity of the panic became evident the clergy gathered and decided that the best way to halt it was to attack "spectral evidence" as a very questionable form of proof. Increase Mather immediately wrote a pamphlet, *Cases of Conscience Concerning Evil Spirits* (selection 4), which the clergy circulated in manuscript to save time, until it could be printed. In it Increase Mather states that he does indeed believe in witches, that the judges are not to be unduly blamed because they "are wise and good men, and have acted with all fidelity according to their light," and concludes "it were better that ten suspected witches should escape, than that one innocent person should be condemned."

With this document and especially its postscript, which was the condemnation by twelve ministers of the use of spectral evidence, Governor Phips brought the trials to an abrupt end. Without spectral evidence the cases fell apart. The accused were set free if they recanted. As sanity gradually returned, so did private and public repentance. Five years later the noblest of the judges, Sewall, stood before his church in Boston and stated his "blame and shame,"

Cotton Mather

asking humble forgiveness for the part he had taken in allowing a procedure that he and the other judges might well know was unsound.

## Select Bibliography

Booth, Sally S. *The Witches of Early America.* New York: Hastings, 1975.

Boyer, Paul, and Stephen Nissenbaum. *Salem Possessed: The Social Origins of Witchcraft.* Cambridge, Mass.: Harvard University Press, 1974.

Danforth, F. L. *New England Witchcraft.* New York: Pageant, 1965.

Haller, William. *The Rise of Puritanism.* 1938; repr., Philadelphia: University of Pennsylvania Press, 1972.

Hansen, Chadwick. *Witchcraft at Salem.* New York: Brazilier, 1969.

Kittredge, George Lyman. *Witchcraft in Old and New England.* 1929; repr., Paterson, N.J.: Atheneum, 1972.

Miller, Perry. *Errand into the Wilderness.* New York: Harper and Row, 1964.

———. *The New England Mind: The Seventeenth Century.* 1961; repr., Cambridge, Mass.: Harvard University Press, 1983.

Morgan, Edmund S., ed. *Puritan Political Ideas, 1558–1794.* Indianapolis: Bobbs-Merrill, 1965.

Upham, C. W. *Salem Witchcraft,* 2 vols. 1867; repr., Williamstown, Mass.: Corner House, 1971.

Wertenbaker, Thomas J. *The Puritan Oligarchy: The Founding of American Civilization.* New York: Grosset and Dunlap, 1947.

Williams, Charles. *Witchcraft.* New York: Meridian, 1959.

Ziff, Larzer. *Puritanism in America: New Culture in a New World.* New York: Viking, 1973.

# The Bloudy Tenent of Persecution

## *Roger Williams (1644)*

First, That the blood of so many hundred thousand soules of Protestants and Papists, spilt in the Wars of present and former Ages, for their respective Consciences, is not required nor accepted by Jesus Christ the Prince of Peace.

Secondly, Pregnant Scripturs and Arguments are throughout the Worke proposed against the Doctrine of persecution for cause of Conscience.

Thirdly, Satisfactorie Answers are given to Scriptures, and objections produced by Mr. Calvin, Beza, Mr. Cotton, and the Ministers of the New English Churches and others former and later, tending to prove the Doctrine of persecution for cause of Conscience.

Fourthly, The Doctrine of persecution for cause of Conscience, is proved guilty of all the blood of the Soules crying for vengeance under the Altar.

Fifthly, All Civill States with their Officers of justice in their respective constitutions and administrations are proved essentially Civill, and therefore not Judges, Governours or Defendours of the Spirituall or Christian state and Worship.

Sixthly, It is the will and command of God, that (since the comming of his Sonne the Lord Jesus) a permission of the most Paganish, Jewish, Turkish, or Antichristian consciences and worships, bee granted to all men in all Nations and Countries: and they are onely to bee fought against with that Sword which is only (in Soule matters) able to conquer, to wit, the Sword of Gods Spirit, the Word of God.

Seventhly, The State of the Land of Israel, the Kings and people thereof in Peace & War, is proved figurative and ceremoniall, and no patterne nor president for any Kingdome or civill state in the world to follow.

Eightly, God requireth not an uniformity of Religion to be inacted and inforced in any civill state; which inforced uniformity (sooner or later) is the greatest occasion of civill Warre, ravishing of conscience, persecution of Christ Jesus is his servants, and of the hypocrisie and destruction of millions of souls.

Source: Roger Williams, *The Bloudy Tenent, of Persecution, for Cause of Conscience, discussed, in A Conference betweene Truth and Peace.* (London, 1644), 60–66, 93–95, passim.

Ninthly, In holding an inforced uniformity of Religion in a civill state, wee must necessarily disclaime our desires and hopes of the Jewes conversion to Christ.

Tenthly, An inforced uniformity of Religion throughout a Nation or civill state, confounds the Civill and Religious, denies the principles of Christianity and civility, and that Jesus Christ is come in the Flesh.

Eleventhly, The permission of other consciences and worships then a state professeth, only can (according to God) procure a firme and lasting peace, (good assurance being taken according to the wisdome of the civill state for uniformity of civill obedience from all sorts.)

Twelfthly, lastly, true civility and Christianity may both flourish in a state or Kingdome, notwithstanding the permission of divers and contrary consciences, either of Jew or Gentile. . . .

## Chap. XL.

But it hath been thought, or said, Shall oppositions against the Truth escape unpunished? will they not prove mischievous, &c.

*Truth.* I answer (as before) concerning the blinde Guides (in case there be no Civill offence committed) the Magistrates, & all men that by the mercy of God to themselves discerne the miserie of such Opposites, have cause to lament and bewaile that fearfull condition wherein such are entangled, to wit, in the snares & chains of Satan, with which they are so invincibly caught and held, that no power in Heaven or Earth, but the Right hand of the Lord in the meeke and gentle dispensing of the Word of Truth, can release and quit them.

Those many false Christs (of whom the Lord Jesus forewarnes, Mat. 24.) have sutably their false bodies, faith, spirit, Baptisme, as the Lord Jesus, hath his true body, faith, spirit, &c. Ephes. 4. correspondent also are their weapons, and the successe, issue, or operation of them. A carnall weapon or sword of steele may produce a carnall repentance, a shew, an outside, an uniformitie through a State or Kingdome: But it hath pleased the Father to exalt the Lord Jesus only, to be a Prince (armed with power and meanes sufficient) to give repentance to Israel, Acts. 5. 31.

Accordingly an unbelieving Soule being dead in sinne (although he be changed from one worship to another, like a dead man shifted into severall changes of apparell) cannot please God, Heb. 11. and consequently, whatever such an unbelieving & unregenerate person acts in Worship or Religion, it is but sinne, Rom. 14. Preaching sinne, praying (though without beads or booke) sinne; breaking of bread, or Lords supper sinne, yea as odious as the oblation of Swines blood, a Dogs neck, or killing of a Man, Isa. 66.

But Faith it is that gift which proceeds alone from the Father of Lights, Phil. 1. 29, and till he please to make his light arise and open the eyes of blind sinners, their soules shall lie fast asleep (and the faster, in that a sword of steele compells them to a worship in hypocrisie) in the dungeons of spirituall darknesse and Sathans slavery.

*Peace.* I adde, that a civill sword (as wofull experience in all ages hath proved) is so far from bringing or helping forward an opposite in Religion to repentance, that Magistrates sinne grievously against the worke of God and blood of Soules, by such proceedings. Because as (commonly) the suffrings of false and Antichristian Teachers harden their followers, who being blind, by this meanes are occasioned to tumble into the ditch of Hell after their blind leaders, with more inflamed zeale of lying confidence. So secondly, violence and a sword of steele begets such an impression in the sufferers, that certainly they conclude (as indeed that Religion cannot be true which needs such instruments of violence to uphold it so) that Persecutors are far from soft and gentle commiseration of the blindnessse of others. To this purpose it pleased the Father of Spirits, of old, to constraine the Emperour of Rome, Antoninus Pius, to write to all the Governours of his Provinces to forbeare to persecute the Christians, because such dealing must needs be so far from converting the Christians from their way, that it rather begat in their mindes an opinion of their crueltie, &c.

## Chap. CXXXVII.

*Peace.* Deare *Truth,* We are now arrived at their last Head: the Title is this, *viz.*

*Their power in the Liberties and Priviledges of these Churches.*

First, all Magistrates ought to be chosen out of Church-members, *Exod. 18. 21. Deut. 17. 15. Prov. 29. 2.* When the Righteous rule, the people rejoyce.

Secondly, that all free men elected, be only Church-members.

1. Because if none but Church members should rule, then others should not choose, because they may elect others beside Church members.

2. From the patterne of *Israel,* where none had power to choose but only Israel, or such as were joyned to the people of God.

3. If it shall fall out, that in the Court consisting of Magistrates and Deputies, there be a dissent between them which may hinder the common good, that

they now returne for ending the same, to their first principles, which are the Free men, and let them be consulted with.

*Truth.* In this *Head* are 2 branches: First concerning the choice of *Magistrates,* that such ought to be chosen as are *Church members:* for which is quoted, *Exod. 18. 21. Dut. 17. 15. Proverbs 19. 29.*

Unto which I answer: It were to be wished, that since the point is so weighty, as concerning the *Pilots* and *Steeresmen* of *Kingdoms* and *Nations,* &c. on whose *abilitie, care* and *faithfulnesse* depends most commonly the *peace* and *safety* of the *commonweales* they sail in: I say it were to be wished that they had more fully explained what they intend by this *Affirmative,* viz. *Magistrates* ought to be chosen out of *Church members.*

For if they intend by this *[Ought to be chosen]* a *necessitie* of *convenience,* viz. that for the greater advancement of *common utilitie* and *rejoycing* of the people, according to the place quoted *(Prov. 29. 2.)* it were to be desired, prayed for, and peaceably endeavored, then I readily assent unto them.

But if by this *[Ought]* they intend such a *necessitie* as those Scriptures quoted imply, viz. that people shall sin by choosing such for *Magistrates* as are not members of *Churches;* as the *Israelites* should have sinned, if they had not (according to *Jethro's* counsell, *Exod. 18.* and according to the *command* of *God,* Deut 18.) chosen their *Judges* and *Kings* within themselves in *Israel:* then I propose these necessary *Queries.*

First whether those are not lawfull *Civill combinations, societies,* and *communions* of men, *Townes, Cities, States* or *Kingdoms,* where no *Church* of *Christ* is resident, yea where his name was never yet heard of: I adde to this, that Men of no small note, skilfull in the *state* of the *World,* acknowledge, that the *World* divided into 30 parts, 25 of that 30 have never yet heard of the name of *Christ:* If their *Civill polities* and *combinations* be not lawfull, (because they are not *Churches,* and their *Magistrates Church* members) then *disorder, confusion,* and all *unrighteousnes* is lawfull, and pleasing to God.

Secondly, whether in such States or Commonweales, where a Church or Churches of Christ are resident, such persons may not lawfully succeed to the Crown or Government, in whom the feare of God (according to *Jethroes* councell) cannot be discerned, nor are brethren of the Church, according to *Deut. 17.)* but only are fitted with Civill and Morall abilities, to manage the Civill affaires of the Civill State.

Thirdly, since not many *Wise* and *Noble* are called, but the *poore* receive the *Gospel,* as *God* hath chosen the *poore* of the *World* to be *rich* in *Faith,* 1 Cor. 1. Jam. 2. Whether it may not ordinarily come to passe, that there may not be found in a true *Church* of *Christ* (which sometimes consisteth but of few persons) persons fit to be either *Kings* or *Governours*, &c. whose *civill office* is no lesse difficult then the office of a *Doctor* of *Physick*, a *Master* or *Pilot* of a *Ship*, or a *Captaine* or *Commander* of a *Band* or *Army* of men: for which services, the children of *God* may be no wayes *qualified*, though otherwise excellent for the *feare* of *God*, and the *knowledge* and *Grace* of the *Lord Jesus*.

4. If *Magistrates* ought (that is, ought only) to be chosen out of the *Church*, I demand if they ought not also to be *dethroned* and *deposed*, when they cease to be of the *Church*, either by voluntary departure from it, or by *excommunication* out of it, according to the bloody *tenents* and *practice* of some *Papists*, with whom the *Protestants* (according to their *principles)* although they seeme to abhor it, doe absolutely agree?

5. Therefore lastly, I ask if this be not to turne the *World* upside down, to turne the *World* out of the *World*, to pluck up the *roots* and *foundations* of all *common societie* in the *World?* to turne the *Garden* and *Paradice* of the *Church* and *Saints* into the *Field* of the *Civill State* of the *World*, and to reduce the *World* to the first *chaos* or *confusion*.

---

## Selection 4

---

# Tests for Witches

### *Increase Mather (1693)*

So odious and abominable is the name of a witch . . . that it is apt to grow up into a scandal for any, so much as to enter some sober cautions against the over hasty suspecting, or too precipitant judging of persons on this account. But certainly, the more execrable the crime is, the more critical care is to be used in the exposing of the names, liberties and lives of men . . . to the imputation of it. The awful hand of God now upon us . . . hath put serious persons into deep musings, and upon curious inquiries what is to be done for the detecting and defeating of this tremendous design of the grand Adversary. . . .

That there are devils and witches, the Scripture asserts, and experience confirms. That they are common enemies of mankind, and set upon mischief, is not to be doubted. That the Devil . . . delights to have the concurrence of witches, and their consent in harming men, is consonant to his native malice

Source: Increase Mather, *Cases of Conscience Concerning Evil Spirits Personating Men* (Boston, 1693).

to man. . . . That witches, when detected and convinced, ought to be exterminated and cut off, we have God's warrant for. . . .

Only the same God who hath said, thou shalt not suffer a witch to live; hath also said, at the mouth of two witnesses, or three witnesses shall he that is worthy of death, be put to death: but at the mouth of one witness, he shall not be put to death. . . .

It is therefore exceeding necessary that in such a day as this, men be informed what is evidence and what is not. It concerns men in point of charity. . . . And it is of no less necessity in point of justice. . . . Evidence supposed to be in the testimony . . . is thoroughly to be weighed, and if it do not infallibly prove the crime against the person accused, it ought not to determine him guilty of it; for so a righteous man may be condemned unjustly. . . .

Among many arguments to evince this, that which is most under present debate, is that which refers to something vulgarly called Specter Evidence, and a certain sort of Ordeal or trial by the sight and touch. The principal plea to justify the convictive evidence in these, is fetched from the consideration of the wisdom and righteousness of God in governing the world, which they suppose would fail, if such things were permitted to befall an innocent person. But it is certain, that. . . . God doth sometimes suffer such things to [happen], that we may thereby know how much we are beholden to Him, for that restraint which He lays upon the Infernal Spirits, who would else reduce a world into a chaos. That the resolutions of such cases as these is proper for the servants of Christ in the ministry cannot be denied; the seasonableness of doing it now, will be justified by the consideration of the necessity there is at this time of a right information of men's judgments about these things, and the danger of their being misinformed. . . .

The first case that I am desired to express my judgment in, is this: Whether it is not possible for the Devil to impose on the imaginations of persons bewitched, and to cause them to believe that an innocent, yea that a pious person does torment them, when the Devil himself doth it . . . ? The answer to the question must be affirmative. . . .

From hence we infer, that there is no outward affliction whatsoever but may befall a good man. Now to be represented by Satan as a tormentor of bewitched or possessed persons, is a sore affliction to a good man. To be tormented by Satan is a sore affliction, yet nothing but what befell Job, and a daughter of Abraham, whom we read of in the Gospel. To be represented by Satan as tormenting others, is an affliction like the former; the Lord may bring such extraordinary temptations on his own children, to afflict and humble them, for some sin they have been guilty of before Him. . . .

This then I declare and testify, that to take away the life of anyone, merely because a specter or devil, in a bewitched or possessed person does accuse them, will bring the guilt of innocent blood on the land. . . . What does such an evidence amount unto more than this: Either such an one did afflict such an one, or the Devil in his likeness, or his eyes were bewitched. . . .

These things being premised, I answer the question affirmatively. There are proofs for the conviction of witches which jurors may with a safe conscience proceed upon, so as to bring them in guilty. . . . But then the inquiry is, what is sufficient proof? . . .

A free and voluntary confession of the crime made by the person suspected and accused after examination, is a sufficient ground of conviction. Indeed, if persons are distracted, or under the power of phrenetic melancholy, that alters the case; but the jurors that examine them, and their neighbors that know them, may easily determine that case; or if confession be extorted, the evidence is not so clear and convictive; but if any persons out of remorse of conscience, or from a touch of God in their spirits, confess and show their deeds . . . nothing can be more clear. . . .

If two credible persons shall affirm upon oath that they have seen the party accused speaking such words, or doing things which none but such as have familiarity with the Devil ever did or can do, that's a sufficient ground for conviction. . . . The Devil never assists men to do supernatural things undesired. When therefore such like things shall be testified against the accused party not by specters which are devils in the shape of persons . . . but by real men or women . . . it is proof enough that such an one has that conversation and correspondence with the Devil, as that he or she, whoever they be, ought to be exterminated from amongst men. This notwithstanding I will add. It were better that ten suspected witches should escape, than that one innocent person should be condemned. . . . I had rather judge a witch to be an honest woman, than judge an honest woman as a witch.

# The Great Awakening

The preceding chapter set forth some of the problems that beset the New England Puritans during the latter half of the seventeenth century—fears of witchcraft, separatism as evidenced in Roger Williams and Anne Hutchinson, the "Half-Way" question, Indian wars, disease, problems with the food supply, and a waning of spiritual ardor. These and other difficulties plagued Christians. But the cooling of religious zeal most troubled many of the leaders, since it had been the primary intention of the founders to establish a tightly knit holy commonwealth, a new Zion, "a city set upon a hill" for all the world to behold what God was newly accomplishing for the redemption of humankind.

From the middle of the century the clergy frequently arraigned the laity for "declension" from the earnestness of their fathers. As embodied in the formula of the jeremiad, this lament for the colony's departing glory was accompanied by stern warnings of God's judgments on a backslidden people. Increase Mather, pastor of the Second Church of Boston, declared in 1678:

> In the last age, in the days of our fathers, in other parts of the world, scarce a sermon preached but some evidently converted, and sometimes hundreds in a sermon. Which of us can say we have seen the like? Clear, sound conversions are not frequent in some congregations. The body of the rising generation is a poor, perishing, unconverted, and (except the Lord pour down his Spirit) an undone generation.

After 1670, still other difficulties came. Massachusetts lost her charter in 1684. Throughout this time Quakers, Baptists, and other dissenting groups were making inroads into the Puritan Zion. What was to be done? Had the early vision of splendid glory come to naught? Had God withdrawn his grace, and, if so, was it irretrievably lost? New England's clergy had many questions and few answers.

## The five harvests

One pastor, however, did more than bemoan the situation and scold his congregation. Solomon Stoddard (1643–1729), a dynamic leader with influence and ideas, pastored the large church at Northampton, which was located far from Boston on the Connecticut River. Because of his influence he was nicknamed "the Pope of the Valley." Following the custom of the time, Stoddard remained in that pulpit for his lifetime, completing an amazing pastorate of sixty years. Due to his failing health, in 1727 the church selected as assistant his own grandson, Jonathan Edwards (1703–1758), who would continue the evangelistic tradition Stoddard had begun. While Stoddard must be recognized as the initiator of mass evangelism and revivalism in America, he was in reality only recalling what had happened earlier in the British Isles, and demanding that it happen in the New World as the obvious answer to New England's spiritual decline. In 1596 a revival had occurred in Edinburgh, and in 1624 through 1630 a series of awakenings had shaken Ulster and Scotland. These had been widely reported.

Was the root cause of New England's problems the declension of the population at large? No, Stoddard answered. The clergy was the ultimate problem, because it was not doing its job. While Puritan pastors were good preachers, their preaching was often misdirected. "We are not sent into the pulpit to shew our wit and eloquence, but to set the consciences of men on fire; not to nourish the vain humors of people, but to lance and wound the consciences of men," Stoddard declared. The clergy was wailing over New England's lost glory, but it had failed to preach for conversions:

> When men don't preach much about the danger of damnation, there is want of good preaching. Some preachers preach much about moral duties and the blessed estate of godly men, but don't seek to awaken sinners and make them sensible of their danger. They cry for reformation. These things are very needful in their places to be spoken unto; but if sinners don't often hear of judgment and damnation, few will be converted. Many men are in a deep sleep and flatter themselves as if there were no hell, or at least that God will not deal so harshly with them as to damn them. Psalm 36:2. Ministers must give them no rest in such a condition. They must pull them as brands out of the burnings. . . . Ministers are faulty when they speak to them with gentleness, as Eli rebuked his sons. Christ Jesus often warned them of the danger of damnation: Matt. 5:29, 30.[1]

Stoddard developed his theology of awakening in other writings. The church must not expect constant revival. God does not work that way. There may be long periods when God allows his people to backslide into sin, even as New England was in the gloom of spiritual darkness. But there also may be periods of renewal. This *law of alternation* operates not only in the church at large, but also in individual Christians. Therefore, Stoddard did not find anything unusual in New England's spiritual deadness; it was simply a trough period. A resurgence of God's power might be expected. In other words, theologians were ignorant of spiritual laws when they thought that the future course was inexorably downward.

Stoddard followed his own advice completely. In response to his strong preaching and pastoral methods, five revivals, or "harvests" as he termed them, came upon the area of Northampton in 1679, 1683, 1696, 1712, and 1718. People turned to Christ in numbers unequaled elsewhere in New England before the Great Awakening. After the 1712 awakening Stoddard preached a powerful sermon on revival and the spiritual law of alternation (selection 5).

After his grandfather's death in 1729 Edwards assumed the pastorate of the Northampton church. He differed with Stoddard regarding some points of theology but was in complete agreement with him regarding the need for evangelism and conversions. In 1734 he preached a series of expository sermons, and suddenly "the Spirit of God began extraordinarily to set in and wonderfully to work among us." In *A Faithful Narrative of the Surprising Work of God* Edwards attempted to objectively report what had happened and why, attributing all to God's doing. It was published in Boston and London, and had a large readership and influence. It reported,

> This work of God, as it was carried on, and the number of true saints multiplied, soon made a glorious alteration in the town. . . . More than 300 souls were savingly brought home to Christ, in this town, in the space of half a year. . . . I hope that by far the greater part of persons in this town, above sixteen years of age, are such as have the saving knowledge of Jesus Christ.[2]

As other pastors began to preach for decisions, awakening spread to two dozen communities in western Massachusetts and Connecticut, lingering for a few years in

Jonathan Edwards

some places. While there had been sporadic revivals in New England previously, never before had so many towns been involved at once.

## "Awakened" Middle Colonies

Even earlier than Jonathan Edwards's Northampton awakening of 1734, a Dutch Reformed pastor in Raritan, New Jersey, Theodore J. Frelinghuysen (1691–1747?), had been preaching searching sermons. The four small, pastorless congregations around Raritan had eagerly welcomed Frelinghuysen upon his arrival from Holland in 1720. These Dutch farmers must have been stunned when their new pastor began his ministry by declaring his principles in no uncertain terms, and demanding a shattering experience of conversion. Frelinghuysen was clearly shocked at their laxity, finding "that while horse-racing, gambling, dissipation, and rudeness of various kinds, were common, the sanctuary was attended at convenience, and religion consisted of the mere formal pursuit of the routine of duty," according to one biographer.[3] Their new pastor regarded many of them as unregenerate, self-righteous, and pharisaical. There were several attempts made to oust Frelinghuysen, but other pastors and the Classis of Amsterdam, which had sent him, supported his evangelistic preaching. Eventually he won out, generating many conversions and beginning a small awakening around Raritan.

In 1726 Gilbert Tennent (1703–1764), a spirited young Presbyterian pastor with an M.A. degree from Yale, came to New Brunswick near Raritan to minister to the English-speaking people there. Tennent saw the effects of Frelinghuysen's evangelism, became friends with him, changed his own pastoral methods, and immediately found success with souls. Tennent's father, William Tennent, Sr., had brought up his sons in classic Calvinism, and began his "Log College" near Neshaminy, Pennsylvania, to train young men for the ministry. William, Sr., was well qualified to educate clergymen, for as a scholar and teacher he was without an equal among the Presbyterians. The men he trained were all convinced evangelists with a vision to begin an awakening throughout the Middle Colonies.

As expectations of a general revival mounted, at this juncture a twenty-five year old Anglican priest, George Whitefield (1714–1770; pronounced "Whîtfield"), came from England on October 30, 1739. Whitefield had a stentorian voice and despite his youth had already achieved phenomenal success in London, Gloucester, and Bristol, with crowds of twenty or thirty thousand being common, and one audience estimated at eighty thousand. Newspapers in America had alerted the colonists to this young revivalist, telling of the awakenings he had begun in Britain, his huge audiences, his hearers' awed silences, and of the people who climbed trees to hear him preach.

When Whitefield arrived in Philadelphia he intended only to stay long enough to pick up supplies for the orphanage he planned to build in Georgia. Surely he had not contemplated a preaching tour through America, and he probably knew little or nothing of the awakenings in New Jersey and New England. But William Tennent, Sr., immediately met him and asked Whitefield to assist in the efforts to spread the awakening. For the revivalist clergy, his coming could not have been more opportune. Nothing imaginable could have created such vast public interest as did Whitefield, for he played down sectarianism, deemphasized his own Anglican ordination, and appealed to all groups.

Whitefield's success in Philadelphia was overwhelming—all that Tennent hoped for. The clergy were uniformly friendly, all churches were open to him, and the public response was so great that he moved to outdoor preaching within a few days. Typical entries in his *Journal* read:

> Monday, November 5 . . . I was visited in the afternoon by the Presbyterian minister, and went afterwards to see the Baptist teacher, who seems to be a spiritual man; and spent part of the evening most agreeably with two Quakers.

> Friday, November 9 . . . preached again at six in the evening, from the Court House steps. I believe there were nearly two thousand more present to-night than last night. Even in London, I never observed so profound a silence.[4]

On November 12, Whitefield left Philadelphia for New Jersey, preached in Gilbert Tennent's church, and went on to New York. Then he resumed his original intention to go to Georgia to set up an orphanage, reaching Savannah on January 10, 1740. All this time he was getting a number of invitations to conduct a tour of New England, and he accepted. Arriving at Boston on September 19, he found a great air of expectancy; local revivals were already in progress and were multiplying. The Boston *News-Letter* reported:

> Last Thursday Evening the Rev'd Mr. Whitefield arrived from Rhode Island. . . . in the Afternoon he preach'd to a vast Congregation in the Rev'd Dr. Colman's Meeting-House. The next Day he preach'd in the Forenoon at the South Church to a Crowded Audience, and in the Afternoon to about 5000 People on the Common: and Lord's-Day in the afternoon having preach'd to a great Number of People at the Old Brick Church, the House not being large enough to hold those that crowded to hear him, when the Exercise was over, He went and preached in the Field, to at least 8000 Persons.[5]

For over a month Whitefield evangelized in the Boston area and as far north as York, Maine. After him Gilbert Tennent conducted an evangelistic tour of New England, attempting to solidify Whitefield's success and to spread the revival still farther. Controversy followed, especially when James Davenport, a Congregational preacher of unsound mind, injected fanaticism into the fray.

## The effects of revival

Sociological and psychological interpretations in the twentieth century have played down New England's Great Awakening or attributed it to other than religious concern. But Edwin S. Gaustad has suggested, "There is, to the contrary, abundant evidence that this religious turmoil in New England was in fact 'great and general,' that it knew no boundaries, social or geographical, that it was both urban and rural, and that it reached both lower and upper classes."[6]

In the Middle Colonies, Gilbert Tennent, ardent and boiling with indignation that any clergymen would oppose what he was convinced was the work of the Holy Spirit, preached one of the most notorious sermons of the period. *The Danger of An Unconverted Ministry,* preached on March 8, 1740, at Nottingham, Pennsylvania, excoriated anti-revivalist "Old Lights." Their opposition to the awakening, Tennent said, proved that they were themselves unregenerate. This spark set the Presbyterian Church on fire. The sermon was both praised and damned in its own day, and estimates of it still differ. Leonard Trinterud has pronounced it "no mere tirade, but a carefully wrought polemic of such devastating efficiency that it accomplished too much,"[7] eventually bringing schism to the Presbyterian Church (selection 6).

After preaching this sermon, Tennent was encouraged by Whitefield to "set out for Boston, in order to blow up the divine fire lately kindled there."[8] In what was to be a bitterly cold winter, Tennent accepted the advice and began, in December 1740, a three-month evangelistic mission to New England, touring through parts of Rhode Island and eastern Connecticut in addition to Boston. Despite the frigid weather, people responded eagerly, made decisions, and came to ministers for spiritual counsel. William Cooper, assistant pastor at Boston's Brattle Street Church, stated that "more came to him in one week in deep concern about their souls, than had come in the whole twenty-four years of his preceding ministry."[9]

Unfortunately for the awakening, the unbalanced pastor at Southold, Long Island, James Davenport, decided to follow up the successes of Whitefield and Tennent in the summer of 1741. Working his way along the coast of Connecticut, in parish after parish he demanded that the clergy recount their spiritual state to him so that he might judge if they were converted. In New Haven he denounced pastor Joseph Noyes as "an unconverted hypocrite and the devil incarnate." All the friends of the awakening were forced to wonder if this was its inevitable result.

With Connecticut bewildered by these events, defenders of the revival needed to clarify much. The most eminent of America's theologians and the intellectual champion of spiritual awakening, Jonathan Edwards, had been invited to speak at the Yale College commencement on September 10, 1741, just a few days after Davenport left town. Well aware of the demand for solid principles of discrimination between sound spirituality and wild fanaticism, Edwards faced the faculty and students and announced his topic: "The distinguishing marks of a work of the Spirit of God, applied to that uncommon operation that has lately appeared on the minds of many of the people of this land: with a particular consideration of the extraordinary circumstances with which this work is attended" (selection 7).

Thus began a critical but sympathetic review of the Great Awakening, which Edwards would continue to refine until 1746 when he published *A Treatise Concerning Religious Affections,* the most profound study of religious psychology to be published in America. Finding nine major problems in the behavior of people like Davenport (but never naming him), he dismissed those problems and demonstrated that they prove nothing, positively or negatively, about the revival. Then he quickly moved on to positive signs that the work is of God, and he found five distinctive marks that could not be duplicated as counterfeit or fraudulent. Determining that the Great Awakening was indeed of God, Edwards warned against hindering or opposing the work of the Holy Spirit, which would be the unpardonable sin.[10]

Meanwhile in New England, Davenport so upset supporters of the awakening that they passed a declaration on July 1, 1742, that he had acted to the "disservice of Religion." The declaration asserted, "We judge it therefore to be our present Duty not to invite Mr. Davenport into our Places of publick Worship." He was jailed, and the court declared him *non compos mentis.* Davenport had singled out for his wild ire the junior pastor of Boston's First Church, Charles Chauncy (1705–1787), who eventually espoused universalism and was increasingly the vocal leader of New England's "Old Lights."

Chauncy was orthodox when he was ordained in 1727, but he soon began to move toward Arminianism, and by 1739 he was entrenched in the ranks of the liberals. When Whitefield preached at the senior pastor's invitation in the First Church pulpit Chauncy had to suffer in silence. But object he must, and in November 1742 he published anonymously *A Letter . . . to Mr. George Wishart* in which he attacked Whitefield. Later, Chauncy was so riled against the awakening that he determined to go on a strenuous three-hundred-mile circuit to gather all the ammunition he could against it. The result of his investigations appeared in the summer of 1743, a huge octavo volume of 424 pages entitled *Seasonable Thoughts on the State of Religion in New England.*

However, Chauncy's book was dated; the Great Awakening had by then largely run its course. Its aftermath: from 25,000 to 50,000 new members for the churches; 150 new churches founded in New England and more in the Middle Colonies; five colleges founded in the surge of energy from the revival (Dartmouth College, the University of Pennsylvania, and Princeton, Rutgers, and Brown universities), and an enlarged understanding throughout the colonies of religious and political liberty.

## Select Bibliography

Edwards, Jonathan. *The Works of Jonathan Edwards*, 7 vols. Vol. 4, *The Great Awakening: A Faithful Narrative*, C. C. Goen, ed. New Haven, Conn.: Yale University Press, 1972.

Gaustad, Edwin S. *The Great Awakening in New England.* New York: Harper, 1957.

Heimert, Alan, and Perry Miller, eds. *The Great Awakening: Documents Illustrating the Crisis and Its Consequences.* Indianapolis: Bobbs-Merrill, 1967.

Miller, Perry. *Errand into the Wilderness.* New York: Harper and Row, 1964.

————. *The New England Mind: From Colony to Province.* 1953; repr., Cambridge, Mass.: Harvard University Press, 1983.

————. *Jonathan Edwards.* 1949; repr., Amherst, Mass.: University of Massachusetts Press, 1981.

Rutman, Darrett B., ed. *The Great Awakening: Event and Exegesis.* New York: Wiley, 1970.

Stout, Harry S. *The Divine Dramatist: George Whitefield and the Rise of Modern Evangelicalism.* Grand Rapids: Eerdmans, 1991.

Tracy, Joseph. *The Great Awakening.* 1841; repr., Edinburgh: Banner of Truth, 1976.

Trinterud, Leonard J. *The Forming of an American Tradition.* Philadelphia: Westminster, 1949.

Westerkamp, Marilyn J. *Triumph of the Laity: Scots-Irish Piety and the Great Awakening, 1625–1760.* New York: Oxford University Press, 1988.

# On the Occasion of an Unusual Outpouring of the Spirit of God

## *Solomon Stoddard (1712)*

Doctrine. There are some special Seasons wherein God doth in a remarkable Manner revive Religion among his People. God doth not always carry on his Work in the Church in the same Proportion. As it is in Nature, there be great Vicissitudes. . . . So there be times wherein there is a plentiful Effusion of the Spirit of God, and Religion is in a more flourishing Condition. Matthew 11.12. . . .

Question. How is it with a People when Religion is revived?

Answer. 1. *Saints are quickened.* It contributes much to the flourishing of Religion, when Righteous men flourish in Holiness, as it is foretold, Psal. 92.12. . . . There be times of Temptation, when godly Men are in a flourishing Condition, Matthew 25.5. "While the Bridegroom tarried, they all slumbered and slept." They grew worldly, and Proud, and Formal, and didn't maintain much of the Life of Godliness. And there be times when their Hearts are lifted up in the ways of God, as is said of Jehoshaphat. 2 Chron. 17:6. When the Weak are as David. When their Souls are in a prosperous Condition, and they are in gracious Frames of Spirit, going on from Strength to Strength. Sometimes they run the ways of God's Commandments, because God enlarges their Hearts. Psal. 119.32. . . . This mightily increaseth Holiness among a People.

2. *Sinners are Converted.* God makes the Gospel at times to be very Powerful. So it was in the Primitive Times. Romans 15.29. . . . There is a mighty Change wrought in a little Time. They that were Dead, are made Alive, and they that were Lost are Found. The Gospel is made a Savour of Life to many. Sometimes there is great Complaint for want of this. . . . At other Times the Number of Saints is greatly multiplied. Acts 9.31. "Then had the churches rest throughout all Judea and Galilee and Samaria, and were edified; and walking in the fear of the Lord, and in the comfort of the Holy Ghost, were multiplied."

3. *Many that are not Converted, do become more Religious.* When Israel went out of Egypt, there was a mixt Multitude that went with them. So when God

Source: Solomon Stoddard, *The Efficacy of the Fear of Hell* (Boston: T. Fleet, 1712), 187–89, 191–94.

is pleased to Convert a Number, there be many others that have a common Work of the Spirit on their Hearts; they are affected with their Condition, Reform their evil Manners, and engage in Religious Duties, and attain to considerable Zeal, and are full of Religious Affections. . . . When God works savingly upon some, it is frequent that others have common Iluminations, whereby great Reformation is wrought, and the Reputation of Religion advanced, and People are disposed to keep the external Covenant; and so much Wrath is prevented. . . .

*This reviving is sometimes of longer, and sometimes of shorter Continuance.* Sometimes Religion flourishes in a Country for a great many years together. So it did for twenty nine Years in the Days of Hezekiah. 2 Chron. 29.1. So when God pours out his Spirit, sometimes the Work continues many Years. . . . But sometimes it is for a less space. We have reason to think that there was much of the converting Presence of God in Corinth for the space of a Year and a half. Acts 18.9, 10. Sometimes it is not so long. Then there is a great stirring for a little Time, and then it fails. . . .

*God is very Arbitrary in this Matter.* The People of God are praying, and Waiting for this Mercy. Habakkuk 3.2. Psal. 85.6. "Wilt thou not revive us again, that thy people may rejoice in thee?" But God will take his own time for this Mercy. . . . No Man can tell beforehand when the Work of God shall Prosper in this or that Place. . . .

Use. 1. *Learn from hence, that the Church of God is subject to great Changes.* Sometimes Religion flourishes, and sometimes it languishes. It is indeed so with particular Souls: sometimes they go on from Strength to Strength, and their Hearts are lifted up in the Ways of God . . . and at other Times they are in a slumbering Condition. They are like sick Men that are unfit for Service, like Trees in Winter. So it is with the Church of God; there is but little of the presence of God among them. There is a great Scarcity of Godly Men. Iniquity abounds, and the Love of many waxes Cold. At other Times Religion is the great thing that is minded; Men are taking the Kingdom of Heaven with Violence. They honour their Profession, and their Light shines before Men, so that they glorify their Father that is in Heaven. . . .

2. We should beg of God, that Religion may revive in this Land. . . . Consider There is a great Need of this. For want of revival, the Land is mightily corrupted, and Sin prevails greatly in all places, and the Profession that Men make is dishonored. It is very acceptable to God to pray for this. There is Encouragement to beg for Revival in the Word of God, when the Church is in a Withering Condition. We must not conclude that it will always be so, and

if we are faithful in Prayer, God will again bring his Church back to a flourishing Condition.

3. Persons should be very careful at such a time, that they do nothing to quench the Spirit. As we must be careful that we do not provoke God to take away his Spirit, so we must be careful that we do not quench the Spirit. 1 Thes. 5.19. This may be done by indulging in different types of Sin. 1. By slighting the Word of God. 2. By making a worldly Cry. 3. By Contention among the Brethren, and a spirit of bickering and strife.

---

## Selection 6

# The Danger of an Unconverted Ministry

### *Gilbert Tennent (1740)*

And Jesus, when he came out, saw much People and was moved with Compassion towards them, because they were as Sheep not having a Shepherd. [Mark 6:34]

As a faithful Ministry is a great Ornament, Blessing and Comfort, to the Church of GOD; even the Feet of such Messengers are beautiful; So on the contrary, an ungodly Ministry is a great Curse and Judgment: These Caterpillars labour to devour every green Thing. . . .

Second General Head of Discourse, is to shew, Why such People, who have no better than the Old Pharisee-Teachers, are to be pitied? And

1. Natural Men have no Call of GOD to the Ministerial Work under the Gospel-Dispensation.

Isn't it a principal Part of the ordinary Call of GOD to the Ministerial Work, to aim at the Glory of GOD, and, in Subordination thereto, the Good of Souls, as their chief Marks in their Undertaking that Work? And can any natural Man on Earth do this? No! no! Every Skin of them has an evil Eye; for no Cause can produce Effects above its own Power. . . .

2. The Ministry of natural Men is uncomfortable to gracious Souls. . . .

Natural Men, not having true Love to Christ and the Souls of their Fellow-Creatures, hence their Discourses are cold and sapless, and as it were freeze

Source: Gilbert Tennent, "The Danger of an Unconverted Ministry" (Boston: Rogers and Fowle, 1742), 2, 7–8, 10–12, 17–20.

between their Lips. And not being sent of GOD, they want that divine Authority, with which the faithful Ambassadors of Christ are clothed, who herein resemble their blessed Master, of whom it is said, That He taught as one having Authority, and not as the Scribes. Mat. 7.29. . . .

Gilbert Tennent (Billy Graham Center Museum, Wheaton, Ill.)

3. The Ministry of natural Men, is for the most part unprofitable; which is confirmed by a three-fold Evidence, viz. of Scripture, Reason, and Experience. . . .

Look into the Congregations of unconverted Ministers, and see what a sad Security reigns there; not a Soul convinced that can be heard of, for many Years together; and yet the Ministers are easy; for they say they do their Duty!

4. The Ministry of natural Men is dangerous, both in respect of the Doctrines, and Practice of Piety. The Doctrines of Original Sin, Justification by Faith alone, and the other Points of Calvinism, are very cross to the Grain of the unrenew'd Nature. And tho' Men, by the Influence of a good Education, and Hopes of Preferment may have the Edge of their natural Enmity against them blunted; yet it's far from being broken or removed: It's only the saving Grace of GOD, that can give us a true Relish for those Nature-humbling Doctrines; and so effectually secure us from being infected by the contrary. Is not the Carnality of the Ministry, one great Cause of the general Spread of Arminianism, Socinianism, Arianism, and Deism, at this Day through the World? . . .

And indeed, my Brethren, we should join our Endeavours to our Prayers. The most likely Method to stock the Church with a faithful Ministry, in the present Situation of Things, the publick Academies being so much corrupted and abused generally, is, To encourage private Schools, or Seminaries of Learning, which are under the Care of skilful and experienced Christians; in which only those should be admitted, who upon strict Examination, have in the Judgment of a reasonable Charity, the plain Evidences of experimental Religion. Pious and experienced Youths, who have a good natural Capacity, and great Desires after the Ministerial Work, from good Motives, might be sought for, and found up and down the Country, and put to Private Schools of the Prophets; especially in such Places, where the Publick ones are not. . . .

The Improvement of the Subject remains. And

1. If it be so, That the Case of those, who have no other, or no better than Pharisee-Teachers, is to be pitied: Then what a Scrole & Scene of Mourning, and Lamentation, and Wo, is opened! because of the Swarms of Locusts, the Crowds of Pharisees, that have as covetously as cruelly, crept into the Ministry, in this adulterous Generation! who as nearly resemble the Character given of the old Pharisees, in the Doctrinal Part of this Discourse, as one Crow's Egg does another. . . .

2. From what has been said, we may learn, That such who are contented under a dead Ministry, have not in them the Temper of that Saviour they profess. . . . And alas! isn't this the Case of Multitudes? If they can get one, that has the Name of a Minister, with a Band, and a black Coat or Gown to carry on a Sabbathdays among them, although never so coldly, and unsuccessfully; if he is free from gross Crimes in Practice, and takes good Care to keep at a due Distance from their Consciences . . . O! think the poor Fools, that is a fine Man indeed; our Minister is a prudent charitable man, he is not always harping upon Terror, and sounding Damnation in our Ears. . . .

3. We may learn, the Mercy and Duty of those that enjoy a faithful Ministry. Let such glorify GOD, for so distinguishing a Privilege, and labour to walk worthy of it, to all Well-pleasuring. . . .

4. If the Ministry of natural Men be as it has been represented; Then it is both lawful and expedient to go from them to hear Godly Persons; yea, it's so far from being sinful to do this, that one who lives under a pious Minister of lesser Gifts, after having honestly endeavor'd to get Benefit by his Ministry, and yet gets little or none, but doth find real Benefit and more Benefit elsewhere; I say, he may lawfully go, and that frequently, where he gets most Good to his precious Soul, after regular Application to the Pastor where he lives, for his Consent, and proposing the Reasons thereof; when this is done in the Spirit of Love and Meekness, without Contempt of any, as also without rash Anger or vain Curiosity. . . .

Again it may be objected, That the aforesaid Practice tends to grieve our Parish-Minister, and to break Congregations in Pieces.

I answer, If our Parish-Minister be grieved at our greater Good, or prefers his Credit before it; then he has good Cause to grieve over his own Rottenness, and Hypocrisie. And as for Breaking of Congregations to Pieces, upon the Account of People's Going from Place to Place, to hear the Word, with a view to get greater Good; that spiritual Blindness and Death, that so generally prevails, will put this out of Danger. It is but a very few, that have got any spiritual Relish; the most will venture their Souls with any Formalist, and be well satisfied with the sapless Discourses of such dead Drones. . . .

And let those who live under the Ministry of dead Men, whether they have got the Form of Religion or not, repair to the Living, where they may be edified. . . . And O! that vacant Congregations would take due care in the Choice of their Ministers! Here indeed they should hasten slowly. The Church of Ephesus is commended, for Trying them which said they were Apostles, and were not; and for finding them Liars. Hypocrites are against all Knowing of others, and Judging, in order to hide their own Filthiness; like Thieves they flee a Search, because of the stolen Goods. But the more they endeavor to hide, the more they expose their Shame. Does not the spiritual Man judge all things? Tho' he cannot know the States of subtil Hypocrites infallibly; yet may he not give a near Guess, who are the Sons of Sceva, by their Manner of Praying, Preaching, and Living? Many Pharisees-Teachers have got a long fine String of Prayer by Heart, so that they are never at a Loss about it; their Prayers and preachings are generally of a Length, and both as dead as a Stone, and without all Savour. . . .

I shall conclude this Discourse with the Words of the Apostle Paul, 2 Cor. 11.14–15.

And no marvel; for Satan himself is transformed into an Angel of Light: Therefore it is no great Thing if his Ministers also be transformed as the Ministers of Righteousness; whose End shall be according to their Works.

---

## Selection 7

---

# The Distinguishing Marks of a Work of the Spirit of God

## *Jonathan Edwards (1741)*

Beloved, believe not every spirit, but try the spirits whether they are of God; because many false prophets are gone out into the world. [1 John 4:1]

The apostolical age, or the age in which the apostles lived and preached the Gospel, was an age of the greatest outpouring of the Spirit of God that ever was; and that both as to the extraordinary influences and gifts of the Spirit, in

Source: Jonathan Edwards, "The Distinguishing Marks Of A Work of the Spirit of God" (Boston: 1741); text is from Jonathan Edwards, *The Great Awakening: A Faithful Narrative,* ed. C. C. Goen (New Haven, Conn.: Yale University Press, 1972), 226, 228–32, 234, 236–37, 248–49, 250–51, 253, 254–55, 260–61.

inspiration and miracles, and also as to his ordinary operations, in convincing, converting, enlightening and sanctifying the souls of men. But as the influences of the true Spirit abounded, so counterfeits did also then abound: the Devil was abundant in mimicking both the ordinary and extraordinary influences of the Spirit of God, as is manifest by innumerable passages of the apostles' writings. This made it very necessary that the church of Christ should be furnished with some certain rules, and distinguishing and clear marks by which she might proceed safely in judging of spirits, and distinguish the true from the false, without danger of being imposed upon. The giving such rules is the plain design of this chapter, where we have this matter more expressly and fully treated of than anywhere else in the Bible. The Apostle here, of set purpose, undertakes to supply the church of God with such marks of the true Spirit as may be plain and safe, and surely distinguishing, and well accommodated to use and practice: and that the subject might be clearly and sufficiently handled, he insists upon it throughout the chapter: which makes it wonderful that what is said in this chapter, is no more taken notice of in this extraordinary day, when that which is so remarkable appears; such an uncommon operation on the minds of people, that is so extensive; and there is such a variety of opinions concerning it, and so much talk about the work of the Spirit. . . .

## Negative signs

But before I proceed particularly to speak to these, I would prepare my way by first observing negatively, in some instances, what are not signs that we are to judge of a work by, whether it be the work of the Spirit of God or no; and especially, what are no evidences that a work that is wrought amongst a people, is not the work of the Spirit of God.

1. Nothing can certainly be concluded from this, that the work that appears is carried on in a way very unusual and extraordinary. 'Tis no sign that a work is not the work of the Spirit of God, that it is carried on in such a way as the same Spirit of God heretofore has not been wont to carry on his work. . . . The Spirit of God is sovereign in his operations; and we know that he uses a great variety; and we can't tell how great a variety he may use, within the compass of the rules he himself has fixed. We ought not to limit God where he has not limited himself. If a work be never so different from the work of God's Spirit that has formerly been, yet if it only agrees in those things that the Word of God has given us as the distinguishing signs of a work of his Spirit, that is sufficient to determine us entirely in its favor.

Therefore 'tis not reasonable to determine that a work is not the work of God's Spirit, because of the extraordinary degree in which the minds of persons

# THE
# Diftinguifhing Marks
## Of a Work of the
# SPIRIT of GOD.

Applied to that uncommon Opération that has lately appeared on the Minds of many of the People of this Land :

With a particular Confideration of the extraordinary Circumftances with which this Work is attended.

# A DISCOURSE

Delivered at *New-Haven, September* 10th 1741. Being the Day after the Commencement ;

And now. Publifhed at the earneft Defire of many Minifters and other Gentlemen that heard it ; with great Enlargements.

# By *Jonathan Edwards*, A. M.

Paftor of the Church of CHRIST at *Northampton.*

With a Preface by the Rev Mr. COOPER of *Bofton.*

Joh 10. 4,5 *And the Sheep follow him, for they know his Voice ; and a Stranger will they not follow, but will flee from him, for they know not the Voice of Strangers.*

BOSTON : Printed andSold by S. KNEELAND and T. GREEN, in Queeñftreet, over againft thePrifon. 1741.

are influenced and wrought upon. If they seem to have an extraordinary conviction of the dreadful nature of sin, and a very uncommon sense of the misery of a Christless condition, or seem to have extraordinary views of the certainty and glory of divine things; and consequent on these apprehensions, are proportionably moved with very extraordinary affections of fear and sorrow, desire, love or joy: or if the change that seems to be made in persons, the alteration in their affections and frames, be very sudden and the work that is wrought on people's minds seems to be carried on with very unusual swiftness, and the persons that are thus strangely affected are very many, and many of them are very young; and also be very unusual in many other circumstances, not infringing upon Scripture marks of a work of the Spirit; these things are no argument that the work is not a work of the Spirit of God. . . .

2. A work is not to be judged of by any effects on the bodies of men; such as tears, trembling, groans, loud outcries, agonies of body, or the failing of bodily strength. The influence the minds of persons are under, is not to be judged of one way or the other, whether it be from the Spirit of God or no, by such effects on the body; and the reason is, because the Scripture nowhere gives us any such rule. . . . There are none of us but what suppose, and would have been ready at any time to say it, that the misery of hell is doubtless so dreadful, and eternity so vast, that if a person should have a clear apprehension of that misery as it is, it would be more than his feeble frame could bear; and especially, if at the same time he saw himself in great danger of it, and to be utterly uncertain whether he should be delivered from it, yea, and to have no security from it one day or hour. If we consider human nature, we need not wonder that when persons have a very great sense of that which is so amazingly dreadful, and also have a great view of their own wickedness and God's anger, that things seem to them to forebode speedy and immediate destruction. . . .

So it may be easily accounted for, that a true sense of the glorious excellency of the Lord Jesus Christ, and of his wonderful dying love, and the exercise of a truly spiritual love and joy, should be such as very much to overcome the bodily strength. We are all ready to own that no man can see God and live; and that 'tis but a very small part of that apprehension of the glory and love of Christ, and exercise of love to him and joy in him, which the saints in heaven are the subjects of, that our present frame can bear: therefore 'tis not at all strange that God should sometimes give his saints such foretastes of heaven, as to diminish their bodily strength. . . .

3. 'Tis no argument that an operation that appears on the minds of a people, is not the work of the Spirit of God, that it occasions a great ado, and a great deal of noise about religion. . . .

4. 'Tis no argument that an operation that appears on the minds of a people, is not the work of the Spirit of God, that many that are the subjects of it, have great impressions on their imaginations. . . .

It is no argument that a work is not the work of the Spirit of God, that some that are the subjects of it, have in some extraordinary frames, been in a kind of ecstasy, wherein they have been carried beyond themselves, and have had their minds transported into a train of strong and pleasing imaginations, and kind of visions, as though they were wrapped up even to heaven, and there saw glorious sights. I have been acquainted with some such instances; and I see no manner of need of bringing in the help of the Devil into the account that we give of these things; nor yet of supposing them to be of the same nature with the visions of the prophets, or St. Paul's rapture into paradise (II Cor. 12:1–4). Human nature, under these vehement and intense exercises and affections of mind, which some persons are the subjects of, is all that need be brought into the account. . . .

Some talk of it as an unreasonable thing to think to fright persons to heaven; but I think it is a reasonable thing to endeavor to fright persons away from hell, that stand upon the brink of it, and are just ready to fall into it, and are senseless of their danger: 'tis a reasonable thing to fright a person out of an house on fire. The word "fright" is commonly used for sudden causeless fear, or groundless surprise; but surely a just fear, that there is good reason for, though it be very great, is not to be spoken against under any such name.

## Positive evidences

Having thus shown, in some instance, what are not evidences that a work that is wrought among a people is not a work of the Spirit of God, I now proceed in the second place, as was proposed, to shew positively, what are the sure, distinguishing, Scripture evidences and marks of a work of the Spirit of God, by which we may proceed in judging of any operation we find in ourselves, or see among a people, without danger of being misled.

And in this, as I said before, I shall confine myself wholly to those marks which are given us by the Apostle in the chapter wherein is my text, where this matter is particularly handled, and more plainly and fully than anywhere else in the Bible. And in speaking to these marks, I shall take them in the order in which I find them in the chapter.

1. When that spirit that is at work amongst a people is observed to operate after such a manner, as to raise their esteem of that Jesus that was born of the Virgin, and was crucified without the gates of Jerusalem; and seems more to confirm and establish their minds in the truth of what the Gospel declares to us of his being the Son of God, and the Saviour of men; 'tis a sure sign that that spirit is the Spirit of God.

2. When the spirit that is at work operates against the interest of Satan's kingdom, which lies in encouraging and establishing sin, and cherishing men's worldly lusts; this is a sure sign that 'tis a true, and not a false spirit. . . .

3. That spirit that operates in such a manner, as to cause in men a greater regard to the Holy Scriptures, and establishes them more in their truth and divinity, is certainly the Spirit of God. . . .

4. Another rule to judge of spirits may be drawn from those opposite compellations given to the two opposite spirits, in the last words of the 6th verse, "The spirit of truth" and "the spirit of error." These words do exhibit the two opposite characters of the Spirit of God, and other spirits that counterfeit his operations. And therefore, if by observing the manner of the operation of a spirit that is at work among a people, we see that it operates as a spirit of truth, leading persons to truth, convincing them of those things that are true, we may safely determine that 'tis a right and true spirit. . . .

5. If the spirit that is at work among a people operates as a spirit of love to God and man, 'tis a sure sign that 'tis the Spirit of God. This sign the Apostle insists upon from the 7th verse to the end of the chapter: "Beloved, let us love one another; for love is of God, and everyone that loveth is born of God, and knoweth God. He that loveth not, knoweth not God, for God is love, etc."

## Application

1. From what has been said, I will venture to draw this inference, viz. that that extraordinary influence that has lately appeared on the minds of people abroad in this land, causing in them an uncommon concern and engagedness

of mind about the things of religion, is undoubtedly, in the general, from the Spirit of God. There are but two things that need to be known in order to such a work's being judged of, viz. facts and rules. The rules of the Word of God we have laid before us; and as to facts, there are but two ways that we can come at them, so as to be in a capacity to compare them with the rules, either by our own observation, or by information from others that have had opportunity to observe.

As to this work that has lately been carried on in the land, there are many things concerning it that are notorious, and known by everybody (unless it be some that have been very much out of the way of observing and hearing indeed) that unless the Apostle John was out in his rules, are sufficient to determine it to be in general, the work of God. 'Tis notorious that the spirit that is at work, takes off persons' minds from the vanities of the world, and engages them in a deep concern about a future and eternal happiness in another world, and puts them upon earnestly seeking their salvation, and convinces them of the dreadfulness of sin, and of their own guilty and miserable state as they are by nature. It is notorious that it awakens men's consciences, and makes 'em sensible of the dreadfulness of God's anger, and causes in them a great desire, and earnest care and endeavor to obtain his favor. It is notorious that it puts them upon a more diligent improvement of the means of grace which God has appointed.

# Concern for Indians and Black Slaves

The story of intolerance and persecution over the centuries is most depressing. Those few souls who demanded an end to the prevailing bigotry of their times were a visionary and a brave lot. In Europe protests against political, religious, and racial intolerance, which was the accepted practice of that age, began to grow toward the end of the sixteenth century.

The sixteenth century in France saw an enormous amount of bloodshed, most notoriously the killing of thousands of French Calvinist Huguenots in the *St. Batholomew's Day Massacre* of 1572. Civil war between the militant Roman Catholics of the House of Guise and the Bourbons continued for years, ending in ironic fashion when the Catholic king, Henry III, was assassinated and the Huguenot leader Henry of Navarre made heir to the throne. To gain it he turned Catholic, saying that "Paris is well worth a Mass." He then ended the civil war in blood-drenched France and issued the *Edict of Nantes* in 1598, granting the Huguenots full toleration, civil rights, and the right to their own fortified towns. Thus the Edict brought in forced toleration, stating, "We permit those of the Pretended Reformed Religion to live and remain in all cities and places without being disturbed, vexed, molested, or forced to do anything against their conscience on the subject of religion." Such a law was hardly able to quell the bitter hatreds.

## The first Indian missions

In the New World tolerance of diversity and concern for people of other origins and persuasions came slowly, but there were some outstanding exceptions. While the Indians were often called "children of Satan," some of the colonists showed genuine concern for their salvation. Peaceful relations with the Indians of Virginia were greatly advanced by the marriage of Pocahontas and John Rolfe in 1613 and by her later social success in England.

In 1613 Alexander Whitaker's *Good Newes from Virginia* (selection 1) called Indians "naked slaves of the divell" but showed real care for them:

> Wherefore my brethren, put on the bowels of compassion, and let the lamen-
> table estate of these miserable people enter in your consideration: One God cre-
> ated us, they have reasonable soules and intellectuall faculties as well as wee. . . .
> If any of us should misdoubt that this barbarous people is uncapable of such
> heavenly mysteries, let such men know that they are farre mistaken in the nature
> of these men. . . . They are a very understanding generation, quicke of appre-
> hension, suddaine in their dispatches, subtile in their dealings, exquisite in their
> inventions, and industrious in their labour. . . . If they stoode in feare of us. . . .
> it were an easie matter to make them willingly to forsake the divell, to embrace
> the faith of Jesus Christ, and to be baptized.

John Eliot (1604–1690), "apostle to the Indians," was the most famous New Englander concerned with the original inhabitants. He came from England to Massachusetts in 1631 and became minister of the church in Roxbury. He learned the Indian dialects and began his work among them in 1646. He soon discovered that they preferred to live by themselves and by 1674 he gathered 3600 "praying Indians" into fourteen self-governing communities. Eliot raised money, even from England, and arranged for the Indians to have housing, jobs, clothes, and land. Then an Indian confederation angered by the expansion of white settlements began what came to be called *King Philip's War* (1675–1676). Much of Massachusetts and Rhode Island were devastated, with several hundred colonists killed and dozens of towns burned. This crippled the cause of missions for a time, but Eliot was so respected that support eventually returned.

Eliot never despaired. In 1687 he gave seventy-five acres of land in Roxbury for the teaching of Indians and blacks. His crowning achievement was the translation of the entire Bible into the Algonkian language in 1663, the first time the Scriptures had been printed in North America. With the Scriptures in their language, Eliot hoped that the Indians could teach their own people, train their own clergy, and be free of constant interference from the colonists. Renowned for learning, piety, evangelistic zeal, and practical wisdom, Eliot lived to a great age. Cotton Mather wrote, "He that writes of Eliot, must write of charity, or say nothing." In 1647 John Winthrop described some of Eliot's methods in his *Journal*.

## Tolerance and a "holy experiment"

No account of the advance of toleration would be complete without discussing the Quakers. Founded in England by George Fox in 1651, this "left-wing" of Puritanism seemed far too extreme for most people, for they had no ministry in the usual sense, no sacraments, no structure, and no liturgy. Plain in speech, plain in dress, and plain in behavior, they gathered in silence for worship until one of their number was moved by the Spirit to speak. While their integrity and industry were admirable, many found them to be offensive, blasphemous, and outrageous because they rejected most of Christianity's forms and sometimes invaded churches to interrupt the sermon with denunciations of false worship. The first Quaker missionaries to Boston, Ann Austin and Mary Fisher, arrived in 1656 and were followed a few weeks later by eight others. They soon were imprisoned and expelled after railing against everything they found objectionable. A number of anti-Quaker measures were passed, one decreeing the death penalty for Quakers who returned after banishment.

This first period of missionary enthusiasm, excesses, and martyrdom gave way by 1680 to a time of organization and consolidation. Emigration to the colonies contributed greatly to the growth of the Quaker movement. By 1674 West Jersey was in Quaker ownership. In 1681 East Jersey was also held by Quakers, with settlement encouraged. Also in 1681 William Penn (1644–1718) received the vast grant of the province of Pennsylvania to pay off a royal debt, and settlement began there the next year. A very different, and quieter, type of Quaker, Penn had a vision of a "holy experiment," where religious freedom was absolute. Three years before the English Toleration Act of 1689, Penn argued against persecution in his booklet, *A Persuasive to Moderation to Church Dissenters in Prudence and Conscience,* writing,

> Moderation, the subject of this discourse, is in plainer English, liberty of conscience to church-dissenters: a cause I have, with all humility, undertaken to plead, against the prejudices of the times.
>
> That there is such a thing as conscience, and the liberty of it, in reference to faith and worship towards God, must not be denied, even by those that are most scandalized at the ill use some seem to have made of such pretences. But to settle the terms: by conscience, I understand, the apprehension and persuasion a man has of his duty to God: by liberty of conscience, I mean, a free and open profession and exercise of that duty; especially in worship.

As targets of persecution, the Quakers were sensitive to prejudices against others and early recognized the awful injustices done to slaves. In 1657 George Fox, while not condemning slavery outright, preached the equality of all people before God and urged Christian teaching and mercy for slaves. In 1671 Fox suggested that slaves should be released. In 1688 four Quakers in Germantown, Pennsylvania, presented a resolution against slavery to their monthly meeting. And in 1693 the first American antislavery tract was published by a Quaker, George Keith. This Quaker concern for blacks continued into the eighteenth century, with Benjamin Lay, John Woolman, and Anthony Benezet being the chief crusaders against the practice. These leaders especially condemned Quakers who held slaves.

Woolman (1720–1772) was born near Burlington, New Jersey, the fourth of thirteen children. He was raised in the simple surroundings of a farming family in which his parents, devout Quakers, saw to it that their children were well instructed in spiritual matters. By age seven Woolman's spiritual concern was awakened, and he "began to be acquainted with the operations of Divine Love." He became a storekeeper, farmer, surveyor, and Quaker minister. A man of deep convictions and sensitive conscience, he made two trips to the South where he observed slavery, two trips to New England, and one voyage to England. He was concerned about numerous social wrongs, among them the treatment of laborers, the causes of war, the effects of poverty, the conditions of sailors at sea, and the treatment of Indians, but his chief concern was slavery. During his two trips to the South, in 1746 and 1757, he made intensive investigations into the situation of the slaves, becoming convinced that the majority of southern blacks lived in wretched conditions while their masters lived in luxury and ease on the labor of their slaves (selection 9).

## Tolerance and the black church

At approximately the same time the great Anglican preacher and revivalist George Whitefield (see pp. 42–44) made a trip through Maryland, Virginia, and the Carolinas. Whitefield was also appalled at the treatment of the blacks. But whereas Woolman tried to alleviate their situation by his quiet persuasion of a few slaveholders, Whitefield publicly excoriated the slaveholders in published letters (selection 8). But Whitefield's thinking on the question of slavery was inconsistent. He had great sympathy for slaves, most of whom he felt, according to this letter, were badly mistreated. And he urged the slaveowners to radically alter their treatment of the slaves. But at the same time Whitefield endorsed slavery in Georgia, where it initially had been prohibited. Nonetheless, he reminded slave owners that the blacks had souls and minds as they had, and that God would hold the owners responsible for their treatment. With that conviction, Whitefield, still a very inexperienced twenty-five, had already established his orphanage in Georgia and wished to do what he could to draw public concern to the condition of southern slaves.

On February 14, 1760, Richard Allen was born a slave to Benjamin Chew of Philadelphia. He was later sold to a slaveholder in Delaware and was converted in his early twenties. He joined the Methodists, who welcomed blacks in their worship. Allen found another reason to like the Methodists in the anti-slavery view of John Wesley. Allen's conversion experience meant much to him, and he referred to it frequently, saying that it gave him assurance that God cared greatly for him and all people. But it gave him more than that. Since slaves were legally property, to be used and sold, Allen could not feel genuine selfhood and status as long as he remained in that condition. He claimed, however, that his conversion broke all shackles; he was free before God, a redeemed soul of infinite worth.

When Allen's slave master also was converted he came to believe that slave-holding was morally wrong. This led him to give Allen the opportunity to work and purchase his freedom. After the Revolutionary War, Allen began an itinerant ministry that took him as far south as South Carolina and as far north as New York.

Richard Allen went to Philadelphia in 1785 to preach to the black members of St. George's Methodist Church. Approximately 1600 blacks in the city at that time worked as domestics, carpenters, and in menial occupations. Few of them attended any church. Allen was distressed at this, and in 1787 founded the Free African Society, a religious mutual aid association. He encouraged as many blacks as possible to attend the services at St. George's, but in 1792 the incident recorded in selection 10 occurred, which caused Allen to leave, vowing to begin a new church. A site at Sixth and Lombard Streets was secured, and against much opposition a church, named Bethel, was erected. White Methodists harassed Allen at every opportunity, and the opposition was especially onerous since it came from the Methodist church itself. The new building was dedicated on July 29, 1794, with Bishop Francis Asbury preaching.

In 1816 Richard Allen gathered representatives from five black congregations (Salem, New Jersey; Attleborough, Pennsylvania; Baltimore, Maryland; Wilmington, Delaware, and Philadelphia) to organize the *African Methodist Episcopal Church*, with Allen elected bishop. He died in 1831.

## Select Bibliography

Allen, Richard. *The Life Experience and Gospel Labors of the Rt. Rev. Richard Allen.* Nashville: Abingdon, 1960.

Cady, Edwin H. *John Woolman.* Great American Thinkers Series. New York: Washington Square, 1965.

Drake, Thomas E. *Quakers and Slavery in America.* New Haven: Yale University Press, 1950.

George, Carol V. R. *Segregated Sabbaths: Richard Allen and the Emergence of Independent Black Churches, 1760–1840.* New York: Oxford University Press, 1973.

McLoughlin, William G. *New England Dissent, 1630–1833: The Baptists and the Separation of Church and State.* Cambridge, Mass.: Harvard University Press, 1971.

Miller, Perry. *Roger Williams: His Contribution to the American Tradition.* Indianapolis: Bobbs-Merrill, 1953.

Morgan, Edmund S., ed. *Puritan Political Ideas.* Indianapolis: Bobbs-Merrill, 1965.

Rosenblatt, Paul. *John Woolman.* New York: Twayne, 1969.

Sernett, Milton C. *Black Religion and American Evangelicalism.* Metuchen, N.J.: Scarecrow, 1975.

Young, Henry J. *Major Black Religious Leaders: 1755–1940.* Nashville: Abingdon, 1977.

Ziff, Larzer. *Puritanism in America: New Culture in a New World.* New York: Viking, 1973.

# Letter . . . to the Inhabitants of Maryland, Virginia, North and South Carolina

## George Whitefield (1740)

As I lately passed through your Provinces in my Way hither, I was sensibly touched with a Fellow-feeling of the Miseries of the poor Negroes. Could I have preached more frequently amongst you, I should have delivered my Thoughts in my publick Discourses; but as my Business here required me to stop as little as possible on the Road, I have no other Way to discharge the Concern which at present lies upon my Heart, than by sending you this Letter: How you will receive it I know not; whether you will accept it in Love, or be offended with me, as the Master of the Damsel was with Paul, for casting the Evil Spirit out of her, when he saw the Hope of his Gain was gone; I am uncertain. Whatever be the Event, I must inform you in the Meekness and Gentleness of Christ, that I think God has a Quarrel with you for your Abuse of and Cruelty to the poor Negroes. Whether it be lawful for Christians to buy Slaves, and thereby encourage the Nations from whom they are bought, to use them as bad, nay worse, than as though they were Brutes; and whatever particular Exceptions there may be (as I would charitably hope there are some) I fear the Generality of you that own Negroes, are liable to such a Charge; for your Slaves, I believe, work as hard if not harder than the Horses whereon you ride.

These, after they have done their work, are fed and taken proper Care of; but many Negroes when wearied with Labour in your Plantations, have been obliged to grind their own Corn after they return home.

Your Dogs are caress'd and fondled at your Tables: But your Slaves, which are frequently stiled Dogs or Beasts, have not an equal Privilege. They are scarce permitted to pick up the Crumbs which fall from their Masters Tables. Nay, some, as I have been informed by an Eye-Witness, have been, upon the most trifling Provocation, cut with Knives, and had Forks thrown into their Flesh—Not to mention what Numbers have been given up to the inhuman

Source: George Whitefield, *Letter . . . to the Inhabitants of Maryland, Virginia, North and South Carolina* [concerning their slaves] in *Three Letters from the Reverend Mr. G. Whitefield* (Philadelphia: B. Franklin, 1740), 13–16.

Usage of cruel Task Masters, who by their unrelenting Scourges have ploughed upon their Backs, and made long Furrows, and at length brought them even to Death itself.

George Whitefield

It's true, I hope there are but few such Monsters of Barbarity suffered to subsist amongst you. Some, I hear, have been lately executed in Virginia for killing Slaves, and the Laws are very severe against such who at any Time murder them.

And perhaps it might be better for the poor Creatures themselves, to be hurried out of Life, than to be made so miserable, as they generally are in it. And indeed, considering what Usage they commonly meet with, I have wondered, that we have not more Instances of Self-Murder among the Negroes, or that they have not more frequently rose up in Arms against their Owners. Virginia has once, and Charlestown more than once been threatened in this way.

And tho' I heartily pray God they may never be permitted to get the upper Hand; yet should such a Thing be permitted by Providence, all good Men must acknowledge the Judgment would be just.—For is it not the highest Ingratitude, as well as Cruelty, not to let your poor Slaves enjoy some Fruits of their Labour?

When, passing along, I have viewed your Plantations cleared and cultivated, many spacious Houses built, and the Owners of them faring sumptuously every Day, my Blood has frequently almost run cold within me, to consider how many of your slaves had neither convenient Food to eat or proper Raiment to put on, notwithstanding most of the Comforts you enjoy were solely owing to their indefatigable Labours.—The Scripture says, "Thou shalt not muzzle the Ox that treadeth out the Corn." Does God take care of Oxen? And will he not take care of the Negroes also? Undoubtedly he will . . . But this is not all—Enslaving or misusing their Bodies would, comparatively speaking, be an inconsiderable Evil, was proper Care taken of their Souls. But I have great reason to believe, that most of you, on Purpose, keep your Negroes ignorant of Christianity; or otherwise, why are they permitted thro' your Provinces, openly to prophane the Lord's Day, by their Dancing, Piping and such like? I know the general Pretence for this Neglect of their Souls is, That teaching them Christianity would make them proud and consequently unwilling to submit to Slavery: But what a dreadful Reflection is this on your Holy Religion? What blasphemous Notions must those that make such an Objection have of the Precepts of Christianity? Do you find any one Command in the Gospel, that has the least Tendency to make People forget their relative Duties? Do you not read that Servants, and as many as are under the Yoke of Bondage, are required to be subject, in all lawful Things, to their Masters; and that not only to the good and gentle, but also to the froward? Nay, may I not appeal to your own Hearts, whether deviating from the Laws of Jesus Christ, is not the Cause of all the Evils and Miseries Mankind now universally groan under, and of all the Vices we find both in ourselves and others? Certainly it is.—And therefore, the Reason why Servants generally prove so bad is, because so little Care is taken to breed them up in the Nurture and Admonition of the Lord.—But some will be so bold perhaps as to reply, That a few of the Negroes have been taught Christianity, and, notwithstanding, have been remarkably worse than others. But what Christianity were they taught? They were baptized and taught to read and write: and this they may do, and much more, and yet be far from the Kingdom of God; for there is a vast Difference between civilizing and Christianizing an Negroe. A Black as well as a white Man may be civilized by outward Restraints, and afterwards break thro' those Restraints again. But I challenge the whole World to produce a single Instance of a Negroe's being made a thorough Christian, and thereby made a worse Servant. It cannot be. But farther, if teaching Slaves Christianity has such a bad Influence upon their Lives, why are you generally desirous of having your Children taught? Think you they are any way better by Nature than the poor Negroes? No, in no wise. Blacks are just as much, and no more, conceived and born in Sin, as White Men are. Both, if born and bred up here, I am persuaded, are naturally capable of the same Improvement. And as for the grown Negroes, I am apt to think, whenever the Gospel is preach'd with Power amongst them, that many will be brought effectually home to God.

Your sincere Well-Wisher and Servant in Christ,

G. Whitefield

Savannah, Jan. 23, 1739–40.

# On the Horrid Treatment of Southern Slaves

## *John Woolman (1757)*

**1757**

The prospect of a road lying open to the same degeneracy in some parts of this newly settled land of America, in respect to our conduct towards the Negroes, hath deeply bowed my mind in this journey; and though to briefly relate how these people are treated is no agreeable work, yet after often reading over the notes I made as I travelled, I find my mind engaged to preserve them.

Many of the white people in those provinces take little or no care of Negro marriages, and when Negroes marry after their own way, some make so little account of those marriages that with views of outward interest they often part men from their wives by selling them far asunder, which is common when estates are sold by executors at vendue. Many whose labour is heavy being followed at their business in the field by a man with a whip, hired for that purpose, have in common little else to eat but one peck of Indian corn and salt for one week with some few potatoes. (The potatoes they commonly raise by their labour on the first day of the week.)

The correction ensuing on their disobedience to overseers or slothfulness in business is often very severe and sometimes desperate. Men and women have many times scarce clothes enough to hide their nakedness, and boys and girls ten and twelve years old are often stark naked amongst their master's children.

Some of our Society and some of the Society called New Lights use some endeavours to instruct those they have in reading, but in common this is not only neglected but disapproved.

These are a people by whose labour the other inhabitants are in a great measure supported, and many of them in the luxuries of life. These are a people who have made no agreement to serve us and who have not forfeited their liberty that we know of. These are souls for whom Christ died, and for our conduct toward them we must answer before that Almighty Being who is no respecter of persons.

Source: John Woolman, *The Works of John Woolman. In Two Parts* (Philadelphia: Joseph Crukshank, 1774), 2:63–66.

They who know the only true God and Jesus Christ whom he hath sent, and are thus acquainted with the merciful, benevolent Gospel Spirit, will therein perceive that the indignation of God is kindled against oppression and cruelty, and in beholding the great distress of so numerous a people will find cause for mourning.

From my lodgings I went to Burleigh Meeting, where I felt my mind drawn into a quiet, resigned state, and after long silence I felt an engagement to stand up, and through the powerful operation of divine love we were favoured with an edifying meeting. Next we had a meeting at Black Water, and so on to the Yearly Meeting at the Western Branch.

When business began some queries were produced by some of their members to be now considered, and if approved, to be answered hereafter by their respective Monthly Meetings. They were the Pennsylvania queries, which had been examined by a committee of Virginia Yearly Meeting appointed the last year, who made some alterations in them, one of which alterations was made in favour of a custom which troubled me. The query was: "Are there any concerned in the importation of Negroes or buying them after imported?", which they altered thus: "Are there any concerned in the importation of Negroes or buying them to trade in?"

John Woolman (Billy Graham Center Museum, Wheaton, Ill.)

As one query admitted with unanimity was: "Are any concerned in buying or vending goods unlawfully imported or prize goods?", I found my mind engaged to say that as we professed the Truth and were there assembled to support the testimony of it, it was necessary for us to dwell deep and act in that wisdom which is pure, or otherwise we could not prosper. I then mentioned their alteration, and referring them to the last mentioned query, added [that] as purchasing any merchandise taken by the sword was always allowed to be inconsistent with our principles, Negroes being captives of war or taken by stealth, those circumstances make it inconsistent with our testimony to buy them, and their being our fellow creatures who are sold as slaves adds greatly to the difficulty. Friends appeared attentive to what was said; some expressed a care and concern about their Negroes; none made any objection by way of reply to what I said. But the query was admitted as they had altered it.

As some of their members have heretofore traded in Negroes as in other merchandise, this query being admitted will be one step further than they have heretofore gone, and I did not see it my duty to press for an alteration, but felt easy to leave all to him who alone is able to turn the hearts of the mighty and make way for the spreading of Truth in the earth by means agreeable to his infinite wisdom. But in regard to those they already had, I felt my mind engaged to labour with them and said that as we believe the Scriptures were given forth by holy men as they were moved by the Holy Ghost, and many of us know by experience that they are often helpful and comfortable and believe ourselves bound in duty to teach our children to read them, I believe that if we were divested of all selfish views the same good Spirit that gave them forth would engage us to learn them to read, that they might have the benefit of them. Some I perceived amongst them who at this time manifested a concern in regard to taking more care in the education of their Negroes.

29th day, 5th month. At the house where I lodged was a meeting of ministers and elders at the ninth hour in the morning, at which time I found an engagement to speak freely and plainly to them concerning their slaves, mentioning how they as the first rank in the Society, whose conduct in that case was much noticed by others, were under the stronger obligations to look carefully to themselves, expressing how needful it was for them in that situation to be thoroughly divested of all selfish views, that living in the pure Truth, and acting conscientiously toward those people in their education, and otherwise, they might be instrumental in helping forward a work so exceeding necessary and so much neglected amongst them. At the 12th hour the meeting of worship began, which was a solid meeting.

---

## Selection 10

# Beginning of the African Methodist Episcopal Church

### *Richard Allen (1831)*

I thought I would stop in Philadelphia a week or two. I preached at different places in the city. My labor was much blessed. I soon saw a large field open in

Source: Richard Allen, *The Life Experience and Gospel Labors of the Rt. Rev. Richard Allen* (Nashville: Abingdon, 1960), 24–35, *passim.*

Richard Allen (Billy Graham
Center Museum, Wheaton, Ill.)

seeking and instructing my African brethren, who had been a long forgotten people and few of them attended public worship. I preached in the commons, in Southwark, Northern Liberties, and wherever I could find an opening. I frequently preached twice a day, at 5 o'clock in the morning and in the evening, and it was not uncommon for me to preach from four to five times a day. I established prayer meetings; I raised a society in 1786 for forty-two members. I saw the necessity of erecting a place of worship for the colored people. I proposed it to the most respectable people of color in this city; but here I met with opposition. . . . We viewed the forlorn state of our colored brethren, and that they were destitute of a place of worship. They were considered as a nuisance.

A number of us usually attended St. George's church in Fourth street; and when the colored people began to get numerous in attending the church, they moved us from the seats we usually sat on, and placed us around the wall, and on Sabbath morning we went to church and the sexton stood at the door, and told us to go in the gallery. He told us to go, and we would see where to sit. We expected to take the seats over the ones we formerly occupied below, not knowing any better. We took those seats. Meeting had begun, and they were nearly done singing, and just as we got to the seats, the elder said, "Let us pray." We had not been long upon our knees before I heard considerable scuffling and low talking. I raised my head up and saw one of the trustees, H— M—, having hold of the Rev. Absalom Jones, pulling him up off of his knees, and saying, "You must get up—you must not kneel here." Mr. Jones replied, "Wait until prayer is over." . . . By this time prayer was over, and we all went out of the church in a body, and they were no more plagued with us in the church. This raised a great excitement and inquiry among the citizens, in so much that I believe they were ashamed of their conduct. But my dear Lord was with us, and we were filled with fresh vigor to get a house erected to worship God in. . . .

We then hired a store-room, and held worship by ourselves. Here we were pursued with threats of being disowned, and read publicly out of meeting if we did continue worship in the place we had hired; but we believed the Lord would be our friend. We got subscription papers out to raise money to build the house of the Lord. By this time we had waited on Dr. Rush and Mr. Robert Ralston, and told them of our distressing situation. We considered it a blessing that the Lord had put it into our hearts to wait upon those gentlemen. They pitied our situation, and subscribed largely towards the church, and were very friendly towards us, and advised us how to go on. . . .

We had no reason to complain of the liberality of the citizens. The first day the Rev. Absalom Jones and myself went out we collected three hundred and sixty dollars. This was the greatest day's collection that we met with. We appointed a committee to look out for a lot—the Rev. Absalom Jones, William Gray, William Wilcher and myself. We pitched upon a lot at the corner of Lombard and Sixth streets. They authorized me to go and agree for it. I did accordingly. The lot belonged to Mr. Mark Wilcox. We entered into articles of agreement for the lot.

We bore much persecution from many of the Methodist connection; but we have reason to be thankful to Almighty God, who was our deliverer. The day was appointed to go and dig the cellar. I arose early in the morning and addressed the throne of grace, praying that the Lord would bless our endeavors. Having by this time two or three teams of my own—as I was the first proposer of the African church, I put the first spade in the ground to dig a cellar for the same. This was the first African Church or meetinghouse that was erected in the United States of America. . . .

Notwithstanding we had been so violently persecuted by the elder, we were in favor of being attached to the Methodist connection; for I was confident that there was no religious sect or denomination would suit the capacity of the colored people as well as the Methodist; for the plain and simple gospel suits best for any people; for the unlearned can understand, and the learned are sure to understand; and the reason that the Methodist is so successful in the awakening and conversion of the colored people; the plain doctrine and having a good discipline. . . .

I bought an old frame that had been formerly occupied as a blacksmith shop, from Mr. Sims, and hauled it on the lot in Sixth near Lombard street, that had formerly been taken for the Church of England. I employed carpenters to repair the old frame, and fit it for a place of worship. In July 1794, Bishop Asbury being in town I solicited him to open the church* for us which he accepted. The Rev. John Dickins sung and prayed, and Bishop Asbury preached. The house was called Bethel, agreeable to the prayer that was made.

---

* This church will at present accommodate between 3,000 and 4,000 persons.

Mr. Dickins prayed that it might be a bethel[†] to the gathering in of thousands of souls. My dear Lord was with us, so that there were many hearty "amen's" echoed through the house. This house of worship has been favored with the awakening of many souls, and I trust they are in the Kingdom, both white and colored. . . .

Many of the colored people in other places were in a situation nearly like those of Philadelphia and Baltimore, which induced us, in April 1816, to call a general meeting, by way of Conference. Delegates from Baltimore and other places which met those of Philadelphia, and taking into consideration their grievances, and in order to secure the privileges, promote union and harmony among themselves, it was resolved: "That the people of Philadelphia, Baltimore, etc., etc., should become one body, under the name of the African Methodist Episcopal Church." We deemed it expedient to have a form of discipline, whereby we may guide our people in the fear of God, in the unity of the Spirit, and in the bonds of peace, and preserve us from that spiritual despotism which we have so recently experienced— remembering that we are not to lord it over God's heritage, as greedy dogs that can never have enough. But with long suffering and bowels of compassion, to bear each other's burdens, and so fulfill the Law of Christ, praying that our mutual striving together for the promulgation of the Gospel may be crowned with abundant success.

† See Genesis Chapter 28.

# Revolution and the New Nation

It was inevitable, many historians hold, that the American colonies would in time revolt against the mother country, England. There were many reasons for this. Prior to the French and Indian War (1754–1763) the colonies had depended heavily on Britain for protection. The British won the war, but the myth of her invincibility was shattered. The colonists realized they needed England less and less. At Fort Duquesne in Pennsylvania General Edward Braddock's British regular soldiers were demoralized and routed, while the American "buckskin" militia fought commendably. The American colonials, baptized by fire, emerged from the war with increased confidence in their military strength. They had borne the brunt of battle at the beginning and had fought valiantly beside the vaunted British Redcoats. At the end of the war perhaps 20,000 American militiamen were under arms. In addition, the colonists resented the arrogant British officers who were supposed to be comrades in arms. General James Wolfe represented the typical British attitude, calling the colonists "in general the dirtiest, most contemptible, cowardly dogs that you can conceive."

The French and Indian War also gave to colonists a new vision of their ultimate destiny. When the British government issued the Proclamation of 1763, prohibiting settlement beyond the Appalachian Mountains, Americans were furious. Flouting royal authority, settlers moved westward in droves and dared the English government to stop them. Their empire had grown so far so fast that England's arrogance knew no bounds. They were in no mood for impertinence from their unruly colonials. The stage was set for a violent family upheaval.

Scholars often point to the Great Awakening of the 1740s as the reason America in the 1760s was so clearly different from the colonies of the 1730s.

The revival was the first spontaneous mass movement of the American people—not as New Englanders or Virginians but as fellow Christians who shared a continent. Perry Miller has written, "Historians have variously pointed out that the decade of the Awakening, 1740 to 1750, is a watershed in American development. . . . you feel, the moment you go to the sources, that after 1750 we are in a 'modern period,' whereas before that, and down to the very outburst, the intellectual world is still medieval, scholastic, static, authoritarian."[1]

## The shape of a new America

While the Great Awakening marked America's final intellectual break with the Middle Ages, politically it signaled her new awareness that the colonies had become a geographic entity. Before 1740 Bostonians had felt more in common with Londoners than with Philadelphians. The Awakening tended to break down both denominational and sectional boundaries. When the preeminent evangelist George Whitefield went from Philadelphia to Boston and made common cause with all Christians, suddenly the people realized their colonial oneness. Winthrop S. Hudson aptly writes:

> And because the Awakening was general, it played an important role in forming a national consciousness among people of different colonies. . . . As a spontaneous movement which swept across all colonial boundaries, generated a common interest and a common loyalty, bound people together in a common cause, and reinforced the conviction that God had a special destiny in store for America, the Awakening contributed greatly to the development of a sense of cohesiveness among the American people.[2]

From North to South at the outbreak of the Revolutionary War the American people were, as a whole, quite devout in most of the colonies. The Sabbath was strictly observed, church attendance was high, and the usual hour-long sermons were avidly heard and discussed by families at home on Sunday afternoons. The Christian ministry was still the profession with the most prestige. The Bible was regarded everywhere as the infallible Word of God and was read, along with John Bunyan's *Pilgrim's Progress* and Richard Baxter's *Call to the Unconverted*.

Growth in the American colonies was impressive. In 1760 the white citizens of the thirteen colonies numbered about 1.6 million. In only fifteen years, by 1775, they totaled about 2.5 million and by 1790, another fifteen years, almost 4 million. There were about 500,000 blacks. The populace was doubling approximately every twenty to twenty-five years.

The overwhelming majority of Americans in 1775 were nominally Protestant, and a high percentage of those—perhaps as high as 74 percent—actually attended church frequently or were claimed as adherents while not holding membership in Protestant churches. Roman Catholics and Jews were still tiny minorities, with approximately 25,000 of the former and only 2000 of the latter. Congregationalists claimed the largest group (580,000), followed by Anglicans (500,000), Presbyterians (410,000), German churches (Reformed, Lutheran, etc., 200,000), Dutch Reformed (75,000), Quakers (40,000), Baptists (25,000), and Methodists (5000).[3]

Much of the population growth owed to a high birthrate, while immigrants poured into the ports of America. In 1770 probably over 90 percent of the people lived in rural districts, and only four communities might deserve the title of *cities*: Philadelphia, the most populous; New York; Boston, and Charleston. Early marriages boosted the birthrate, and widows usually remarried quickly. Babies came with regularity to most families, and eight to twelve children in a family was common because the rate of infant mortality was also high. A governor of Massachusetts, William Phips, had twenty-six brothers and sisters, all by the same mother.

## A future without limits

Since so many Americans were sincere Christians, a theological interpretation was frequently given to the break with England. Victory in the Revolutionary War was interpreted as great opportunity for the new nation's self-determination, and a proof of God's blessing on her independence. Conrad Cherry has written, "The achievement of constitutional government was seen as the first step in a bold experiment that would assure basic human freedoms; it was also understood as a serious effort to erect an American model for the Old World."[4]

Once the colonies had decided to declare their independence, most Protestant clergy swung behind the Congress and incessantly rallied support for the war from their pulpits. Much of their success was due to their ability to arouse in the people a sense of American destiny under God. There were clergy and laypeople in most denominations who either stayed neutral or sided (usually as quietly as possible) with the mother country, but they were very much in the minority, and the strongest support for revolution came from Congregationalists, Presbyterians, and Baptists. Ambrose Serle, a representative of England's Lord Dartmouth, wrote to him in April 1777, "When the war is over, there must be a great Reform established, ecclesiastical as well as civil; for, though it has not been much considered at Home, Presbyterianism is really at

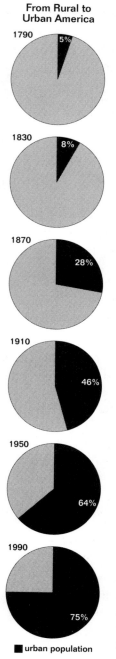

**From Rural to Urban America**

1790 — 5%

1830 — 8%

1870 — 28%

1910 — 46%

1950 — 64%

1990 — 75%

■ urban population

*Source: U.S. Census*

the Bottom of this whole Conspiracy, has supplied it with Vigour, and will never rest, till something is decided upon it."[5] By "Presbyterianism" Serle meant Calvinism, to which Congregationalists, Baptists, and Presbyterians all adhered.

When Charles Cornwallis surrendered his British force to George Washington on October 19, 1781, at Yorktown, Virginia, Americans were jubilant. Shortly thereafter, in 1783, Governor Jonathan Trumbull asked the president of Yale, Ezra Stiles (1727–1795), to preach the Connecticut election sermon. Stiles was given the opportunity to be expansive regarding national optimism and ebullience, and the resultant sermon, *The United States Elevated to Glory and Honor* (selection 11), went to over 100 pages in print. Stiles delivered it before the state legislature, but he actually intended to address his remarks to far flung places. According to Edmund S. Morgan, Stiles "was talking over their heads, to the world that lay three thousand miles over the water. America, he was saying, had not merely conquered George III; America had conquered monarchy. America was the future of Europe. In the coming years, as American ships carried the flag around the globe, the power of freedom would everywhere become apparent."[6]

And the years rolled on. America grew with incredible speed, and her future seemed secure and magnificently bright. In 1803, President Thomas Jefferson authorized his envoy in Paris to offer $10 million to the French to purchase the city of New Orleans and land to the *east*. Without any warning, the French foreign minister asked the envoy how much he would give for *all* Louisiana. This was astonishing; it had never been imagined that France would sell this colony. After a week of haggling, a figure of $15 million was agreed to, giving the United States enough area to the *west* to more than double the existing nation. So came about the most magnificent real estate bargain in history—828,000 square miles of excellent land and phenomenal resources for about three cents an acre. By its bargain with France, Americans got the western half of the richest river valley on the face of the globe and set the foundations for a major world power. Almost immediately settlers poured across the Mississippi River into the new territory, areas were cleared, and towns formed. Nine new frontier states joined the original thirteen between 1791 and 1819. Tens of thousands moved west.

The movement toward the setting sun became so massive that almost the entire populations of towns in Connecticut and other states moved out. The mass migration was extremely worrisome to many. The West was a raw and vast wilderness, and there was a real danger that new settlers, finding no Christian influence there, would revert to paganism. Many, especially the clergy, were worried that Christian missions and the founding of new churches could never keep up with settlement.

One of those most worried was a Congregational pastor who led a number of significant causes to advance Christianity. Lyman Beecher (1775–1863), "father of more brains than any man in America," was the parent of Harriet Beecher Stowe and Henry Ward Beecher, and he had inherited the mantle of Timothy Dwight as the evangelical leader of the Second Great Awakening. Beecher exerted enormous labors for years in innumerable organizations and reform efforts and became president of Lane Theological Seminary in Cincinnati, Ohio, in 1832. He considered Lane to be at the heart of the West and a pivot point on which to swing the effort to Christianize it. His famous sermon, "A Plea for the West," was written in 1835 (selection 12).

## Select Bibliography

Beecher, Lyman. *The Autobiography of Lyman Beecher*, 2 vols., edited by Barbara M. Cross. Cambridge, Mass.: Harvard University Press, 1961.

Handy, Robert T. *A Christian America: Protestant Hopes and Historical Realities.* New York: Oxford University Press, 1974.

Hudson, Winthrop S., ed. *Nationalism and Religion in America: Concepts of American Identity and Mission.* New York: Harper and Row, 1970.

Morgan, Edmund S. *The Gentle Puritan: A Life of Ezra Stiles, 1727–1795.* 1962; repr. , New York: Norton, 1983.

Niebuhr, H. Richard. *The Kingdom of God in America.* New York: Harper and Row, 1937.

_____. *The Social Sources of Denominationalism.* Cleveland: World, 1929.

Tuveson, Ernest L. *Redeemer Nation: The Idea of America's Millennial Role.* Chicago: University of Chicago Press, 1968.

Wright, Esmond. *Fabric of Freedom, 1763–1800*, rev. ed. The Making of America Series. New York: Hill and Wang, 1978.

# The United States Elevated to Glory and Honour

## *Ezra Stiles (1783)*

And to make thee high above all nations which he hath made, in praise,
and in name, and in honour; and that thou mayest be an holy people unto
the Lord thy God. [Deut. 26:19]

Taught by the omniscient Deity, Moses foresaw and predicted the capital events
relative to Israel, through the successive changes of depression and glory, until
their final elevation to the first dignity and eminence among the empires of the
world. These events have been so ordered as to become a display of retribution
and sovereignty; for while the good and evil, hitherto felt by this people, have
been dispensed in the way of exact national retribution, their ultimate glory and
honour will be of the divine sovereignty, with a "not for your sakes, do I this,
saith the Lord, be it known unto you—but for mine holy name's sake." . . .

. . . I shall enlarge no further upon the primary sense and literal accom-
plishments of this and numerous other prophecies respecting both Jews and
Gentiles, in the latter day glory of the church. For I have assumed the text only
as introductory to a discourse upon the political welfare of God's American
Israel, and as allusively prophetick of the future prosperity and splendour of
the United States.

Already does the new constellation of the United States begin to realize this
glory. It has already risen to an acknowledged sovereignty among the republicks and kingdoms of the world. And we have reason to hope, and I believe
to expect, that God has still greater blessings in store for this vine which his
own right hand hath planted, to make us "high among the nations in praise,
and in name, and in honour." The reasons are very numerous, weighty, and
conclusive.

Liberty, civil and religious, has sweet and attractive charms. The enjoyment of this, with property, has filled the English settlers in America with a

Source: Ezra Stiles, *A Sermon Preached Before Governor Jonathan Trumbull and the Connecticut
General Assembly* . . . (2d ed., Worcester, Mass.: Isaiah Thomas, 1785), 5–7, 58–62, 95–98.

most amazing spirit, which has operated, and still will operate, with great energy. Never before has the experiment been so effectually tried, of every man's reaping the fruits of his labour and feeling his share in the aggregate system of power. The ancient republicks did not stand on the people at large; and therefore no example or precedent can be taken from them. Even men of arbitrary principles will be obliged, if they would figure in these states, to assume the patriot so long that they will at length become charmed with the sweets of liberty.

Our degree of population is such as to give us reason to expect that this will become a great people. It is probable that within a century from our independence the sun will shine on fifty million of inhabitants in the United States. This will be a great, a very great nation, nearly equal to half Europe. Already has our colonization extended down the Ohio and to Koskaseah on the Mississippi. And if the present ratio of increase should be rather diminished in some of the elder settlements, yet an accelerated multiplication will attend our general propagation and overspread the whole

Ezra Stiles

territory westward for ages. So that before the Millennium, the English settlements in America may become more numerous millions than that greatest dominion on earth, the Chinese empire. Should this prove a future fact, how applicable would be the text, when the Lord shall have made his American Israel "high above all nations which he hath made," in numbers, "and in praise, and in name, and in honour!"

I am sensible some will consider these as visionary Utopian ideas. And so they would have judged had they lived in the apostolick age and been told that by the time of Constantine the empire would have become Christian. As visionary that the twenty thousand souls which first settled New-England should be multiplied to near a million in a century and a half. As visionary that the Ottoman empire must fall by the Russian. As visionary to the Catholicks is the certain downfall of the Pontificate. As Utopian would it have been to the loyalists, at the battle of Lexington, that in less than eight years the independence and sovereignty of the United States should be acknowledged by four European sovereignties, one of which should be Britain herself. How wonderful the revolutions, the events of Providence! We live in an Age of Wonders. We have lived an age in a few years. We have seen more wonders accomplished in eight years than are usually unfolded in a century. . . .

This great American revolution, this recent political phenomenon of a new sovereignty arising among the sovereign powers of the earth, will be attended to and contemplated by all nations. Navigation will carry the American flag around the globe itself and display the Thirteen Stripes and New Constellation at Bengal and Canton on the Indus and Ganges, on the Whang-ho and the Yang-tse-kiang; and with commerce will import the wisdom and literature of the east. That prophecy of Daniel is now literally fulfilling—there shall be an universal travelling "too and fro, and knowledge shall be increased." This knowledge will be brought home and treasured up in America: and being here digested and carried to the highest perfection, may reblaze back from America to Europe, Asia and Africa, and illumine the world with TRUTH and LIBERTY.

That great Civilian, Dr. John Adams, the learned and illustrious American Ambassadour, observes thus, "But the great designs of Providence must be accomplished;—great indeed! The progress of society will be accelerated by centuries by this revolution. The Emperour of Germany is adopting, as fast as he can, American Ideas of toleration and religious liberty: And it will become the fashionable system of Europe very soon. Light spreads from the day-spring in the west; and may it shine more and more until the perfect day." So spreading may be the spirit for the restoration and recovery of long lost national rights, that even the Cortes of Spain may re-exist and resume their ancient splendour, authority, and control of royalty. The same principles of wisdom and enlightened politicks may establish rectitude in publick government throughout the world. . . .

Here will be no bloody tribunals, no cardinals inquisitors-general, to bend the human mind, forcibly to control the understanding, and put out the light of reason, the candle of the Lord, in man; to force an innocent Galileo to renounce truths demonstrable as the light of day. Religion may here receive its last, most liberal, and impartial examination. Religious liberty is peculiarly friendly to fair and generous disquisition. Here deism will have its full chance; nor need libertines more to complain of being overcome by any weapons but the gentle, the powerful ones of argument and truth. Revelation will be found to stand the test to the ten thousandth examination.

There are three coetaneous events to take place whose fruition is certain from prophecy, the annihilation of the Pontificate, the reassembling of the Jews, and the fulness of the Gentiles. That liberal and candid disquisition of Christianity, which will most assuredly take place in America, will prepare

Europe for the first event, with which the other will be connected, when, especially on the return of the twelve tribes to the Holy Land, there will burst forth a degree of evidence hitherto unperceived and of efficacy to convert a world. More than three quarters of mankind yet remain heathen. Heaven put a stop to the propagation of Christianity when the church became corrupted with the adoration of numerous deities and images, because this would have been only exchanging an old for a new idolatry. Nor is Christendom now larger than it was nine centuries ago. The promising prospects of the *Propaganda fide* at Rome are coming to nothing: and it may be of the divine destiny that all other attempts for gospelizing the nations of the earth shall prove fruitless, until the present Christendom itself be recovered to the primitive purity and simplicity. At which time, instead of the Babel confusion of contradicting missionaries, all will harmoniously concur in speaking one language, one holy faith, one apostolick religion to an unconverted world. At this period, and in effecting this great event, we have reason to think that the United States may be of no small influence and consideration. It was of the Lord to send Joseph into Egypt, to save much people, and to shew forth his praise. It is of the Lord that "a woman clothed with the sun, and the moon under her feet," and upon "her head a crown of twelve stars," (not to say thirteen) should "flee into the wilderness, where she hath a place prepared of God" (Rev. xii. 1 & 6), and where she might be the repository of Wisdom, and "keep the commandments of God, and have the testimony of Jesus." It may have been of the Lord that Christianity is to be found in such great purity in this church exiled into the wilderness of America; and that its purest body should be evidently advancing forward, by an augmented natural increase and spiritual edification, into a singular superiority—with the ultimate subserviency to the glory of God, in converting the world.

# A Plea for the West

## *Lyman Beecher (1835)*

Who hath heard such a thing? who hath seen such things? Shall the earth be made to bring forth in one day? or shall a nation be born at once? for as soon as Zion travailed, she brought forth her children. [Isa. 66:8]

. . . But if this nation is, in the providence of God, destined to lead the way in the moral and political emancipation of the world, it is time she understood her high calling, and were harnessed for the work. For mighty causes, like floods from distant mountains, are rushing with accumulating power, to their consummation of good or evil, and soon our character and destiny will be stereotyped forever.

It is equally plain that the religious and political destiny of our nation is to be decided in the West. There is the territory, and there soon will be the population, the wealth, and the political power. The Atlantic commerce and manufactures may confer always some peculiar advantages on the East. But the West is destined to be the great central power of the nation, and under heaven, must affect powerfully the cause of free institutions and the liberty of the world.

The West is a young empire of mind, and power, and wealth, and free institutions, rushing up to a giant manhood, with the rapidity and a power never before witnessed below the sun. And if she carries with her the elements of her preservation, the experiment will be glorious—the joy of the nation—the joy of the whole earth, as she rises in the majesty of her intelligence and benevolence, and enterprise, for the emancipation of the world.

It is equally clear, that the conflict which is to decide the destiny of the West, will be a conflict of institutions for the education of her sons, for purposes of superstition, or evangelical light; of despotism, or liberty. . . .

The thing required for the civil and religious prosperity of the West, is universal education, and moral culture, by institutions commensurate to that result—the all-pervading influence of schools, and colleges, and seminaries, and pastors, and churches. When the West is well supplied in this respect,

Source: Lyman Beecher, *A Plea for the West,* 2d ed. (Cincinnati: Truman and Smith, 1835), 11–40, passim.

though there may be great relative defects, there will be, as we believe, the stamina and the vitality of a perpetual civil and religious prosperity.

By whom shall the work of rearing the literary and religious institutions of the West be done?

Not by the West alone.

The West is able to do this great work for herself,—and would do it, provided the exigencies of her condition allowed to her the requisite time. The subject of education is no where more appreciated; and no people in the same time ever performed so great a work as has already been performed in the West. Such an extent of forest never fell before the arm of man in forty years, and gave place, as by enchantment, to such an empire of cities, and towns, and villages, and agriculture, and merchandise, and manufactures, and roads and rapid navigation, and schools, and colleges, and libraries, and literary enterprise, with such a number of pastors and churches, and such

Lyman Beecher

a relative amount of religious influence, as has been produced by the spontaneous effort of the religious denominations of the West. The later peopled states of New-England did by no means come as rapidly to the same state of relative, intellectual and moral culture as many portions of the West have already arrived at, in the short period of forty, thirty, and even twenty years.

But this work of self-supply is not complete, and by no human possibility could have been completed by the West, in her past condition.

No people ever did, in the first generation, fell the forest, and construct the roads, and rear the dwellings and public edifices, and provide the competent supply of schools and literary institutions. New-England did not. Her colleges were endowed extensively by foreign munificence, and her churches of the first generation were supplied chiefly from the mother country;—and yet the colonists of New-England were few in number, compact in territory, homogeneous in origin, language, manners, and doctrines; and were coerced to unity by common perils and necessities; and could be acted upon by immediate legislation; and could wait also for their institutions to grow with their growth and strengthen with their strength. But the population of the great West is not so, but is assembled from all the states of the Union, and from all the nations of Europe, and is rushing in like the waters of the flood, demanding for its moral preservation the immediate and universal action of those institutions which discipline the mind, and arm the conscience and the heart. And so various are the opinions and habits, and so recent and imperfect is the acquaintance, and so sparse are the settlements of the West, that no homogeneous public sentiment can be formed to legislate immediately into being the requisite institutions. And yet they are all needed immediately, in their utmost perfection and power. A nation is being "born in a day," and all the nurture of schools and literary institutions is needed, constantly and universally, to rear it up to a glorious and unperverted manhood. . . .

Whence, then, shall the aid come, but from those portions of the Union where the work of rearing these institutions has been most nearly accomplished, and their blessings most eminently enjoyed? And by whom, but by those who in their infancy were aided; and who, having freely received, are now called upon freely to give, and who, by a hard soil and habits of industry and economy, and by experience are qualified to endure hardness as good soldiers and pioneers in this great work? And be assured that those who go to the West with unostentatious benevolence, to identify themselves with the people and interests of that vast community, will be adopted with a warm heart and an unwavering right hand of fellowship. . . .

But how shall this aid be extended to our brethren of the West in the manner most acceptable and efficacious?

Not by prayers and supplications only, nor by charities alone. . . .

Nor is it by tracts, or Bibles, or itinerating missions, that the requisite intellectual and moral power can be applied. There must be permanent, powerful, literary and moral institutions, which, like the great orbs of attraction and light, shall send forth at once their power and their illumination, and without them all else will be inconstant and ephemeral. Let it not, however, for a moment be supposed, that the schools of the West are to be sustained by the emigration of an army of instructors from the East. For though for the present *necessity*, the aid of qualified instructors is not to be repelled, but invited; yet for any permanent reliance, it is but a drop of the bucket to the ocean. . . .

Nothing is more certain, than that the great body of the teachers of the West must be educated at the West. It is by her own sons chiefly, that the great work is to be consummated which her civil, and literary, and religious prosperity demands.

But how shall the requisite supply of teachers for the sons and daughters of the West be raised up? It can be accomplished by the instrumentality of a learned and pious ministry, educated at the West. . . .

We must educate! We must educate! or we must perish by our own prosperity. If we do not, short from the cradle to the grave will be our race. If in
our haste to be rich and mighty, we outrun our literary and religious institutions, they will never overtake us; or only come up after the battle of liberty is
fought and lost, as spoils to grace the victory, and as resources of inexorable
despotism for the perpetuity of our bondage. And let no man at the East quiet
himself, and dream of liberty, whatever may become of the West. Our alliance
of blood, and political institutions, and common interests, is such, that we cannot stand aloof in the hour of her calamity, should it ever come. Her destiny
is our destiny; and the day that her gallant ship goes down, our little boat sinks
in the vortex!

It was to meet these exigences of our common country in the West, that the
Lane Seminary was called into being by the munificence of the sons of the
West; first by a donation from the two gentlemen whose name it bears, followed by the gift of sixty acres of land, on which the institution is located, by
Mr. Elnathan Kemper, and the sale of fifty more at a reduced price and long
credit by the same benefactor; to which have been added fifteen thousand dollars by the citizens of Cincinnati and the West, for the construction of two college buildings and two professors' houses. To this has been added by our friends
on this side of the mountains, twenty thousand dollars from one individual,
for the endowment of the professorship of Theology; and by others, thirty
thousand, for the endowment of the two professorships of Biblical Literature
and Ecclesiastical History.

What we now need is a chapel for the accommodation of students and a
fast increasing community with a place of worship; the endowment of a professorship of Sacred Rhetoric, and a library. For the first, we have dared to rely
on our friends in Boston and its vicinity. The library we hope to receive from
our friends in New-York; and for the Professorship of Sacred Rhetoric we look
up, hoping and believing that God will put into the heart of one or more individuals to endow it. . . .

This vast territory is occupied now by ten states and will soon be by twelve.
Forty years since it contained only about one hundred and fifty thousand souls;
while it now contains little short of five millions. At the close of this century,
if no calamity intervenes, it will contain, probably, one hundred millions—a
day which some of our children may live to see; and when fully peopled, may
accommodate three hundred millions. It is half as large as all Europe, four
times as large as the Atlantic states, and twenty times as large as New-England.
Was there ever such a spectacle—such a field in which to plant the seeds of an
immortal harvest!—so vast a ship, so richly laden with the world's treasures

and riches, whose helm is offered to the guiding influence of early forming institutions!

The certainty of success calls us to immediate effort. If we knew not what to do, if all was effort and expense in untried experiments, there might be some pretext for the paralysis of amazement and inaction. But we know what to do: the means are obvious, and well tried, and certain. The sun and the rain of heaven are not more sure to call forth a bounteous vegetation, than Bibles, and Sabbaths, and schools, and seminaries, are to diffuse intellectual light and warmth for the bounteous fruits of righteousness and peace. The corn and the acorn of the East are not more sure to vegetate at the West than the institutions which have blessed the East are to bless the West.

# Threats to Christian Orthodoxy

If Christians in America expected their faith to be challenged, they were not disappointed. A diverse group of eighteenth-century "infidels"—*antinomians, universalists, deists, unitarians, Socinians,* and *Arminians*—were all European in origin, and most of them claimed to be Christian. They stemmed from the rise of rationalism in Europe, which emphasized the rational capacity of the human mind, and considered it the source of truth both about humanity and about the world.

While most of these movements did not reject supernatural revelation, at least at the start, in time they came to question basic Christian doctrines and to have such confidence in the power of the human mind that it was able to select which doctrines to accept or reject. For some of these groups the mind rejected a number of basic Christian teachings, usually dealing with sin and the need for a divine Savior.

## Deism

Deism first seemed to pose the greatest threat to American Christianity. Lord Herbert of Cherbury (1583–1648), often called "the father of deism," taught five points that later deists generally adhered to: (1) There is a supreme and good God. (2) This sovereign should be worshiped. (3) Virtue is the human religious duty. (4) Humans must repent of wickedness. (5) There is reward or punishment in the life to come. Herbert felt that all religions could agree upon these common principles, and he rarely mentioned Jesus, certainly not as the Son of God and the Savior of the world.

Many Christians condemned Herbert's *De Veritate,* published in 1624, and saw his influence in the philosophy of John Locke (1632–1704) and the *latitudinarian party* in the Church of England, led by Archbishop of Canterbury John Tillotson (1630–1694). Tillotson and the latitudinarians were not overtly deist, but they were very inclined toward rationalistic ideas. The controversy over deism in England became more heated when John Toland (1670–1722), influenced heavily by Locke, published *Christianity Not Mysterious* in 1696, and his ideas began to filter to the New World. In 1739 Jonathan Edwards wrote,

> The Deists wholly cast off the Christian religion, and are professed infidels. . . . They own the being of God; but deny that Christ was the son of God, and say he was a mere cheat; and so they say all the prophets and apostles were: and they deny the whole Scripture. They deny that any of it is the word of God. They deny any revealed religion, or any word of God at all; and say that God has given mankind no other light to walk by but their own reason.[1]

Other Christians might differ from Edwards in details, but the general outlines of deism and the profound horror of Edwards's denunciation were shared by almost all within the church.

The anger of Christians toward foreign sources of such thinking was heightened when Americans began to espouse it. Thomas Jefferson was preeminently the representative of deism in the popular mind. His religious concepts were expressed in his 1781 work, *Notes on the State of Virginia.* Religion to Jefferson meant a utilitarian moral code, not an actual divine revelation. Many details in the Bible seemed dubious to Jefferson, and where uncertainty prevails, "Ignorance is preferable to error; and he is less remote from the truth who believes nothing, than he who believes what is wrong."[2] Jefferson was strongly influenced by the French *philosophes* during his years in France from 1783 to 1789 and thereafter became even more an opponent of Christianity and an exponent of deism. Jefferson frequently expressed his doubts as to God's existence or the deity of Christ in the years leading to his election as President in 1800. This convinced many Federalist clergy and laypeople that, as a leading spokesman for infidelity, he deserved their unremitting attacks. He, in turn, became more avowedly anticlerical.

Then in 1784 Ethan Allen (1738–1789), the Revolutionary War hero who captured Fort Ticonderoga, published *Reason the Only Oracle of Man, or a Compendious System of Natural Religion.* It was a poorly written and repetitious 477-page work (as Allen well knew),[3] and it shocked many that such a frontal attack on spiritual truth could be published in America. Timothy Dwight declared that this was the first book against Christianity published in the New

World.[4] Adolf Koch says of the book, "The long sentences lack clarity and emphasis and the repetition of his favorite ideas is tiresome."[5]

In the book, Allen says he is generally "denominated a Deist, the reality of which I never disputed, being conscious I am no Christian, except mere infant baptism makes me one; and as to being a Deist . . . I have never read their writings."[6] Throughout, Allen tore away at the very vitals of the Christian faith as savagely as he could:

> Was it not that we were rational creatures, it would have been as ridiculous to have pretended to have given us a Bible, for our instruction in matters of religion or morality, as it would to a stable of horses.[7]

> That Jesus Christ is not God is evident from his own words . . . besides being impossible and contradictory . . . for God and man are not and cannot be one and the same.[8]

> The doctrine of the Trinity is destitute of foundation, and tends manifestly to superstition and idolatry.[9]

There is no way to know how widely the work was read, but it likely had a significant distribution throughout New England.[10]

Others who took Allen's lead in attacking Christianity were Joel Barlow (1754–1812), a Revolutionary War chaplain who went to France and became a thoroughgoing deist, and Elihu Palmer (1764–1806), a former Congregational, Baptist, and then universalist preacher. In his *Principles of Nature,* Palmer denounced the entire Christian plan of salvation. "Sophistry and folly united cannot exhibit a greater specimen of nonsense and irrationality. This story of the virgin and the ghost, to say no more of it, does not wear the appearance of much religion."[11] The Bible is "a book, whose indecency and immorality shock all common sense and common honesty."[12]

Of all the deistic writings that infuriated Christians, those of Thomas Paine (1737–1809) probably aroused the most ire. Born in Norfolk, England, he sailed to America in 1774, and in 1776 wrote *Common Sense,* in which he appealed to the ordinary citizen to declare his or her independence. Later he penned a series of pamphlets entitled *The American Crisis,* which did much to encourage the patriots during the war. Returning to England in 1787, he wrote *The Rights of Man* and was indicted for treason for attacking British institutions. He fled to France, where he was greatly influenced by French deism. After the Reign of Terror he was imprisoned by the Jacobins for a year, and during this period he wrote *The Age of Reason.*

The United States, as a new nation eager to take a place in the councils of the world, was especially open to foreign notions and influences. Seizing this opportunity, France and other nations exported deism. *The Encyclopedia,* a large number of volumes written by Voltaire and other Frenchmen, the *System de la Nature,* and Paine's *Age of Reason* (selection 13) were shipped to America in great quantity. An enormous edition of *The Age of Reason* could be sold for a few cents a copy in the United States.[13] Where it could not be sold it was to be given away.

These works were not, on the whole, closely reasoned arguments for thinkers or scholars. They were designed to baffle and amuse, not to convince or teach. They were addressed to the unthinking and to those inclined to loose morals or a dislike for Christianity. People well recalled how good a friend Paine had been to America during the Revolution, so many were willing to read his new book. They found that he used much invective and ridicule. Ashbel Green, a distinguished pastor, said that *The Age of Reason* was "a book in which the most contemptible ignorance, the grossest falsehood, the most vulgar buffoonery, the most unblushing impudence, and the most daring profaneness are united."[14] Jeremy Belknap, a Congregationalist of Boston, said of the volume that it was a "species of vulgar infidelity, founded partly in pedantry, partly in debauchery and partly in ill manners."[15]

## The natures of God and humanity

In addition to deism, other challenges to Christian orthodoxy appeared during the eighteenth century. Most of these also were influenced by European thinking. Two tendencies toward unitarianism had been around for centuries: *Arianism* and *Socinianism.* Arius, presbyter of Alexandria (d. 336), created a huge controversy over Christology in the early church, was attacked by Athanasius, and pronounced heretical at the Council of Nicea in 325. Essentially Arius denied the eternality of Jesus Christ the Son of God as the *Logos,* saying that, because Christ was "begotten," he must have had a beginning, and is therefore a being of intermediate status between the Creator and the creature. Arianism continued to be the commonest form of unitarianism in New England until well into the nineteenth century. Socinianism, following the thought of Lelio Sozzini (1525–1562), a more extreme form of antitrinitarianism, taught that Jesus was a revelation of God but strictly a man.

Books published in England had spread antitrinitarian ideas for decades; Samuel Clarke's *Scripture Doctrine of the Trinity* (1712) and Thomas Emlyn's *An Humble Inquiry into the Scripture-Account of Jesus Christ* (1702) were read by clergymen with liberal tendencies, especially in New England. By the 1760s a number of pastors in the Boston area were drifting toward Arianism, prominent among them Jonathan Mayhew and Charles Chauncy. In 1787 King's Chapel became the first church in America to declare itself Unitarian.

This was the situation in New England for a number of years, during which there was enough antitrinitarianism "to alarm the orthodox, but its exact nature and extent remained uncertain," as Conrad Wright declares.[16] Two vital institutions were at stake in the forthcoming battle between trinitarianism and unitarianism: the churches of New England, and the nation's oldest college, Harvard.

While Yale College in Connecticut was under the control of orthodox Calvinists, Massachusetts' Harvard had long been problematic. A number of pastors around Boston were liberals, and they were largely in control of Harvard; there had been tension for decades. Both the president and the Hollis professor of Divinity, Joseph Willard and David Tappan, were moderate Calvinists, and they died within a year of each other. This gave the liberals the opportunity they had been waiting for. In 1805 they elected Henry Ware, a liberal, to the chair of divinity. A year later another liberal, Samuel Webber, was named president. The conflict was now launched in earnest.

Ware wasted no time. He began, not by addressing the trinitarian controversy, but by speaking out on another issue that had been festering for some time: the question of original sin, radical depravity, and the guilt inherited from the first human parents. This argument had continued for centuries. Pelagius (b. 409) held that God imputes to humans only those acts they personally perform. Arminius (1560–1609) argued that humans have an evil tendency that may be called sin, but it does not involve guilt or punishment; certainly humans are sick, but they are not accounted guilty of Adam's sin.

On the other hand, Augustine (354–430), Luther (1483–1546), Calvin (1509–1564), and other Reformers regarded Scripture as clearly teaching that the race was united in Adam, either organically or by federal headship. Innate depravity, then, was imputed to humanity in the same way Christ's righteousness was imputed to the Christian. This is in addition to the urge to sin—a total corruption of the will—that Adam bequeathed to all his posterity.

All of New England had, from its founding, accepted this latter, *Augustinian* view, which was regarded as orthodox and fully in accord with Scripture. But the winds of change had been blowing against this doctrine, especially in the thinking of such liberals as Charles Chauncy.

Ware entered this controversy with a lively tract that defended, not the more moderate view of Arminius as might have been expected, but the extreme view of Pelagius! This theory had been condemned by the Council of Carthage in 418, and frequently thereafter. In his tract, *Letters Addressed to Trinitarians and Calvinists,* Ware argued that a person is by nature "innocent and pure, free from all moral corruption, as well as destitute of all positive holiness; and, until he has, by the exercise of his faculties, actually formed a character either good or bad, an object of the divine complacency and favour." Ware's conclusion was that a person is "by nature no more inclined or disposed to vice than to virtue."

Obviously Ware was declaring that he intended to steer Harvard in an entirely new theological direction, far from the intentions of its founders.

Within a short time a new, rigorously orthodox seminary was founded at Andover, Massachusetts, to counter Harvard, and an increasingly acrimonious debate began between various partisans. Now out in the open for all to see, the debate raged until two events of great significance occurred. In 1819 the pastor of Boston's Federal Street Church, William Ellery Channing (1780–1842), was invited to preach the ordination sermon of Jared Sparks as minister of a Unitarian society in Baltimore. Channing took as his subject "Unitarian Christianity," and the sermon (selection 14) received national publicity. It came to be regarded as the classic statement of American Unitarianism.

The second event of major importance happened the next year, 1820. With many New England congregations being torn apart in the controversy swirling about them, the orthodox Congregationalists went to the courts to prevent Unitarians from getting title to church property previously held by trinitarians. In the famous "Dedham decision" of 1820, written by Unitarian Chief Justice Isaac Parker, the Massachusetts Supreme Court ruled that church property was vested in the voters of the parish—even if a majority of the communicant members of the church were opposed. Thus the property of more than sixty churches was transferred to the Unitarians, and the churches of the Standing Order, the term commonly used for the settled churches of New England Congregationalism, were irrevocably split asunder.

Against these and other expressions of heterodoxy the orthodox protested loudly and often in vain, it seemed. Involved theological conflicts, adroit ecclesiastical maneuvering and complex legal battles resulted. Would Christianity, as the founding fathers knew it, disappear from their beloved New England? For a time it seemed so.

While many protested and some leaders emerged, the first dominant champion of the New England orthodox came to national prominence in 1795. Timothy Dwight (1752–1817) came with much promise. A grandson of Jonathan Edwards and a precocious lad, as might be expected, he was graduated from Yale in 1769. Two years later he became a tutor at Yale and at age nineteen was younger than many of those he taught. During the Revolution he served as an army chaplain and in 1795 was elected president of Yale College. Public opinion throughout Connecticut hailed him as the obvious choice for the post.

At that time Yale was not a thriving college, and Dwight was not certain he wanted the job. "I do not court the appointment; let those who do, take it," he said. "To build up a ruined college is a difficult task." Discipline was notoriously slack, and the overwhelming majority of students were infidels who delighted in the arguments of Paine and Allen. But Dwight possessed, at forty-three, a great deal of experience, boundless energy, and an openness to new ideas. Perhaps most important, he had abundant common sense and no intention of alienating the students. He won their respect by his own example of Christian integrity and dignity. Then he began a sledge-hammer attack on infidelity through the unexpected tactic of free and open debate with Christianity's opponents at the college. To their surprise, students were encouraged to openly discuss their religious doubts and difficulties. President Dwight prepared a great four-year series of sermons for the college chapel. Since students usually attended for four years the sermon series was repeated, and most heard Dwight's comprehensive system of theology in which the entire philosophy of skepticism was answered.

Soon change began to be noticeable. Already in 1796 one student wrote home, "We now see the advantage of having an able director at the head of affairs, one whose commands are energetic, respected, and obeyed. . . . It is surprising to see what a difference there is in the behavior of the students since last year; at present there is no card playing . . . breaking glass bottles, etc. but all is order and quietness."[17] Early in 1802 two seniors were overwhelmed with conviction of their sins, and soon made a confession of faith. This impressed others, and the number under conviction multiplied. In the week preceding vacation fifty young men declared themselves "serious inquirers." Some feared the spiritual concern would evaporate over the school break. The reverse occurred. Colleges throughout New England heard of the revival at Yale, and the impulse spread. Half of the seniors were by then professing conversion, and one-third of the class eventually entered the ministry.

Timothy Dwight was preeminent in his day in leading a renewed assault on all that seemed to threaten Christian principles. He wrote voluminously (selection 15), served as president of Yale till his death, and raised up younger, able lieutenants such as Lyman Beecher (selection 11), Nathaniel William Taylor (selection 18), and Asahel Nettleton, to further the cause.

# The Ninteenth Century

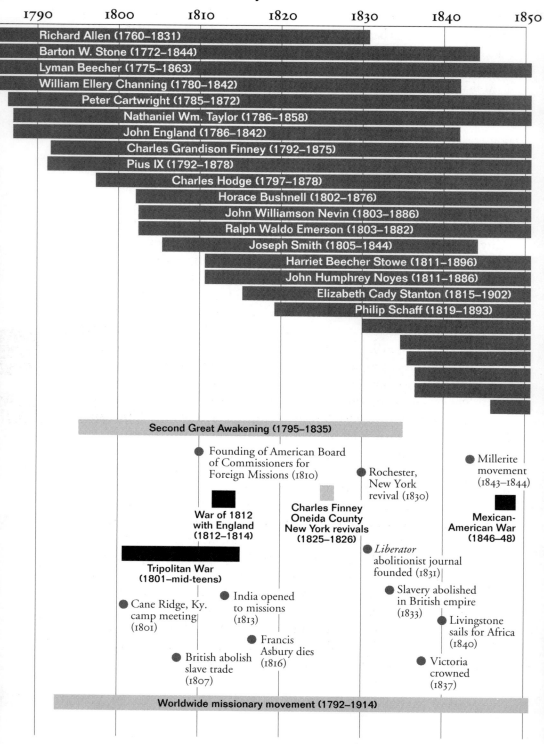

1790　1800　1810　1820　1830　1840　1850

Richard Allen (1760–1831)
Barton W. Stone (1772–1844)
Lyman Beecher (1775–1863)
William Ellery Channing (1780–1842)
Peter Cartwright (1785–1872)
Nathaniel Wm. Taylor (1786–1858)
John England (1786–1842)
Charles Grandison Finney (1792–1875)
Pius IX (1792–1878)
Charles Hodge (1797–1878)
Horace Bushnell (1802–1876)
John Williamson Nevin (1803–1886)
Ralph Waldo Emerson (1803–1882)
Joseph Smith (1805–1844)
Harriet Beecher Stowe (1811–1896)
John Humphrey Noyes (1811–1886)
Elizabeth Cady Stanton (1815–1902)
Philip Schaff (1819–1893)

Second Great Awakening (1795–1835)

Founding of American Board of Commissioners for Foreign Missions (1810)

Millerite movement (1843–1844)

Rochester, New York revival (1830)

War of 1812 with England (1812–1814)

Charles Finney Oneida County New York revivals (1825–1826)

Mexican-American War (1846–48)

Liberator abolitionist journal founded (1831)

Tripolitan War (1801–mid-teens)

India opened to missions (1813)

Slavery abolished in British empire (1833)

Cane Ridge, Ky. camp meeting (1801)

Livingstone sails for Africa (1840)

Francis Asbury dies (1816)

British abolish slave trade (1807)

Victoria crowned (1837)

Worldwide missionary movement (1792–1914)

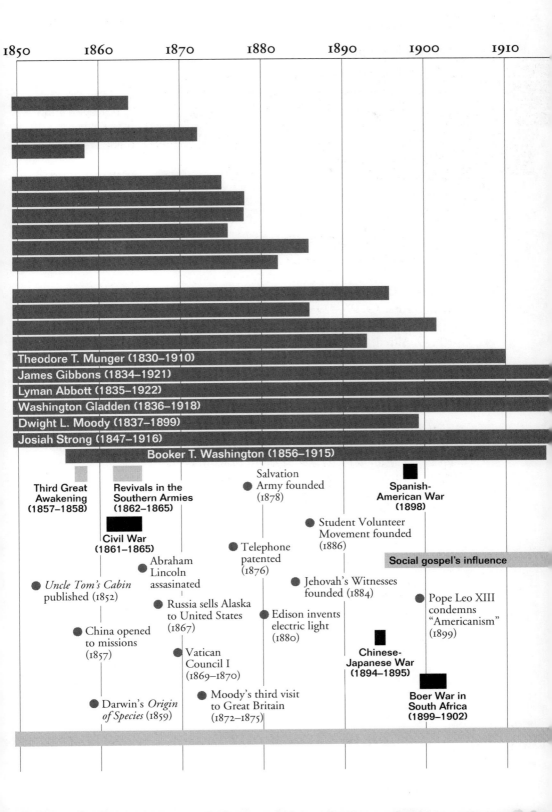

| 1850 | 1860 | 1870 | 1880 | 1890 | 1900 | 1910 |

Theodore T. Munger (1830–1910)
James Gibbons (1834–1921)
Lyman Abbott (1835–1922)
Washington Gladden (1836–1918)
Dwight L. Moody (1837–1899)
Josiah Strong (1847–1916)
Booker T. Washington (1856–1915)

**Salvation
Army founded
(1878)**

**Spanish-
American War
(1898)**

**Third Great
Awakening
(1857–1858)**

**Revivals in the
Southern Armies
(1862–1865)**

**Student Volunteer
Movement founded
(1886)**

**Civil War
(1861–1865)**

Telephone
patented
(1876)

**Social gospel's influence**

Abraham
Lincoln
assassinated

*Uncle Tom's Cabin*
published (1852)

Jehovah's Witnesses
founded (1884)

Pope Leo XIII
condemns
"Americanism"
(1899)

Russia sells Alaska
to United States
(1867)

Edison invents
electric light
(1880)

China opened
to missions
(1857)

Vatican
Council I
(1869–1870)

**Chinese-
Japanese War
(1894–1895)**

Darwin's *Origin
of Species* (1859)

Moody's third visit
to Great Britain
(1872–1875)

**Boer War in
South Africa
(1899–1902)**

## Select Bibliography

Brown, Arthur W. *Always Young for Liberty: A Biography of William Ellery Channing.* Syracuse, N.Y.: Syracuse University Press, 1956.

Cassirer, Ernst. *The Philosophy of the Enlightenment,* trans. by F. Koelln and J. Pettegrove. Boston: Beacon, 1951.

Channing, William E. *Works of William Ellery Channing,* 6 vols. 1882; repr., New York: B. Franklin, 1971.

Cragg, Gerald R. *The Church and the Age of Reason, 1648–1789.* Baltimore: Penguin, 1970.

Cuningham, Charles E. *Timothy Dwight, 1752–1817: A Biography.* New York: Macmillan, 1942.

Dwight, Timothy. *Travels; in New England and New York,* 4 vols. 1821–22; repr., Barbara Solomon, ed. Cambridge, Mass.: Harvard University Press, 1969.

Gay, Peter. *Deism: An Anthology.* Princeton, N.J.: Van Nostrand, 1968.

Hatch, Nathan O. *The Democratization of American Christianity.* New Haven, Conn.: Yale University Press, 1989.

Koch, G. Alfred. *Religion of the American Enlightenment.* New York: Crowell, 1968.

Purcell, Richard J. *Connecticut in Transition: 1775–1818,* rev. ed. Middletown, Conn.: Wesleyan University Press, 1963.

Wilbur, Earl Morse. *A History of Unitarianism,* 2 vols.: Vol. 2, *Unitarianism in Transylvania, England and America.* 1952; repr., Boston: Beacon, 1965.

Willey, Basil. *The Eighteenth Century Background: Studies on the Idea of Nature in the Thought of the Period.* Boston: Beacon, 1961.

Wright, Conrad. *The Beginnings of Unitarianism in America,* 1955; repr., Hamden, Conn.: Shoe String, 1976.

# The Age of Reason

## *Thomas Paine (1794)*

I believe in one God, and no more; and I hope for happiness beyond this life.

I believe in the equality of man; and I believe that religious duties consist in doing justice, loving mercy, and endeavoring to make our fellow creatures happy.

But lest it should be supposed that I believe in many other things in addition to these, I shall in the progress of this work, declare the things I do not believe, and my reasons for not believing them

I do not believe in the creed professed by the Jewish church, by the Roman church, by the Greek church, by the Turkish church, by the Protestant church, nor by any church that I know of. My own mind is my own church. . . .

It is curious to observe how the theory of what is called the Christian church sprung out of the tail of the heathen mythology. A direct incorporation took place in the first instance, by making the reputed founder to be celestially begotten. The trinity of gods that then follow was no other than a reduction of the former plurality, which was about twenty or thirty thousand; the statue of Mary succeeded the statue of Diana of Ephesus; the deification of heroes changed into the canonization of saints; the mythologists had gods for everything; the Christian mythologists had saints for everything; the church became as crowded with one as the Pantheon had been with the other, and Rome was the place of both. The Christian theory is little else than the idolatry of the ancient mythologists accommodated to the purpose of power and revenue, and it yet remains to reason and philosophy to abolish the amphibious fraud.

Nothing that is here said can apply, even with the most distant disrespect, to the real character of Jesus Christ. He was a virtuous and an amiable man. The morality that he preached and practiced was of the most benevolent kind; and though similar systems of morality had been preached by Confucius and by some of the Greek philosophers many years before, by the Quakers since, and by many good men in all ages, it has not been exceeded by any. . . .

Source: Moncure D. Conway, ed., *The Writings of Thomas Paine*, 6 vols. (New York: G. P. Putnam, 1894–96), 1:14–127, passim.

In the former part of this essay I have spoken of revelation; I now proceed further with that subject, for the purpose of applying it to the books in question.

Revelation is a communication of something which the person to whom that thing is revealed did not know before. For if I have done a thing or seen it done, it needs no revelation to tell me I have done it or seen it, nor to enable me to tell it or to write it.

Revelation, therefore, cannot be applied to anything done upon earth, of which man himself is the actor or the witness; and, consequently, all the historical and anecdotal parts of the Bible, which is almost the whole of it, is not within the meaning and compass of the word "revelation," and, therefore, is not the word of God.

When Samson ran off with the gateposts of Gaza, if he ever did so (and whether he did or not is nothing to us), or when he visited his Delilah, or caught his foxes, or did anything else, what has revelation to do with these things? If they were facts, he could tell them himself, or his secretary, if he kept one, could write them if they were both either telling or writing; and if they were fictions, revelation could not make them true; and whether true or not, we are neither the better nor the wiser for knowing them. When we contemplate the immensity of the Being who directs and governs the incomprehensible whole of which the utmost ken of human sight can discover but a part, we ought to feel shame at calling such paltry stories the word of God.

As to the account of the Creation, with which the Book of Genesis opens, it has all the appearances of being a tradition which the Israelites had among them before they came into Egypt; and after their departure from that country they put it at the head of their history, without telling (as it is most probable) that they did not know how they came by it. The manner in which the account opens shows it to be traditionary. It begins abruptly; it is nobody that speaks; it is nobody that hears; it is addressed to nobody; it has neither first, second, nor third person; it has every criterion of being a tradition; it has no voucher. Moses does not take it upon himself by introducing it with the formality that he uses on other occasions, such as that of saying, "The Lord spake unto Moses, saying. . . ."

Why it has been called the Mosaic account of the Creation, I am at a loss to conceive. Moses, I believe, was too good a judge of such subjects to put his name to that account. He had been educated among the Egyptians, who were a people as well skilled in science and particularly in astronomy as any people of their day; and the silence and caution that Moses observes in not authenticating the account is a good negative evidence that he neither told nor believed it. The case is that every nation of people has been worldmakers, and the

Israelites had as much right to set up the trade of worldmaking as any of the rest; and as Moses was not an Israelite, he might not choose to contradict the tradition. The account, however, is harmless; and this is more than can be said of many other parts of the Bible.

Whenever we read the obscene stories, the voluptuous debaucheries, the cruel and torturous executions, the unrelenting vindictiveness, with which more than half the Bible is filled, it would be more consistent that we call it the word of a demon than the word of God. It is a history of wickedness that has served to corrupt and brutalize mankind; and for my part I sincerely detest it, as I detest everything that is cruel.

We scarcely meet with anything, a few phrases excepted, but what deserves either our abhorrence or our contempt, till we come to the miscellaneous parts of the Bible. In the anonymous publications, the Psalms and the Book of Job, more particularly in the latter, we find a great deal of elevated sentiment reverentially expressed of the power and benignity of the Almighty; but they stand on no higher rank than many other compositions on similar subjects, as well before that time as since.

---

## Selection 14

# Unitarian Christianity

## *William Ellery Channing (1819)*

1. In the first place, we believe in the doctrine of God's UNITY, or that there is one God, and one only. To this truth we give infinite importance, and we feel ourselves bound to take heed, lest any man spoil us of it by vain philosophy. The proposition, that there is one God, seems to us exceedingly plain. We understand by it, that there is one being, one mind, one person, one intelligent agent, and one only, to whom underived and infinite perfection and dominion belong. We conceive, that these words could have conveyed no other meaning to the simple and uncultivated people, who were set apart to be the depositories of this great truth, and who were utterly incapable of understanding those hair-breadth distinctions between being and person, which the sagacity of later ages has discovered. We find no intimation, that this language was to

Source: *The Works of William E. Channing,* 6th ed. (Boston: J. Munroe and Co., 1846), 69–78, passim.

be taken in an unusual sense, or that God's unity was a quite different thing from the oneness of other intelligent beings.

We object to the doctrine of the Trinity, that, whilst acknowledging in words, it subverts in effect, the unity of God. According to this doctrine, there are three infinite and equal persons, possessing supreme divinity, called the Father, Son, and Holy Ghost. Each of these persons, as described by theologians, has his own particular consciousness, will, and perceptions. They love each other, converse with each other, and delight in each other's society. They perform different parts in man's redemption, each having his appropriate office, and neither doing the work of the other. The Son is mediator and not the Father. The Father sends the Son, and is not himself sent; nor is he conscious, like the Son, of taking flesh. Here, then, we have three intelligent agents, possessed of different consciousnesses, different wills, and different perceptions, performing different acts, and sustaining different relations; and if these things do not imply and constitute three minds or beings, we are utterly at a loss to know how three minds or beings are to be formed. . . .

We do, then, with all earnestness, though without reproaching our brethren, protest against the irrational unscriptural doctrine of the Trinity. . . .

2. Having thus given our views of the unity of God, I proceed in the second place to observe, that we believe in the unity of Jesus Christ. We believe that Jesus is one mind, one soul, one being, as truly one as we are, and equally distinct from the one God. We complain of the doctrine of the Trinity, that, not satisfied with making God three beings, it makes Jesus Christ two beings, and thus introduces infinite confusion into our conceptions of his character. This corruption of Christianity, alike repugnant to common sense and to the general strain of Scripture, is a remarkable proof of the power of a false philosophy in disfiguring the simple truth of Jesus. . . .

Surely, if Jesus Christ felt that he consisted of two minds, and that this was a leading feature of his religion, his phraseology respecting himself would have been colored by this peculiarity. The universal language of men is framed upon the idea, that one person is one person, is one mind, and one soul; and when the multitude heard this language from the lips of Jesus, they must have taken it in its usual sense, and must have referred to a single soul all which he spoke, unless expressly instructed to interpret it differently. But where do we find this instruction? Where do you meet, in the New Testament, the phraseology which abounds in Trinitarian books, and which necessarily grows from the doctrine of two natures in Jesus? Where does this divine teacher say, "This I speak as God, and this as man; this is true only of my human mind, this only of my divine"? Where do we find in the Epistles a trace of this strange phraseology? Nowhere. It was not needed in that day. It was demanded by the errors of a later age.

We believe, then, that Christ is one mind, one being, and, I add, a being distinct from the one God. That Christ is not the one God, not the same being with the Father, is a necessary inference from our former head, in which we saw that the doctrine of three persons in God is a fiction. But on so important a subject, I would add a few remarks. We wish, that those from whom we differ, would weigh one striking fact. Jesus, in his preaching, continually spoke of God. The word was always in his mouth. We ask, does he, by this word, ever mean himself? We say, never. On the contrary, he most plainly distinguishes between God and himself, and so do his disciples. How this is to be reconciled with the idea, that the manifestation of Christ, as God, was a primary object of Christianity, our adversaries must determine. . . .

3. Having thus given our belief on two great points, namely, that there is one God, and that Jesus Christ is a being distinct from, and inferior to, God, I now proceed to another point, on which we lay still greater stress. We believe in the *moral perfection of God.* We consider no part of theology so important as that which treats of God's moral character; and we value our views of Christianity chiefly as they assert his amiable and venerable attributes. . . .

We believe that God is infinitely good, kind, benevolent, in the proper sense of these words; good in disposition, as well as in act; good, not to a few, but to all; good to every individual, as well as to the general system. . . .

4. Having thus spoken of the unity of God; of the unity of Jesus, and his inferiority to God; and of the perfections of the Divine character; I now proceed to give our views of the mediation of Christ, and of the purposes of his mission. With regard to the great object which Jesus came to accomplish, there seems to be no possibility of mistake. We believe that he was sent by the Father to effect a moral, or spiritual deliverance of mankind; that is, to rescue men from sin and its consequences, and to bring them to a state of everlasting purity and happiness. We believe, too, that he accomplishes this sublime purpose by a variety of methods; by his instructions respecting God's unity, parental character, and moral government, which are admirably fitted to reclaim the world from idolatry and impiety, to the knowledge, love, and obedience of the Creator; by his promises of pardon to the penitent, and of divine assistance to those who labor for progress in moral excellence; by the light which he has thrown on the path of duty; by his own spotless example, in which the loveliness and sublimity of virtue shine forth to warm and quicken, as well as guide us to perfection; by his threatenings against incorrigible guilt; by his glorious discoveries of immortality; by his sufferings and death; by that signal event,

the resurrection, which powerfully bore witness to his divine mission, and brought down to men's senses a future life; by his continual intercession, which obtains for us spiritual aid and blessings; and by the power with which he is invested of raising the dead, judging the world, and conferring the everlasting rewards promised to the faithful. . . .

We farther agree in rejecting, as unscriptural and absurd, the explanation given by the popular system, of the manner in which Christ's death procures forgiveness for men. This system used to teach as its fundamental principle, that man, having sinned against an infinite Being, has contracted infinite guilt, and is consequently exposed to an infinite penalty. We believe, however, that this reasoning, if reasoning it may be called, which overlooks the obvious maxim, that the guilt of a being must be proportioned to his nature and powers, has fallen into disuse. Still the system teaches, that sin, of whatever degree, exposes to endless punishment, and that the whole human race, being infallibly involved by their nature in sin, owe this awful penalty to the justice of their Creator. It teaches, that this penalty cannot be remitted, in consistency with the honor of the divine law, unless a substitute be found to endure it or to suffer an equivalent. It also teaches, that, from the nature of the case, no substitute is adequate to this work, save the infinite God himself; and accordingly, God, in his second person, took on him human nature, that he might pay to his own justice the debt of punishment incurred by men, and might thus reconcile forgiveness with the claims and threatenings of his law. Such is the prevalent system. Now, to us, this doctrine seems to carry on its front strong marks of absurdity; and we maintain that Christianity ought not to be encumbered with it, unless it be laid down in the New Testament fully and expressly. We ask our adversaries, then, to point to some plain passages where it is taught. We ask for one text, in which we are told, that God took human nature that he might make an infinite satisfaction to his own justice; for one text, which tells us, that human guilt requires an infinite substitute; that Christ's sufferings owe their efficacy to their being borne by an infinite being; or that his divine nature gives infinite value to the sufferings of the human. Not *one word* of this description can we find in the Scriptures; not a text, which even hints at these strange doctrines. They are altogether, we believe, the fictions of theologians. Christianity is in no degree responsible for them. We are astonished at their prevalence. What can be plainer, than that God cannot, in any sense, be a sufferer, or bear a penalty in the room of his creatures? How dishonorable to him is the supposition, that his justice is now so severe, as to exact infinite punishment for the sins of frail and feeble men, and now so easy and yielding, as to accept the limited pains of Christ's human soul, as a full equivalent for the endless woes due from the world?

---

## Selection 15

---

# Travels; in New England and New York

## *Timothy Dwight (1817)*

The present state of our moral and religious character cannot perhaps be more advantageously illustrated than by a comparison of it with that of our ancestors. The religion of former times was more zealous, rigid, scrupulous, and uniform. At the same time it was less catholic, gentle, indulgent in lawful cases, graceful, and amiable. The strictness, the energy, the commanding character of their religion, we have in a great measure lost. Where they stood firmly against the blast, we bend to escape its force. Where they watched, we are asleep. Where they fought manfully, we are employed in parleying. Where they triumphed, we are satisfied with a drawn battle. On the other hand we have in some respects advantageously relaxed from their austerity and rigor. We live more kindly and evangelically with Christians of other denominations. Our religious controversies are less violent, and we regard fewer things as fundamental grounds of difference. On the other hand, they educated their families more virtuously, regulated society with greater skill, executed laws with more exactness, and settled the affairs of men on a more solid foundation. They chiefly exhibited the magnanimous, we the gentler virtues. Ours are more amiable, but less firm. Theirs were rough and uninviting, but more to be relied on. In justice to these excellent men, it ought to be added that to them we are indebted for almost everything in our character which merits commendation. In some respects we have polished, but upon the whole, instead of improving, we have impaired their system. Formerly New England was inhabited almost exclusively by two classes of men: public professors of religion, and men of decent moral characters. The latter class universally believed without a doubt in divine revelation, and intended one day to become religious. All of them also regularly attended the public worship of God, and almost all of them observed in their conduct a respectful conformity to the precepts of his word. Every immorality was regarded

Source: Timothy Dwight, *Travels; in New England and New York*, 4 vols. (New Haven: S. Converse, 1822), 4:254, 267–68, 321–22, 340–42.

as a crime, and confessed to be incapable of justification or defense. When crimes were committed at all, they were committed with a consciousness of guilt, in secrecy and solitude, without a hope that principles could be found to palliate them, and with a certainty of shame and censure in every case of detection. They were committed only under the pressure of sudden or powerful temptations, when gain bewildered, when provocation stung, and when the mind was goaded by passion or appetite. After the perpetration, as he himself perfectly foresaw, the criminal was declared by the universal voice to be an offender against law and a sinner against God. He might be pitied, but he was never excused. He went, therefore, to the perpetration with trembling, and shrunk from the universal frown whenever he was detected.

Timothy Dwight

In such a state of society, you will readily believe, crimes were rare. Capital convictions were scarcely known, and a capital punishment was a prodigy. In almost all instances also, the persons convicted were foreigners. Inferior offenses, though more frequent, were few; and the stocks and the whipping post had little other use besides that which was monitory. Few infidels existed, and hardly one of them avowed his principles.

The present state of our society is in some respects the same with that which has been here described. In others the variations are marked by small shades of difference; in others still, the diversity is sufficiently evident. From the middle or neutral class of men, infidelity has received a considerable accession of recruits. You will not suppose that these men have been convinced of the truth of infidel principles, or of the falsehood of those which are contained in the Scriptures. They are merely men who love sin, and without conviction or evidence hail whatever will enable them to perpetrate it in peace. They are men who conclude without reasoning and resolve without inquiry. . . .

Let me solicit you to take a cursory view of the care and caution used from the beginning in introducing a candidate into the ministry. Let me then ask you whether in any business of human life you have known more prudent or more effectual expedients employed. Is not the utmost security here attained of receiving only the proper candidates? If these measures will not insure a learned, pious, and faithful ministry, what will?

The ministry here is safe also from the temptations presented in several other countries by rank and opulence. I am far from believing that rank and opulence necessarily conduct those by whom they are possessed to criminal conduct. I well know that many such persons have been distinguished for their wisdom and piety. But you will agree with me that these splendid objects involve serious temptations. You will also admit that, where they are annexed to places of any kind, the votaries of wealth and splendor will covet, and not unfrequently obtain, these places. It is here believed, and I think with no small appearance of reason, that great secular enjoyments would open the desk in spite of every precaution to the intrusion of loose and worldly men. But no devotee to wealth or honor will be allured into this office by the salary connected with it, or the tenure on which it is holden. I neither deny, nor doubt, that the former is too small, and the latter too precarious. As both are, however, there is probably no class of men more unblamable than the clergy of Connecticut.

You are not to conclude from anything which I have here said that ministers do not in the great body of instances continue firmly fixed in the places where they are originally settled. Almost all of them continue in their stations during life, unless when they are voluntarily exchanged for others. This fact, however, has its foundation *chiefly in the manners and habits of the people*. Ministers and schoolmasters to a great extent form the manners, and the manners support the ministers and schoolmasters. Hence the situation of ministers is justly asserted to be stable and permanent: as great a proportion of their whole number probably terminating life where they were originally settled as in most parts and perhaps in any part of the Christian world. The greatest source of separation between ministers and their people is the smallness of their salaries: and this, I confess, threatens, at the present expensive period, a more numerous train of evils than have hitherto been known of a similar nature in New England.

I am, Sir, yours, etc.

. . . The Christian Observer,[18] speaking with reference to this part of the subject, says, "These are times in which we must sorrowfully own that the ministry of the established church are held in a disrespect unknown in former days. There is but little or no respect to their office, as such."

I have chosen to appeal to these papers for two reasons. One is that, living in a distant country, and having never been in Great Britain, it cannot be supposed that I am personally acquainted with the state of the established church.

Whatever knowledge I possess of this subject, derived from books and men, whether Englishmen or Americans, you, or others, might perhaps be disposed to question; and thus my remarks, however just, might be left in a state of uncertainty, or perhaps absolutely discredited. The other is that, as I am a Presbyterian, you might believe me less candid with respect to this subject than I intend to be.[19]

To the present appeal no objection can, I presume, be reasonably made. Permit me then to say, with the exception heretofore made, that in the collection of churches in New England which are Presbyterian or Congregational such clergymen as are here described are unknown. We have some bad ministers, they are, however, *rarae aves.* But a minister who spent his time, or any part of it, in the dissipation specified by this letter writer would here be regarded as a prodigy. I never knew one who in this country could have these things said of him with truth. Few have I known, very few, who were not believed to be persons of piety. No minister belonging to these churches thinks of such a thing as selecting sermons. Every minister preaches two sermons every Sabbath, and always composes them both himself. Let me add, the great body of them are of course religious, fraught with the spirit of the Gospel, and very generally judicious. Many of them are excellent. It is impossible that a man who devotes himself at all to his study, or his parochial concerns, should compose so many sermons and get them by heart. They are, therefore, generally read; and the inhabitants are so far persuaded that written discourses, taken together, are more instructive and profitable than extemporaneous ones that they are well satisfied with this manner of preaching, and usually prefer it. There is, however, a considerable exception to what I have here asserted. A number of ministers, and not a very small one, when they have arrived to middle life, and have become familiarized to the doctrines and duties of theology, preach either from short notes, or extemporaneously: studying their discourses, however, more laboriously perhaps than when they are written. Instruction is here the ruling character of preaching, rather than addressing the feelings or the imagination. In behalf of this mode I allege three reasons. One is that religion has nowhere more prevailed than in the old settlements of New England. Another is that the people are nowhere less blown about by every wind of doctrine. The third is that sound instruction is more satisfactory to an audience, and generally more popular. . . .

. . . There are 869 Presbyterian congregations[20] and eighty-one Episcopal in the states of New Hampshire, Massachusetts, Vermont, and Connecticut. Every one of these has a church. Almost every church is decent and in good repair. Almost all are painted, except such as are of brick or stone; and nineteen out of twenty have steeples. A great number have been built in the new settlements; and many others, in the places of such as have been pulled down because the proprietors have wished for larger or handsomer buildings. A multitude of these churches may be pronounced handsome, not indeed in the same sense in which the fine specimens of architecture exhibited by various churches in the city of London are styled handsome. Still, though not answering the demands of the taste and science of a connoisseur in that art, they are beautiful objects to the eye. Nor can anything be more delightful to a traveler than the continual succession of these buildings at intervals of three, four, five, and six miles throughout all the ancient settlements of this country, where, drest in snowy white, they appear like stars amid the universal verdure, unless perhaps his agreeable surprise at finding the same objects in settlements so new as to forbid even the hope, and much more the expectation of seeing them at a period apparently premature. It ought to be added that the spirit which prompts to the settlement of ministers, and to the rebuilding and repairing of churches, is rapidly increasing. . . .

*Dear Sir,*

There is another view in which the religion of this, and indeed of every other country, ought to be considered by him who would either describe or understand it in a comprehensive manner. To this I will now proceed.

The original planters of New England, viz. the Plymouth colonists, held:

1. That the Scriptures only contain the true religion, and that nothing which is not contained in them is obligatory upon the conscience;

2. That every man has the right of judging for himself, of trying doctrines by them, and of worshipping according to his apprehensions of their meaning;

3. That the doctrinal articles of the Reformed Churches of England, Scotland, Ireland, France, the Palatinate, Geneva, Switzerland, and the United Provinces are agreeable to the holy oracles;

4. That the pious members of all these churches were to be admitted to their communion;

5. That no particular church ought to consist of more members than can conveniently watch over one another, and usually meet and worship in one congregation;

6. That every such church is to consist of those only who appear to believe in Christ and to obey him;

7. That any competent number of such persons have a right to embody themselves in a church for their mutual edification;

8. That this ought to be done by an *express covenant;*

9. That, when embodied, they have a right to choose all their officers;

10. That these officers are pastors or teaching elders, ruling elders, and deacons;

11. That pastors are to oversee, rule, teach, and administer the sacraments, and that they are to be maintained. . . .

20. That the Lord's day was to be strictly observed throughout, and that fasts and thanksgivings are to be observed as the state of providence requires.

With these tenets the first colonists of New Hampshire, Massachusetts, and Connecticut generally agreed.

The great body of the present inhabitants of New England hold them in substance at the present time. In a few particulars, the Hopkinsians have super-added to the doctrinal part of this system. A considerable number of Armini-ans and perhaps a greater number of Unitarians inhabit the eastern parts of New England, especially of Massachusetts. A few of both are found elsewhere. In Connecticut I do not know a single Unitarian clergyman among the Con-gregationalists, and scarcely half a dozen Arminian.

# 7

# Revivalism and the Second Great Awakening

As the eighteenth century drew to a close, America's decline in religious interest, and the rise of infidelity, were pronounced. In the East, a number of prominent people espoused deism and renounced Christianity. As already noted, President Thomas Jefferson, elected in 1800, was a deist, and his secretary of war, Henry Dearborn (1751–1829), so hated the churches that he once said, "So long as these temples stand we cannot hope for good government." General Charles Lee (1731–1782) also detested Christianity, and in his will he demanded not to be buried "in any church or church-yard, or within a mile of any Presbyterian or Anabaptist meeting-house."[1] In the West and South, where churches were just getting a foothold, antireligious sentiment was especially high. The early settlers of Kentucky frequently named their towns or counties after famous French infidels such as Rousseau, LaRue, Bourbon, and Altamont. In 1793 the Kentucky legislature voted to do away with the services of a chaplain, as no longer wanted.

For years the annual General Assembly of the Presbyterian Church in the U.S.A.[2] had sent pastoral letters to all of its congregations lamenting the decline of morals and zeal, but the pastoral letter of 1798 showed more alarm than any of its predecessors:

> Dear Friends and Brethren: The aspect of divine providence, and the extraordinary situation of the world, at the present moment, indicate, that a solemn admonition by the ministers of religion and other church-officers in General Assembly convened, has become our indispensable duty. . . . We perceive, with pain and fearful apprehension, a general dereliction of religious principle and

practice amongst our fellow citizens; a great departure from the faith and simple purity of manners for which our fathers were remarkable; a visible and prevailing impiety and contempt for the laws and institutions of religion, and an
abounding infidelity which in many instances tends to Atheism itself. . . . God
hath a controversy with us—Let us prostrate ourselves before Him![3]

It is remarkable that only one year later, the General Assembly's pastoral
letter for 1799 had a very different tone:

> Notwithstanding there is still cause to deplore the prevalence of vice and
> immorality . . . amidst this generally unfavourable aspect, there are several par-
> ticular circumstances peculiarly comforting and encouraging. . . . We have
> heard from different parts the glad tidings of the outpourings of the Spirit, and
> of times of refreshing from the presence of the Lord. We have heard from sev-
> eral parts of our church, and elsewhere, of the late hopeful conversion of many.
> From the east, from the west, and from the south, have these joyful tidings
> reached our ears.[4]

In 1801 the General Assembly wrote, "From many of their churches, the
Assembly have heard the most pleasing accounts of the state of vital piety.
Revivals, of a more or less general nature, have taken place in many parts, and
multitudes have been added to the church."[5] In 1802 the Assembly stated, "In
some parts of the states of Virginia and North Carolina, the Spirit of God
has, we trust, been poured out in an extraordinary manner; and by accounts
received from Kentucky and Tennessee, the unusual work there, of which the
Assembly have been heretofore informed, appears, during the last year, to
have been progressive."[6] And in 1803 the Assembly was positively joyful as it
surveyed the nation:

> Since an inquiry of this nature has become part of the annual business of
> the Assembly, it may be confidently asserted, that no result was ever presented
> to our body so favourable, and so gratifying to the friends of truth and piety. . . .
> In most of the northern and eastern Presbyteries, revivals of religion of a more
> or less general nature, have taken place. Sinners have been convinced and con-
> verted . . . without any remarkable bodily agitations, or extraordinary affec-
> tions. In this calm and ordinary manner, many hundreds have been added to
> the church in the course of the last year. In many of the southern and western
> Presbyteries, revivals more extensive, and of a more extraordinary nature, have
> taken place. The Assembly . . . are constrained to acknowledge with thankful-
> ness, that the last year, while it presented a continuance and great extension of

this extraordinary work, furnished also increasing evidence that it is indeed the work of God. . . .

Information of a very pleasing nature was also communicated . . . of a work of divine grace in various parts of Connecticut, especially in Yale College; in which important institution many of the youth have hopefully become pious. The probable influence of such an event, in so respectable a seminary of learning, on the church of Christ generally . . . cannot but make a very pleasing impression on the friends of piety.

On the whole, the Assembly cannot but declare with joy, that the state and prospect of vital religion in our country are more favourable and encouraging than at any period within the last forty years.[7]

## A different sort of awakening

The commissioners to the Assembly had a right to be hopeful. What was happening around them was the beginning of the *Second Great Awakening*, a movement that would be far longer in duration (from approximately 1795 to 1835), and far wider in influence than the first awakening of the 1740s. A number of points need to be noted to compare the First and Second great awakenings:

First, in the 1740s the colonies were mostly still strung in a narrow band along the eastern seacoast, and the frontier had not yet moved far inland. This would tend to make the character of the Great Awakening rather homogeneous. By 1800, the frontier of the United States already extended many hundreds of miles inland and, as the General Assembly noted above, the nation was divided into a number of parts, each with its own distinctive character. Therefore the Second Awakening would take on different aspects. Such was indeed the case; the awakening in the West, with its camp meetings and more emotional tone, differed markedly from the awakening in the colleges and cities of the East.

Second, over its long life the Second Awakening, particularly under Charles G. Finney, first developed the modern concept of urban mass evangelism with a city-wide ecumenical "crusade" or "campaign," in which a highly organized advance and follow-up organization works through a number of churches.

Third, the observer can follow development of techniques of evangelism during the Second Great Awakening that alter markedly the entire concept of awakenings or revivals—from Solomon Stoddard's (selection 5) and Jonathan Edwards' astonishment at the "surprising work of God," to Finney's carefully calculated methods embodied in his revolutionary statement, "A revival is not a miracle. . . . It is a purely philosophical result of the right use of the constituted means."[8] While Finney quickly added that God's blessing was necessary for any revival to occur, he was declaring that revivals are not unpredictable movings of the Holy Spirit's power, but the result of human manipulation of God-given methods for bringing about spiritual renewal.

Fourth, while the Great Awakening of the 1740s had its by-products, especially in the founding of churches and colleges, the Second Great Awakening is especially noteworthy for generating innumerable reform causes: antislavery, women's rights, prison reform, temperance, world peace, education, Sabbath observance, and many more. Finney first effectively wedded evangelism and reform. Through thousands of voluntary reform societies, which sprang up across America, multitudes of women and men toiled mightily for God to alleviate the conditions that bred sin and prevented humans from realizing their full potential under God. In our cynical time, when we look back on this dedicated effort that dwarfs anything today, such a dynamic and altruistic spirit is almost inconceivable.

Obviously, in the first half of the nineteenth century America was rapidly changing. The nation's secular and religious situations included the following:

1. The shift from Calvinist election and predestination, and an inertia sometimes induced by "hyper-Calvinism," to an Arminian view that humans have free will to choose or reject Jesus Christ.
2. An upward mobility through which common people could assume more power in civil and church life.
3. Liberal tendencies of "the New Divinity" and evangelistic "tools" used by Protestants (sometimes called "means" and "measures") to hasten conversion and church growth.
4. The search for social panaceas, which bore a host of reform movements and experiments in perfectionistic and communitarian living.

In the 1740s the Great Awakening abated in New England and the Middle Colonies, but it continued throughout the rural South for some decades. The Methodists under Bishop Francis Asbury had singular success in Delaware, Maryland, and Brunswick County, Virginia, after the Revolution. Local revivals also broke out in some Connecticut towns: Norfolk in 1767; Killingly in 1776; Lebanon in 1781; New Britain in 1784; East Haddam and Lyme in 1792; Farmington and New Hartford in 1795, and Milford in 1796. Revivals occurred in western Pennsylvania, in the towns north of Pittsburgh, and in the western portion of New York during the 1790s. While there was no general revival from 1745 to 1795, local awakenings kept the spirit of revival aflame.

The Second Great Awakening in the West began decisively under the ministry of James McGready (1762?–1817), a fiery Presbyterian preacher who in 1796 became pastor of three small churches in Logan County, Kentucky (for a description of this area at that time, see selection 16). The frontier was rough-and-tumble, sparsely populated, and lawless. Most people had never attended a school, and Peter Cartwright reported that he knew of men forty-five years old who had never seen a wagon. McGready's intense, direct preaching and thunderous voice thrilled his backwoods audiences and brought results. At Red River in June 1800 four or five hundred members of McGready's church gathered at a four-day Communion service. Four other preachers joined McGready for the extensive preaching that the people expected. On the first three days the meetings were solemn and reverent, but on the final day, while Methodist John McGee was preaching, the congregation joyously and frantically began to shout and cry. As McGee wrote, "The floor was soon covered with the slain; their screams for mercy pierced the heavens."

In the frontier wilderness, with its bleak, lonely, and dangerous life devoid of any social outlets, the people asked for more such meetings, and McGready and the others planned another sacramental service for July 1800 at Gasper River. They expected a similar attendance. To their astonishment unprecedented crowds began to arrive from distances as great as 100 miles. Tents were set up everywhere, wagons with provisions were brought in, and the underbrush far beyond the church cleared. The response to the preaching was as excited as before. In camp meeting after camp meeting similar revivals broke out, until the area affected spread into Tennessee.

But the full force of the new work was yet to be felt. Barton W. Stone (1772–1844), a Presbyterian pastor in Bourbon County, Kentucky, heard of McGready's work and traveled across the state in 1801 to observe it, writing, "The scene was new to me and passing strange. It baffled description." Much impressed, he returned home and made plans for a similar protracted meeting at Cane Ridge in August 1801. Being better publicized than its predecessors, the *Cane Ridge Camp Meeting* drew far greater numbers. The multitude was estimated between 10,000 and 25,000, many coming long distances. Even 10,000 was an astonishing figure at a time when Lexington, the largest town in Kentucky, had fewer than 1800 inhabitants. Stone, dumbfounded at the numbers pouring in, realized that the extensive arrangements already made would be strained to the breaking point. Invitations had been sent to all the Methodist, Presbyterian and Baptist clergy for miles around, and, once things got underway, Stone rejoiced that "all appeared cordially united in it. They were of one mind and soul: the salvation of sinners was the one object. We all engaged in singing the same songs, all united in prayer, all preached the same things."[9]

After the first years of the awakening in the West one of the most eminent frontier evangelists was Peter Cartwright (1785–1872), a Methodist circuit rider who was a frontiersman himself and knew the West as did few others (selection 16). A stalwart and enormously dedicated man, he lived a life that was never dull, finding himself often in difficult situations where he had to use his powerful fists to handle rowdies. Contemporaries reported that Cartwright's booming voice made women weep and strong men tremble. One of the few battles he lost was in 1846 when he ran for an Illinois seat in Congress; the winner was a lawyer from Springfield named Abraham Lincoln. Cartwright's vivid descriptions of life on the frontier and the expansion of Christianity make the times come alive for us.

## Charles Finney and new measures

The second phase of the Second Great Awakening was led by an apprentice lawyer, Charles Grandison Finney (1792–1875). After Finney's birth in Connecticut his parents followed the mass migration of people seeking free land and riches on the New York State frontier. After growing up on the remote shores of Lake Ontario, Finney tried being a schoolteacher and then a lawyer. On October 10, 1821, he was so overwhelmed by spiritual need that he went to the woods north of Adams, New York, and experienced one of the more famous conversions of that century. He had promised that "If I am ever converted, I will preach the gospel," and he turned about to do just that.

After a rudimentary education in divinity, Finney was ordained in 1824 and became a missionary in rural Jefferson County, where he conducted revival meetings with much success. In early October 1825 Finney and his wife Lydia went to Western, a town near Utica, New York, when an unforeseen occurrence catapulted him from backwoods missionary to nationally known evangelist. The following eight years were probably the most spectacular evangelistic activity the country has ever seen. At Western he was persuaded to begin evangelistic meetings, which became sensationally successful. The *Oneida County revivals* were conducted in its eager towns for the next year and one-half, producing large numbers of converts and making Finney a much sought-after preacher.

Though ordained a Presbyterian minister, Finney always had trouble with doctrines of Calvinism. Election and predestination seemed to stultify action in those who would be saved. As a lawyer he had been trained in free will and personal responsibility, and these seemed to contradict Finney's rather superficial understanding of Calvin's concept that one could do little to change his or her ultimate destiny. Finney increasingly furthered his belief in free will, and the sinner's opportunity to choose. Therefore, he was fearful of holding meetings in Philadelphia, the bastion of historic or *Old School Presbyterianism*. But in 1828 he was invited to preach there. Despite his differences with some preachers he met with little resistance and eventually spent a full year in its numerous churches.

Finney's greatest revival was conducted in Rochester, New York, from September 1830 to March 1831. Whitney Cross has written,

> No more impressive revival has occurred in American history. Sectarianism was forgotten and all churches gathered in their multitudes. . . . But the exceptional feature was the phenomenal dignity of this awakening. No agonizing souls fell in the aisles, no raptured ones shouted hallelujahs. Rather, despite his doses of hell-fire, the great evangelist, "in an unclerical suit of gray," acted "like a lawyer arguing . . . before a court and jury," talking precisely, logically, but with wit, verve, and informality. Lawyers, real-estate magnates, millers, manufacturers, and commercial tycoons led the parade of the regenerated. The theatre became a livery stable. Taverns closed.[10]

In 1832, for the first time, Finney became a settled pastor, of the Second Free Presbyterian Church (Chatham Street Chapel) in New York City. Utterly disdainful of the Old School faction in his Presbyterian denomination, Finney railed at them and drew huge crowds to hear him preach and practice his "*new measures*," which were thought objectionable by many: public praying by women in mixed audiences; protracted series of evangelistic meetings (i.e., daily services); colloquial language used by the preacher; the anxious seat or bench (where concerned people could come at the sermon's end on the preacher's invitation); the practice of praying for people by name, and immediate membership for converts.

On December 5, 1834, Finney began a long series of talks in Chatham Street Chapel which eventually became an enormously successful book entitled *Lectures on Revivals of Religion* (selection 17). In it, Finney was not just mounting a reaction to Old School Calvinism. *Lectures* also declared the principles of the revival program he had employed, principles he confidently assumed (correctly) would become the standard for much of American Protestantism.

The tumultuous nature of the buoyant young nation was reflected in the number of conflicts within the rapidly-growing Protestant churches after 1800. Appearing increasingly were tendencies among church leaders to veer toward Old School or high church sentiments, or toward *New School* or low church views. One must be careful in assigning labels of a later day to that time, but in general it may be said that the former were conservatives who maintained historic doctrines and the latter were the liberalizing party. This division occurred for many years in a number of denominations, and much of it was a protest against the rampant revivalism of the nineteenth century. Reacting to the influence of mergers between Congregational and Presbyterian churches on the frontier, Finney's new measures and the doctrinal sentiments of Nathaniel W. Taylor's *New Divinity* at Yale (selection 19), Presbyterian conservatives formed the Old School party and brought a series of heresy trials, culminating in the Old School-New School division of 1837.

Differing views on whether the individual or the corporate Christian church were of primary importance underlaid the controversies. Obviously revivalism stressed the importance of the individual, and many felt that the corporate church, its confessions, and its sacramental life were being undervalued in the excitement of mass evangelism. High church sentiments, supporting the latter view, were represented in the Episcopal church by John H. Hobart (1775–1830), bishop of New York, and among the Presbyterians and Reformed by John W. Nevin (1803–1886), a graduate of Princeton and professor at the German Reformed seminary in Mercersburg, Pennsylvania.[11]

The German Reformed churches had been under Dutch Reformed jurisdiction until 1793 and, since then, had tried to make themselves an autonomous group. They remained small and struggling, founding a feeble seminary at Carlisle, Pennsylvania, in 1825 that moved ten years later to Mercersburg. In 1840 Nevin accepted a post in this seminary, and in 1843 he was joined by an eminent church historian, Philip Schaff (1819–1893), who shared his high church sentiments to a great degree. Against those who understood (as in revivalism) that the Christian faith was a relationship of individuals to Jesus Christ, who are only later brought together to form the church, Nevin stressed the ecumenical unity of all believers. The church, he said, is not a loose association to which a Christian can affiliate. Rather, membership is crucial to faith, for in the church the believer joins in living union with Christ. The mystical body of Christ and believers—one holy, catholic, and apostolic church—remains united through all time. Christ's "real spiritual presence" is expressed in the Lord's Supper, which should be the center of worship.

Nevin's views, called the *Mercersburg theology* or *evangelical catholicism,* countered prevailing practices at numerous points, but he especially attacked new measures revivalism, which had greatly infiltrated German Reformed churches. In *The Anxious Bench* (selection 18) Nevin stated that the national preoccupation with these measures was "unfavorable to deep, thorough, and intelligent piety" and "fatal to the true idea of devotion." A far more profound work, *The Mystical Presence; or a Vindication of the Reformed or Calvinistic Doctrine of the Holy Eucharist,* was published in 1846. The Mercersburg romantic longing for an ideal Christian union of all Reformed, Lutheran, and Roman Catholic believers contributed to a violent confrontation with both revivalists and conservatives. Partly as a result, Nevin's health was broken, and Schaff narrowly escaped conviction in a heresy trial. Despite this, they contributed to a fresh diversity in viewpoints in a number of denominations.

## Select Bibliography

Boles, John B. *The Great Revival, 1787–1805: The Origins of the Southern Evangelical Mind.* Lexington: University of Kentucky Press, 1972.

Conkin, Paul K. *Cane Ridge: America's Pentecost.* Madison, Wis.: University of Wisconsin Press, 1990.

Cross, Whitney R. *The Burned-over District: The Social and Intellectual History of Enthusiastic Religion in Western New York, 1800–1850.* 1950; repr., Los Angeles: Octagon, 1981.

Dupuis, Richard A. G., and Garth M. Rosell, eds. *The Memoirs of Charles G. Finney: The Complete Restored Text, Critical Edition.* Grand Rapids: Zondervan, 1989.

Foster, Charles I. *An Errand of Mercy: The Evangelical United Front, 1790–1837.* Chapel Hill: University of North Carolina Press, 1960.

Hardman, Keith J. *Charles Grandison Finney, 1792–1875: Revivalist and Reformer.* Syracuse: Syracuse University Press, 1987.

Johnson, Charles A. *The Frontier Camp Meeting: Religion's Harvest Time.* Dallas: Southern Methodist University Press, 1955.

Johnson, Paul E. *A Shopkeeper's Millennium: Society and Revivals in Rochester, New York, 1815–1837.* New York: Hill and Wang, 1978.

Smith, Timothy L. *Revivalism and Social Reform: American Protestantism on the Eve of the Civil War.* New York, Harper, 1965.

# The Backwoods Preacher

### *Peter Cartwright (1856)*

## Parentage

I was born September 1st, 1785, in Amherst County, on James River, in the State of Virginia. My parents were poor. My father was a soldier in the great struggle for liberty, in the Revolutionary war with Great Britain. He served over two years. My mother was an orphan. Shortly after the united colonies gained their independence, my parents moved to Kentucky, which was a new country. It was an almost unbroken wilderness from Virginia to Kentucky at that early day, and this wilderness was filled with thousands of hostile Indians, and many thousands of the emigrants to Kentucky lost their lives by these savages. There were no roads for carriages at that time, and although the emigrants moved by thousands, they had to move on pack-horses. Many adventurous young men went to this new country. The fall my father moved, there were a great many families who joined together for mutual safety, and started for Kentucky. Besides the two hundred families thus united, there were one hundred young men, well armed, who agreed to guard these families through, and, as a compensation, they were to be supported for their services. After we struck the wilderness we rarely travelled a day but we passed some white persons, murdered and scalped by the Indians while going to or returning from Kentucky. . . .

In the fall of 1793 my father determined to move to what was then called the Green River country, in the southern part of the State of Kentucky. He did so, and settled in Logan County, nine miles south of Russellville, the county seat, and within one mile of the state line of Tennessee. . . .

Logan County, when my father moved to it, was called "Rogues' Harbour." Here many refugees from almost all parts of the Union fled to escape justice or punishment; for although there was law, yet it could not be executed, and it was a desperate state of society. Murderers, horse-thieves, highway robbers and counterfeiters fled here, until they combined and actually formed a majority. The honest and civil part of the citizens would prosecute these wretched

Peter Cartwright, *The Backwoods Preacher; Being the Autobiography of Peter Cartwright* (London: Wesleyan-Methodist Book Room, 1865), 1–8, 15–16, 32–33, 41, 51–52, *passim*.

banditti, but they would swear each other clear; and they really put all law at defiance, and carried on such desperate violence and outrage, that the honest part of the citizens seemed to be driven to the necessity of uniting and combining together, and taking the law into their own hands, under the name of Regulators. This was a very desperate state of things.

Shortly after the Regulators had formed themselves into a society, and established their code of by-laws, on a court day at Russellville, the two bands met in town. Soon a quarrel commenced, and a general battle ensued between the rogues and Regulators, and they fought with guns, pistols, dirks, knives, and clubs. Some were actually killed, many wounded, the rogues proved victors, kept the ground, and drove the Regulators out of town. The Regulators rallied again, hunted, killed. and lynched many of the rogues, until several of them fled, and left for parts unknown. Many lives were lost on both sides, to the great scandal of civilised people. This is but a partial view of frontier life.

When my father settled in Logan County, there was not a newspaper printed south of Green River, no mill short of forty miles, and no schools worth the name. Sunday was a day set apart for hunting, fishing, horse-racing, card-playing, balls, dances, and all kinds of jollity and mirth. We killed

Peter Cartwright

our meat out of the woods, wild; and beat our meal and hominy with a pestle and mortar. We stretched a deer skin over a hoop, burned holes in it with the prongs of a fork, sifted our meal, baked our bread, eat it, and it was first-rate eating too. We raised, or gathered out of the woods, our own tea. We had sage, bohea, cross-vine, spice, and sassafras teas in abundance. As for coffee, I am not sure that I ever smelled it for ten years. We made our sugar out of the water of the maple-tree, and our molasses too. These were great luxuries in those days.

## Cane Ridge Camp-Meeting

Time rolled on, population increased fast around us, the country improved, horse-thieves and murderers were driven away, and civilisation advanced considerably. Ministers of different denominations came in and preached through the country; but the Methodist preachers were the pioneer messengers of salvation in these ends of the earth. Even in Rogues' Harbour there was a Baptist Church, a few miles west of my father's, and a Presbyterian congregation a few miles north, and the Methodist *Ebenezer* a few miles south.

Somewhere between 1800 and 1801, in the upper part of Kentucky, at a memorable place called "Cane Ridge," there was appointed a sacramental meeting by some of the Presbyterian ministers, at which meeting, seemingly unexpected by ministers or people, the mighty power of God was displayed in a very extraordinary manner; many were moved to tears, and bitter and loud crying for mercy. The meeting was protracted for weeks. Ministers of almost all denominations flocked in from far and near. The meeting was kept up by night and day. Thousands heard of the mighty work, and came on foot, on horseback, in carriages, and waggons. It was supposed that there were in attendance at times during the meeting from twelve to twenty-five thousand people. Hundreds fell prostrate under the mighty power of God, as men slain in battle. Stands were erected in the woods from which preachers of different Churches proclaimed repentance toward God and faith in our Lord Jesus Christ, and it was supposed, by eye and ear witnesses, that between one and two thousand souls were happily and powerfully converted to God during the meeting. It was not unusual for one, two, three, and four to seven preachers to be addressing the listening thousands at the same time from the different stands erected for the purpose. The heavenly fire spread in almost every direction. It was said by truthful witnesses, that, at times, more than one thousand persons broke out into loud shouting all at once, and that the shouts could be heard for miles around.

From this camp-meeting, for so it ought to be called, the news spread through all the Churches, and through all the land, and it excited great wonder and surprise; but it kindled a religious flame that spread all over Kentucky and through many other states. And I may here be permitted to say, that this was the first camp-meeting ever held in the United States, and here our camp-meetings took their rise. . . .

## The Great Revival

From 1801 for years a blessed revival of religion spread through almost the entire inhabited parts of the West, Kentucky, Tennessee, the Carolinas, and many other parts, especially through the Cumberland country, which was so called from the Cumberland River, which headed and mouthed in Kentucky, but in its great bend circled south through Tennessee, near Nashville. The Presbyterians and Methodists in a great measure united in this work, met together, prayed together, and preached together.

In this revival originated our camp-meetings, and in both these denominations they were held every year, and, indeed, have been ever since, more or less. They would erect their camps with logs, or frame them, and cover them with clapboards or shingles. They would also erect a shed, sufficiently large to protect five thousand people from wind and rain, and cover it with boards or shingles; build a large stand, seat the shed, and here they would collect together from forty to fifty miles around, sometimes further than that. Ten, twenty, and sometimes thirty ministers, of different denominations, would come together and preach night and day, four or five days together; and, indeed, I have known these camp-meetings to last three or four weeks, and great good resulted from them. I have seen more than a hundred sinners fall like dead men under one powerful sermon, and I have seen and heard more than five hundred Christians all shouting aloud the high praises of God at once; and I will venture to assert that many happy thousands were awakened and converted to God at these camp-meetings. Some sinners mocked, some of the old dry professors opposed, some of the old starched Presbyterian preachers preached against these exercises, but still the work went on, and spread almost in every direction, gathering additional force, until our country seemed all coming home to God.

In this great revival the Methodists kept moderately balanced; for we had excellent preachers to steer the ship or guide the flock. But some of our members ran wild, and indulged in some extravagances that were hard to control.

The Presbyterian preachers and members, not being accustomed to much noise or shouting, when they yielded to it went into great extremes and downright wildness, to the great injury of the cause of God. Their old preachers licensed a great many young men to preach, contrary to their Confession of Faith. That Confession of Faith required their ministers to believe in unconditional election and reprobation, and the unconditional and final perseverance of the saints. But in this revival they, almost to a man, gave up these points of high Calvinism, and preached a free salvation to all mankind. The Westminster Confession required every man, before he could be licensed to preach, to have a liberal education; but this qualification was dispensed with, and a great many fine men were licensed to preach without this literary qualification or subscribing to those high-toned doctrines of Calvinism. . . .

Just in the midst of our controversies on the subject of the powerful exercises among the people under preaching, a new exercise broke out among us, called the *jerks*, which was overwhelming in its effects upon the bodies and minds of the people. No matter whether they were saints or sinners, they would be taken under a warm song or sermon, and seized with a convulsive jerking all over, which they could not by any possibility avoid, and the more they resisted the more they jerked. If they would not strive against it and pray in good earnest, the jerking would usually abate. I have seen more than five hundred persons jerking at one time in my large congregations. Most usually persons taken with the jerks, to obtain relief, as they said, would rise up and dance. Some would run, but could not get away. Some would resist; on such the jerks were generally very severe. . . .

Methodism in Europe this day would have been as a thousand to one, if the Wesleyans had stood by the old landmarks of John Wesley: but no; they must introduce pews, literary institutions, and theological institutes, till a plain, old-fashioned preacher, such as one of Mr. Wesley's "lay preachers," would be scouted, and not allowed to occupy one of their pulpits. Some of the best and most useful men that were ever called of God to plant Methodism in this happy republic were among the early pioneer preachers, east, west, north, and south; and especially in our mighty West. We have no such preachers now as some of the first ones who were sent out to Kentucky and Tennessee.

The Presbyterians, and other Calvinistic branches of the Protestant Church, used to contend for an educated ministry, for pews, for instrumental music, for a congregational or stated salaried ministry. The Methodists universally opposed these ideas; and the illiterate Methodist preachers actually set the world on fire (the American world at least) while they were lighting their matches!

## Itinerant Life

At the close of this Conference year, 1806, I met the Kentucky preachers at Lexington, and headed by William Burke, about twenty of us started for Conference, which was held in East Tennessee, at Ebenezer Church, Nollichuckie, September 15th. Our membership had increased to twelve thousand six hundred and seventy; our net increase was about eight hundred. . . .

I think I received about forty dollars this year; but many of our preachers did not receive half that amount. These were hard times in those Western wilds; *many,* very *many,* pious and useful preachers were literally starved into a location. I do not mean that they were starved for want of food; for, although it was rough, yet the preachers generally got enough to eat. But they did not generally receive in a whole year money enough to get them a suit of clothes; and if people, and preachers too, had not dressed in home-spun clothing, and the good sisters had not made and presented their preachers with clothing, they generally must retire from itinerant life, and go to work and clothe themselves. Money was very scarce in the country at this early day, but some of the best men God ever made breasted the storms, endured poverty, and triumphantly planted Methodism in this Western world. . . .

Our increase for 1809–10 was 1,950. Increase of travelling preachers, fifteen.

At this Conference I was returned to Livingston Circuit, Cumberland District; Learner Blackman presiding elder. At the close of this year, 1810–11, we met at New Chapel, Shelby County, Kentucky, November 1st, 1810. Our increase of members, this Conference year, 4,264; increase of travelling preachers, thirteen.

The Western Conference met the last time as the Western Conference at Cincinnati, October 1st, 1811, and our increase this year was 3,600. Our increase in preachers was ten. Our strength of membership in the entire Western Conference at its last session as a Western Conference, was 30,741. In 1787 we had but ninety members that were officially reported from the West; and if, as we have elsewhere stated, that at the General Conference of 1st May, 1800, in Baltimore, the Western Conference was regularly organized, with about two thousand members, the reader will plainly see that God wrought in eleven years by the pioneer fathers that planted Methodism in this vast Western wilderness; and of the little band of travelling preachers that then ploughed the wilderness, say twelve men, none are now living save Mr. Henry Smith. In the fall of 1804, when I joined the Conference, there was a little over 9,000 members in the Western Conference; in 1811, 30,741. There were then a little over forty travelling preachers, and in 1810 over one hundred; and yet, at this time, there are not more than six of us left lingering on the shores of time to look back, look around, and look forward to the future of the Methodist Episcopal Church for weal or for woe. Lord, save the Church from desiring to have pews, choirs, organs, or instrumental music, and a congregational ministry, like other heathen Churches around them.

In 1804, the membership of the whole Church was 119,945, travelling preachers 433, throughout the United States territories and Canada. Their increase this year, throughout the Union, was 6,811. In 1812, when the Western Conference was divided into Ohio and Tennessee Conferences, our entire membership had increased to 184,567; increase of members in eight years, near 65,000. Travelling ministers in 1804, 433; in 1812, 688.

# Lectures on Revivals of Religion

## *Charles Grandison Finney (1835)*

### I. A Revival of Religion Is Not a Miracle

1. A miracle has been generally defined to be, a Divine interference, setting aside or suspending the laws of nature. It is not a miracle, in this sense. All the laws of matter and mind remain in force. They are neither suspended nor set aside in a revival.

2. It is not a miracle according to another definition of the term miracle—*something above the powers of nature.* There is nothing in religion beyond the ordinary powers of nature. It consists entirely in the *right exercise* of the powers of nature. It is just that, and nothing else. When mankind become religious, they are not *enabled* to put forth exertions which they were unable before to put forth. They only exert the powers they had before in a different way, and use them for the glory of God.

3. It is not a miracle, or dependent on a miracle, in any sense. It is a purely philosophical result of the right use of the constituted means—as much so as any other effect produced by the application of means. There may be a miracle among its antecedent causes, or there may not. The apostles employed miracles, simply as a means by which they arrested attention to their message, and established its Divine authority. But the miracle was not the revival. The miracle was one thing; the revival that followed it was quite another thing. The revivals in the apostles' days were connected with miracles, but they were not miracles.

I said that a revival is the result of the *right* use of the appropriate means. The means which God has enjoyed for the production of a revival, doubtless have a natural tendency to produce a revival. Otherwise God would not have enjoined them. But means will not produce a revival, we all know, without the blessing of God. No more will grain, when it is sowed, produce a crop without the blessing of God. It is impossible for us to say that there is not as direct an influence or agency from God, to produce a crop of grain, as there is to pro-

Source: Charles G. Finney, *Lectures on Revivals of Religion* (Boston: C. H. Pierce, 1848), 14–20, 357–81, *passim.*

duce a revival. What are the laws of nature, according to which, it is supposed, that grain yields a crop? They are nothing but the constituted manner of the operations of God. In the Bible, the word of God is compared to grain, and preaching is compared to sowing seed, and the results to the springing up and growth of the crop. And the result is just as philosophical in the one case, as in the other, and is as naturally connected with the cause.

I wish this idea to be impressed on all your minds, for there has long been an idea prevalent that promoting religion has something very peculiar in it, not to be judged of by the ordinary rules of cause and effect; in short, that there is no connection of the means with the result, and no tendency in the means to produce the effect. No doctrine is more dangerous than this to the prosperity of the church, and nothing more absurd. . . .

## II. I Am to Show What a Revival Is

Charles Grandison Finney, 1834
(Allen Memorial Art Museum,
Oberlin [Ohio] College)

It presupposes that the church is sunk down in a backslidden state, and a revival consists in the return of the church from her backslidings, and in the conversion of sinners.

1. A revival always includes conviction of sin on the part of the church. Backslidden professors cannot wake up and begin right away in the service of God, without deep searchings of heart. The fountains of sin need to be broken up. In a true revival, Christians are always brought under such convictions; they see their sins in such a light, that often they find it impossible to maintain a hope of their acceptance with God. It does not always go to that extent; but there are always, in a genuine revival, deep convictions of sin, and often cases of abandoning all hope.

2. Backslidden Christians will be brought to repentance. A revival is nothing else than a new beginning of obedience to God. Just as in the case of a converted sinner, the first step is a deep repentance, a breaking down of heart,

a getting down into the dust before God, with deep humility, and forsaking of sin.

3. Christians will have their faith renewed. While they are in their backslidden state they are blind to the state of sinners. Their hearts are as hard as marble. The truths of the Bible only appear like a dream. They admit it to be all true; their conscience and their judgment assent to it; but their faith does not see it standing out in bold relief, in all the burning realities of eternity. But when they enter into a revival, they no longer see men as trees walking, but they see things in that strong light which will renew the love of God in their hearts. This will lead them to labor zealously to bring others to him. They will feel grieved that others do not love God, when they love him so much. And they will set themselves feelingly to persuade their neighbors to give him their hearts. So their love to men will be renewed. They will be filled with a tender and burning love for souls. They will have a longing desire for the salvation of the whole world. They will be in agony for individuals whom they want to have saved; their friends, relations, enemies. They will not only be urging them to give their hearts to God, but they will carry them to God in the arms of faith, and with strong crying tears beseech God to have mercy on them, and save their souls from endless burnings.

4. A revival breaks the power of the world and of sin over Christians. It brings them to such vantage ground that they get a fresh impulse towards heaven. They have a new foretaste of heaven, and new desires after union to God; and the charm of the world is broken, and the power of sin overcome.

5. When the churches are thus awakened and reformed, the reformation and salvation of sinners will follow, going through the same stages of conviction, repentance, and reformation. Their hearts will be broken down and changed. Very often the most abandoned profligates are among the subjects. Harlots, and drunkards, and infidels, and all sorts of abandoned characters, are awakened and converted. The worst part of human society are softened, and reclaimed, and made to appear as lovely specimens of the beauty of holiness.

### Instructions to Converts

6. Young converts should be taught *to do all their duty*. They should never make a compromise with duty, nor think of saying "I will do *this* as an offset for neglecting *that*." They should never rest satisfied till they have done their duty of every kind, in relation to their families, the church, Sabbath Schools, the impenitent around them, the disposal of their property, the conversion of the world. Let them do their duty, as they feel it when their hearts

are warm; and never attempt to pick and choose among the commandments of God. . . .

9. They should set out with a determination to *aim at being useful in the highest degree possible.* They should not rest satisfied with merely being useful, or remaining in a situation where they can do *some* good. But if they see an opportunity where they can do more good, they must embrace it, whatever may be the sacrifice to themselves. No matter what it may cost them, no matter what danger or what suffering, no matter what change in their outward circumstances, or habits, or employments it may lead to. If they are satisfied that they will on the whole do more good, they should not even hesitate. How else can they be like God? How can they think to bear the image of Jesus Christ, if they are not prepared to do all the good that is in their power? When a man is converted he comes into a new world, and should consider himself as a new man. If he finds he can do the most good by remaining in his old employment, let it be so. But if he can do more good in some other way, he is bound to change. It is for the want of attention to this subject, in the outset, that Christians have got such low ideas on the subject of duty. And that is the reason why there are so many useless members in our churches.

10. They must be taught *not to aim at comfort but usefulness in religion.* There are a great many spiritual epicures in the churches, who are all the while seeking to be happy in religion, while they take very little pains to be useful. They had much rather spend their time in singing joyful hymns, and in pouring out their happy feelings in a gushing tide of exultation and triumph, than to spend it in agonizing prayer for sinners, or in going about and pulling dying men out of the fire. They seem to feel as if they were born to enjoy themselves. But I do not think such Christians show such fruits as to make their example one to be imitated. Such was not the temper of the apostles. They travailed for souls, and laboured in weariness and painfulness, and in deaths oft, to save sinners. Nor is it safe. Ordinarily, Christians are not qualified to drink deep at the fountain of joy. In ordinary cases, a deep agony of prayer for souls is more profitable than high flights of joy. Let young converts be taught, plainly, not to calculate upon a life of joy and triumph. They may be called to go through fiery trials. Satan may sift them like wheat. But they must go forward, not calculating so much to be happy as to be useful, not talking about comfort but duty, not desiring flights of joy and triumph, but hungering and thirsting after righteousness, not studying how to create new flights of rapture, but how to know the will of God, and do it. They will be happy enough in heaven. . . .

### Instruction of Young Converts

(3.) Teach them that religion does not consist in raptures, or ecstacies, or high flights of feeling. There may be a great deal of these where there *is* religion. But it ought to be understood that they are all involuntary emotions, and may exist in full power where there *is no* religion. They may be the mere workings of the imagination, without any truly religious affection at all. Persons may have them to such a degree as actually to swoon away with ecstacy, even on the subject of religion, without having any religion. I have known one person almost carried away with rapture, by a mere view of the natural attributes of God, his power and wisdom, as displayed in the starry heavens, and yet the person had no religion. Religion is obedience to God, the voluntary submission of the soul to the will of God. . . .

## Remarks

1. The church is verily guilty for her past neglect, in regard to the instruction of young converts.

Instead of bringing up their young converts to be working Christians, the churches have generally acted as if they did not know how to employ young converts, or what use to make of them. They have acted like a mother, who has a great family of daughters, and knows nothing how to set them to work, and so suffers them to grow up idle and untaught, useless and despised, and to be the easy prey of every designing villain.

If the church had only done her duty in training up young converts to work, and labour for Christ, the world would have been converted long ago. But instead of this, how many churches even oppose young converts, when they attempt to set themselves at work for Christ. Multitudes of old professors look with suspicion upon every movement of young converts, and talk against them, and say, "They are too forward, they ought not to put themselves forward, but *wait* for those who are older." There is *waiting* again. Instead of bidding young converts "God speed," and cheering them on when they take hold with warm hearts and strong hands, very often they hinder them and perhaps put them down. How often have young converts been stopped from going forward, and turned in behind a formal, lazy, inefficient church, till their spirit is crushed, and their zeal extinguished, and after a few ineffectual struggles to throw off the cords, they conclude to sit down with the rest and WAIT. In many places, young converts cannot even attempt to hold a prayer-meeting by themselves, but what the pastor, or some of the deacons, rebukes them for being so forward, and charges them with spiritual pride. "Oh, ho! you are *young converts,* are you? and so you want to get together and call all the neighbors together to look at you, because you are young converts." You had better turn preachers at once. A celebrated Doctor of Divinity in New England boasted at a public table of his success in keeping all his converts still. He had great difficulty, he said, for they were in a terrible fever to do something, to talk, or pray, or get up meetings, but by the greatest vigilance he had kept it all down, and now his church was just as quiet as it was before the revival. Wonderful achievement for a minister of Jesus Christ! Was that what the blessed Savior meant when he told Peter, "Feed my lambs"?

2. Young converts should be *trained to labour,* just as carefully as young recruits in an army are trained for war.

Suppose a captain in the army should get his company enlisted, and then take no more pains to teach and train and discipline them, than are taken by many pastors to train and lead forward their young converts. Why, the enemy would laugh at such an army. Call them soldiers! Why, as to any effective service, they are in a mere state of babyhood, they know nothing what to do or how to do it, and if you bring them up to the CHARGE, where are they? Such an army would resemble the church that does not train her young converts. Instead of being trained to stand shoulder to shoulder in the onset, they feel no practical confidence in their leaders, no confidence in their neighbors, no confidence in themselves, and they scatter at the first shock of battle. Look at the church now. Ministers are not agreed as to what shall be done, and many of them will turn and fight back against their brethren, quarreling about New Measures, or the Act and Testimony, or something. And as to the members, they cannot feel confidence when they see their leaders so divided. And then if they attempt to do any thing—Alas! alas! what ignorance, what awkwardness, what discord, what weakness, what miserable work they make of it. And so it must continue, until the church shall train up young converts to be intelligent, single-hearted, self-denying, working Christians. Here is an enterprise now going on in this city, which I rejoice to see. I mean the *Tract* enterprise—a blessed work. And the plan is to train up a body of devoted Christians to do—what?—why to do what all the church ought to have been trained to do long ago, to know how to pray, and how to converse with people about their soul's salvation, and how to attend anxious meetings, and how to deal with inquirers, and how to SAVE SOULS.

# The Anxious Bench

## John Williamson Nevin (1844)

It has been already stated, that the Anxious Bench is made the direct object of regard in this tract, rather than New Measures in general, for the very purpose of cutting off occasion, as much as may be, from those who seek occasion, for confounding in this way things that are entirely distinct. The particular is made to stand for the general, in the way of specimen or type, so as to exclude all that is not of the same complexion and spirit. If any choose notwithstanding to take the idea of New Measures in a wider sense, they have a right to please themselves in so doing, if they see proper; but they can have no right surely to obtrude their own arbitrary view on the present discussion. There is a broad difference between New Measures in the one sense, and New Measures in the other sense. It is overbearing impudence to pretend, that a protracted meeting, or a meeting for social prayer, is of the same character with the anxious bench, or the various devices for theatrical effect with which this is so frequently linked. Such meetings lie in the very conception of Christian worship, and are as old as the Church. The assertion sometimes heard, that the idea of protracted meetings, now so familiar and so generally approved, is one of recent origin, for which we indebted to the system of New Measures, serves only to expose the ignorance of those by whom it is made. It is no less an abuse of terms, as well as of common sense, to include in this system tract societies, the cause of missions, and the benevolent agencies in general, by which the Church is endeavoring to diffuse the knowledge of the truth throughout the world. All these things are natural, direct utterances of the spirit of Christianity itself, and have no affinity whatever with the order of action represented by the Anxious Bench. The same thing may be said of revivals. They are as old as the gospel itself. Special effusions of the Spirit, the Church has a right to expect in every age, in proportion as she is found faithful to God's covenant; and where such effusions take place, an extraordinary use of the ordinary means of grace will appear, as a matter of course. But still a revival is one thing, and a Phrygian

Source: John Williamson Nevins, *The Anxious Bench* (Chambersburg, Penn.: German Reformed Church, 1844), 19–84, *passim*.

dance another; even though the Phrygian dance should be baptized into Christian Montanism. Life implies action, but all action is not life. It is sheer impudence to say, that new measures and revival measures are the same thing.

And there is good reason to believe, that the confusion which is said to prevail with regard to the whole subject, is much less in fact than is sometimes represented. As a general thing, people know very well that there is no affinity or connection, between the system represented by the Anxious Bench, and such evangelical interests as have now been mentioned. Even in those sections, where it has been found convenient to stretch the idea of New Measures over this hallowed territory, there is a better knowledge of the true state of the case probably than is often supposed.

John Williamson Nevin

But allowing the confusion to be as complete, among the German Churches, as it is represented, shall no effort be made to correct it, and put things in their proper light? Admit that the best practices, and most important interests, are in the eyes of many identified with the system of New Measures, in the proper sense, so that to assault the latter is considered an assault at the same time upon the former; still is that a reason for sparing and sheltering the system, under its own bad form? Is there no help for the German Churches, in this predicament? Must they have revivals, in the way of the Anxious Bench, or no revivals at all? Must it be with them Finneyism, Methodism, Winebrennerism, or open war with serious religion, and the spirit of missions, under every form? Is the necessary alternative, in their case, quackery or death? Rather, in these circumstances, it becomes a solemn duty to take the difficulty by the horns, and reduce it to its proper posture. We owe it to the German Churches, not to suffer things so different, in a case of such vast moment, to be so deplorably confounded. The case is one that calls loudly for light, and it is high time that light should be extended to it without reserve. If it be a reigning error, to involve light and darkness in this way, under a common term, in the same sweeping censure, that is not a reason surely why we should try to uphold the darkness for the sake of the light, but a sacred requisition upon us rather, to insist on a clear, full discrimination of the one element from the other. If Finneyism and Winebrennerism, the anxious bench, revival machinery, solemn tricks for effect, decision displays at the bidding of the preacher, genuflections and prostrations in the aisle or around the altar, noise and disorder, extravagance and rant, mechanical conversions, justification by feeling rather than faith, and encouragement ministered to all fanatical impressions: if these things, and things in the same line indefinitely, have no connection in fact with true serious religion and the cause of revivals, but tend only to bring them into discredit, let the fact be openly proclaimed. Only in this way, may it be hoped that the reproach put upon revivals and other evangelical interests by some, under cover of their pretended connection with this system of New Measures in the true sense, will be in due time fairly rolled away.

The mourner strives of course to *feel* faith. The spiritual helpers standing round are actively concerned, to see him brought triumphantly through. Excitement rules the hour. No room is found either for instruction or reflection. A sea of feeling, blind, dark and tempestuous, rolls on all sides. Is it strange, that souls thus conditioned and surrounded, should become the victims of spiritual delusion? All high wrought excitement must, in its very nature, break, when it reaches a certain point. How natural that this relaxation, carrying with it the sense of relief as compared with the tension that had place before, should be mistaken on such an occasion for the peace of religion, that mysterious something which it is the object of all this process to fetch into the mind. And how natural that the wearied subject of such experience, should be hurried into a wild fit of joy by this imagination, and stand prepared, if need by, to clap his hands and shout hallelujah, over his fancied deliverance. Or even without this mimic sensation, how natural that the mourner, at a certain point, should allow himself to be persuaded by his own wishes, or by the authority of the minister perhaps, and other friends, telling him how easy it is to believe and urging him at last to consider the thing done; so as to take to himself the comfort of the new birth, as it were in spite of his own experience, and be counted among the converted. Altogether the danger of delusion and mistake, where this style of advancing the cause of religion prevails, must be acknowledged to be very great. The measure of the danger will vary of course, with the extent to which the characteristic spirit of the system is allowed to work. A Winebrennerian camp meeting, surrendering itself to the full sway of this spirit, will carry with it a more disastrous operation, than the simple Anxious Bench in a respectable and orderly Church. But in any form, the system is full of peril, as opening the way to spurious conversions, and encouraging sinners to rest in hopes that are vain and false.

# Redefining the Christian Message

Yale president Timothy Dwight (selection 15) founded the *New Haven theology* or *New Divinity* to help lead New England's orthodox against the threats of deism and infidelity. While he maintained great respect for his grandfather, Jonathan Edwards, Dwight reasoned that ideas a half-century old were inadequate to confront the new problems. Where Edwards had preferred the philosophy of John Locke, Dwight chose the Scottish Common-Sense Realism of Thomas Reid and Dugald Stewart, and he deviated from his grandfather in other ways as well.

However, it was Dwight's student, Nathaniel William Taylor (1786–1858), who was the real architect of the New Divinity. Educated at Yale, Taylor became the pastor of New Haven's First Church and then, in 1822, professor of Theology at Yale Divinity School. He is probably the best representative of the changing humor among the heirs of New England Puritanism and Calvinism. Grappling with challenges to the doctrine of original sin, Taylor was willing to modify a part of the doctrine he considered to be indefensible—the idea that people should be adjudged guilty by God for the sin of Adam. Not that this reduced the guilt of humans by one whit, Taylor held; people are completely responsible and utterly guilty of their own sins. Therefore the guilt of humans is actual, not imputed, as earlier theologians of the eminence of Tertullian, Augustine, Luther, and Calvin had taught.

In concert with Charles Finney (selection 17) and others, Taylor furthered New School views which insisted that the moral depravity of humans does not "consist in a sinful nature, which they have corrupted by being *one* with Adam, and by *acting in his act.* . . . Nor does the moral depravity of men consist in *any disposition or tendency* to sin. . . . " Rather, Taylor declared, this moral depravity *"is man's own act, consisting in a free choice of some object rather than God, as his chief good."* No human will avoid sinning, and though this is inevitable, it is not—as with Edwards—causally necessary. "Sin is in the sinning," Taylor stated in his two famous phrases, and humans possess "power to the contrary."

When Taylor preached these views in *Concio ad Clerum* (selection 19) before the General Association of Connecticut in 1828, he infuriated followers of Edwards, but he was enunciating views that were already shaping part of the ethos of mainstream Protestantism. Sydney Ahlstrom has written that, as expounded by various Presbyterian, Congregational, Baptist, and Methodist theologians, "New Schoolism" became virtually the theology of nonsectarian revivalism, the Sunday school movement, foreign and domestic missions, and much more. "One can almost speak of it as the theology of American Evangelical Protestantism during its nineteenth-century heyday," Ahlstrom writes.[1] Certainly it was amazingly consonant with the mood of freedom-loving Jacksonian America, which fondly held that rational decision and upward mobility, in matters both spiritual and secular, were within the power of every human. Meanwhile many others, such as Old School Calvinists across the nation and Presbyterians at Princeton Theological Seminary in particular (selections 32, 35), were certain that the New Divinity had not merely made some minor capitulations to the liberals but had caved in at a very crucial point.

## Romanticism and the transcendentalists

While Yale College was developing the New Divinity, over at Harvard Ralph Waldo Emerson (1803–1882) was attending the divinity school. He was born in Boston, received a formal classical education at Harvard, and in 1829 was ordained to the ministry at Boston's Second Church. After three years there he resigned as pastor because the congregation was unwilling to discontinue the communion service. By this time Emerson was beginning to display a brilliance he had not previously shown, and he was drawing much inspiration from romantic thinkers such as Jean-Jacques Rousseau (1712–1778), Samuel Taylor Coleridge (1772–1834), and Thomas Carlyle (1795–1881). In 1833 Emerson began his lifelong career as a lecturer, essayist, and poet. In 1836 he wrote *Nature,* an essay broaching his revolutionary ideas, and joined the Transcendental Club, made up mostly of rebellious young Unitarian clergymen, which included George Ripley, Theodore Parker, Orestes Brownson, and James Freeman Clarke, and laymen such as Henry David Thoreau.

It is difficult to summarize the ideas of these *Transcendentalists,* but they did agree on "the spiritual principle," which enshrined several concepts: (1) a rejection of any external authority; (2) a conviction of divine love, and (3) a determination to cultivate the intuitions of the soul. Emerson himself taught that imagination, insight, and instinct all go together to make up the religious intuition, through which each soul is linked to God. Once the soul has learned to utilize the gift of intuition, it can break through the materialistic layers of life and achieve union with God by enjoying the life of the "oversoul." Since these ideas were close to *pantheism*, Emerson had no use in his system for evil as an ontological reality, and therefore no need for salvation from sin or for a Savior.

Rather than please many of the old-line Unitarians or prove itself to be a logical development of their doctrinal drift, Transcendentalism appalled men like Andrews Norton, who called it the "latest form of infidelity." And Emerson retaliated by speaking of the "corpse-cold Unitarianism of Boston and Harvard College," glad that he had gone far beyond it, in his view, into a warm idealism which had shed any last vestiges of sectarianism.

On July 15, 1838, Emerson was invited to address the senior class at the Harvard Divinity School. His sermon (selection 20) became the most controversial and event-making utterance of his entire career.[2] To understand it, the sermon needs to read in its entirety.[3] It brought down the fury of many Unitarians, and rocked that denomination to its roots.

## The "Nurture" of American liberalism

Emerson and the Transcendentalists were strongly affected by the romantic movement, and their chief influence was in the nation's schoolrooms and parlors. Horace Bushnell (1802–1876), dubbed "the father of American religious liberalism," was also strongly influenced by romanticism, and more directly affected the seminaries and pulpits. Bushnell was born in Connecticut, the son of a Congregationalist pastor who was an Arminian. Already prejudiced against orthodox Calvinism, he graduated from Yale and tried teaching, business, and the law for a time, until a conversion experience of sorts made him decide to try the ministry. Returning to Yale Divinity School at the very time the debate over the New Haven Theology was raging, he studied under Taylor for a time but later confessed that he was more influenced by reading Friedrich Schleiermacher (1768–1834) and Coleridge than by Taylor. Veering ever further to the theological left, he stated that Taylor was overly concerned with logic, while he was less interested in logic than in life. In 1833 Bushnell became the pastor of the North Congregational Church in Hartford, Connecticut, which was riven with controversy. It took him some years to deal with that situation. He remained in that pulpit until his retirement.

Bushnell's first book, *Christian Nurture* (1847), gave him immediate notoriety and, as Winthrop S. Hudson writes, "was one of the most influential books ever to be published in America."[4] Parents usually taught a child that he or she was lost in sin until the Holy Spirit gave grace. Salvation would come through a datable conversion experience, probably during a revival. That evangelistic conversion, it was taught, was the most important point of a person's life. But Bushnell, arguing against original sin and the revival tradition of New England, said that if a child has been properly instructed and seen faith modeled by parents, it may be impossible to point to a specific conversion date. Bushnell declared that a child is susceptible to good even though plagued by sinful tendencies from birth. Parents should, therefore, raise their children within the household of faith, so that children will grow up never having known a time when they were not Christians.

In the light of New England's tradition of evangelism through revivals, this was a revolutionary idea, and provoked a wide reaction. Bushnell was accused of ignoring the Holy Spirit's crucial agency in human conversion and of bringing Christianity down to a form of religious naturalism. He insisted he did not, declaring that he supported revivals. Gradually, however, the idea of Christian nurture caught on across America. In time, it established an entirely different concept of Christian education in many churches, while not necessarily erasing the validity of evangelism and a datable conversion.

In 1849 Bushnell published *God in Christ,* in which he presented his "Dissertation on Language," which was accused of robbing language of its precision and making it merely poetic in form. In *Vicarious Sacrifice* (selection 21), published in 1865, he held that the most appropriate concept of the atonement is not that Christ was the *ransom* paid to Satan for the souls of the saints, nor was his death, as Anselm of Canterbury (1033–1109) taught, a satisfaction of the curse of the law that was rendered to God's justice and honor. Rather, Bushnell developed a theory similar to Peter Abelard's (1079–1142) *subjectivist* or *moral influence* theory. Abelard taught that the death of Christ is a *moral influence* in that it awakens in people gratitude to and love for God. Bushnell wrote that Christ's death evokes a *moral response* in humans, allowing them to respond to God's love in repentance and amendment of life. Abelard's theory has been widely criticized over the centuries, and Bushnell's modification of it received more criticism. However, by the turn of the century his ideas had become quite popular in liberal Protestant circles.

## Select Bibliography

Bishop, Jonathan. *Emerson on the Soul.* 1964; repr. ed., New York: AMS, n.d.

Brown, Jerry W. *The Rise of Biblical Criticism in America, 1800–1870: The New England Scholars.* Middletown, Conn.: Wesleyan University Press, 1969.

Carpenter, Frederic I. *Emerson Handbook.* New York: Hendricks House, 1957.

Cross, Barbara M. *Horace Bushnell: Minister to a Changing America.* Chicago: University of Chicago Press, 1958.

Griffin, Clifford S. *Their Brothers' Keepers: Moral Stewardship in the United States, 1800–1865.* 1960; repr. ed., Westport, Conn.: Greenwood, 1983.

Miller, Perry, ed. *The American Transcendentalists: Their Prose and Poetry.* Garden City, N.Y.: Doubleday, 1957.

Myers, A. J. William. *Horace Bushnell and Religious Education.* Boston: Little, Brown, 1937.

# Concio ad Clerum: A Sermon On Human Nature, Sin, and Freedom

## Nathaniel William Taylor (1828)

Ephesians 2:3. "And were by nature the children of wrath, even as others."

## I. Moral Depravity Defined

By the moral depravity of mankind I intend generally, the entire sinfulness of their moral character—that state of the mind or heart to which guilt and the desert of wrath pertain. I may say then negatively,

This depravity does not consist in any essential attribute or property of the soul—not in *any thing created* in man by his Maker. On this point, I need only ask—does God create in men a sinful nature, and damn them for the very nature he creates? Believe this, who can.

Nor does the moral depravity of men consist in a sinful nature, which they have corrupted by being *one* with Adam, and by *acting in his act.* To believe that I am one and the same being with another who existed thousands of years before I was born, and that by virtue of this identity I truly acted in his act, and am therefore as truly guilty of his sin as himself—to believe this, I must renounce the reason which my Maker has given me; I must believe it also, in face of the oath of God to its falsehood, entered upon the record. . . .

The question then still recurs, what is this moral depravity for which man deserves the wrath of God? I answer—*it is man's own act, consisting in a free choice of some object rather than God, as his chief good—or a free preference of the world and of worldly good, to the will and glory of God.* . . .

## II. Depravity Is by Nature

What then are we to understand, when it is said that mankind are depraved *by nature?* I answer—*that such is their nature, that they will sin and only sin in all the appropriate circumstances of their being.* . . .

Source: Nathaniel William Taylor, *Concio ad Clerum. A Sermon Delivered in the Chapel of Yale College, September 10, 1828* (New Haven: Hezekiah Howe, 1828), 5–38, passim.

So of mankind, change their circumstances as you may; place them where you will within the limits of their being; do what you will to prevent the consequence, you have one uniform result, entire moral depravity. No change of condition, no increase of light nor of motives, no instructions nor warnings, no any thing, within the appropriate circumstances of their being, changes the result. Unless there be some interposition, which is not included in these circumstances, unless something be done which is above nature, the case is hopeless. Place a human being any where within the appropriate limits and scenes of his immortal existence, and such is his nature, that he will be a depraved sinner.

When therefore I say that mankind are entirely depraved *by nature,* I do not mean that their nature is *itself* sinful, nor that their nature is the *physical* or *efficient* cause of their sinning; but I mean that their nature is the occasion, or reason of their sinning—that *such is their nature, that in all the appropriate circumstances of their being, they will sin and only sin. . . .*

Nathaniel W. Taylor

The message we are to deliver to men is a message of wrath, because they are the perpetrators of the deed that deserves wrath. It is a message of mercy to men who by acting, are to comply with the terms of it, and who can never hope to comply even through God's agency, without putting themselves to the doing of *the very thing* commanded of God. And it is only by delivering such a message, that we, Brethren, can be "workers together with God." Let us then go forth with it; and clearing God, throw all the guilt of sin with its desert of wrath, upon the sinner's single self. Let us make him see and feel that he can go to hell only as a self-destroyer—that it is this fact, that will give those chains their strength to hold him, and those fires the anguish of their burning. Let us if we can, make this conviction take hold of his spirit, and ring in his conscience like the note of the second death. If he trembles at the sound in his ears, then let us point him to that mercy which a dying Jesus feels for him, and tell him with the sympathies of men who have been in the same condemnation, that he need but to love and trust HIM, and heaven is his inheritance. Without derogating from the work of God's Spirit let us urge him to his duty—*to his duty—to his duty,* as a point-blank direction to business now on hand and now to be done. With the authorised assurance that "peradventure God may give him repentance," let us make known to him the high command of God, "*strive* to enter in at the strait gate," and make him hear every voice of truth and mercy in heaven and on earth, echoing the mandate.

Then shall the ministers of reconciliation be clad with truth as with a garment, and delivering their message not only in its substance but in its true manner and form, shall commend themselves to every man's conscience in the sight of God. Having his strength perfected in their weakness, they shall go forth "as archangels strong," and bidding the wide earth receive God's salvation, the bands of hell shall break, and a redeemed world return to the dominion of its God.

Finally, I cannot conclude without remarking, how fearful are the condition and prospects of the sinner. His sin is his own. He yields himself by his own free act, by his own choice, to those propensities of his nature, which under the weight of God's authority he *ought to govern*. The gratification of these he makes his chief good, immortal as he is. For this he lives and acts—this he puts in the place of God—and for this, and for nothing better he tramples on God's authority and incurs his wrath. Glad would he be, to escape the guilt of it. Oh—could he persuade himself that the fault is not his own—this would wake up peace in his guilty bosom. Could he believe that God is bound to convert and save him; or even that he could make it certain that God will do it, this would allay his fears, this would stamp a bow on the cloud that thickens, and darkens, and thunders damnation on his guilty path. But his guilt is all his own, and a just God may leave him to his choice. He is going on to a wretched eternity, the self-made victim of its woes. Amid sabbaths and Bibles, the intercessions of saints, the songs of angels, the intreaties of God's ambassadors, the accents of redeeming love, and the blood that speaketh peace, he presses on to death. God beseeching with tenderness and terror—Jesus telling him he died once and could die again to save him—mercy weeping over him day and night—heaven lifting up its everlasting gates—hell burning, and sending up its smoke of torment, and the weeping and the wailing and the gnashing of teeth, within his hearing—and onward still he goes. See the infatuated immortal! Fellow sinner,—IT IS YOU.

Bowels of divine compassion—length, breadth, height, depth of Jesus' love—Spirit of all grace, save him—Oh save him—or he dies forever.

## Excursus on Sin, Human Freedom, and God's Moral Government

The difficulties on this difficult subject as it is extensively regarded, result in the view of the writer from two very common but groundless assumptions—

assumptions which so long as they are admitted and reasoned upon, *must* leave the subject involved in insuperable difficulties.

The assumptions are these; First, *that sin is the necessary means of the greatest good and as such, so far as it exists, is preferable on the whole to holiness in its stead.* Secondly, *that God could in a moral system have prevented all sin or at least the present degree of sin.*

In further explanation of the ground taken in answering the above objection, the following enquiries are submitted to the consideration of the candid.

Is not the assumption that the degree of sin which exists, or even any degree of sin, is on the whole preferable to holiness in its stead, inconsistent alike with the benevolence and the sincerity of God? With his benevolence. If such be the nature of God, of man, of holiness, of sin, of all things, that sin is the necessary means of the greatest good, ought it not to be made the subject of precept—would it not be, by a benevolent moral Governor? For how can it be consistent with the benevolence of a moral governor, to require of his subjects that moral conduct which is not on the whole for the best?

The second assumption now claims our notice; viz. *that God could have prevented all sin, or at least the present degree of sin, in a moral system.*

If holiness in a moral system be preferable on the whole to sin in its stead, why did not a benevolent God, were it possible to him, prevent all sin and secure the prevalence of universal holiness? Would not a moral universe of perfect holiness, and of course of perfect happiness, be happier and better than one comprising sin and its miseries? And must not infinite benevolence accomplish all the good it can? Would not a benevolent God then, *had it been possible to him in the nature of things,* have secured the existence of universal holiness in his moral kingdom? . . .

But the main enquiry on this point remains—does the supposition that God could not prevent sin in a moral system, limit his power at all? To suppose or affirm that God cannot perform what is *impossible in the nature of things,* is not properly to limit his power. Is there then the least particle of evidence, that the entire prevention of sin in moral beings is possible to God in the nature of things? If not, then what becomes of the very common assumption of such possibility?

All evidence of the truth of this assumption must be derived either from the *nature of the subject,* or from *known facts.* Is there such evidence from *the nature of the subject?* It is here to be remarked, that the prevention of sin by any influence that destroys the *power to sin,* destroys moral agency. Moral agents then must possess the power to sin. Who then can prove *a priori* or from the nature of the subject, *that a being who* CAN *sin, will* NOT *sin?* How can it be proved *a priori* or from the nature of the subject, that a thing *will not be*, when for aught that appears, it *may* be? On this point, is it presumptuous to bid defiance to the powers of human reason? . . .

The writer hopes he shall not be charged *without proof*, with denying what he fully believes—that the providential purposes or decrees of God extend to all actual events, sin not excepted. God may really purpose the existence of sin, whether he purposes it for one reason or for another; he may, as the example shows, as really purpose sin though wholly an evil, considered as *incidental*, so far as his power of prevention is concerned, to the best moral system, as purpose it considered as so excellent in its nature and relations as to be the necessary means of the greatest good. And while the theory now proposed exhibits the providential government of God as the basis of submission, confidence and joy, under all the evils that befall his dependent creatures; it also presents, as no other theory in the view of the writer does present, the Moral Government of God in its unimpaired perfection and glory, to deter from sin and allure to holiness his accountable subjects.

---

## Selection 20

---

# The Divinity School Address

## *Ralph Waldo Emerson (1838)*

Jesus Christ belonged to the true race of prophets. He saw with open eye the mystery of the soul. Drawn by its severe harmony, ravished with its beauty, he lived in it, and had his being there. Alone in all history, he estimated the greatness of man. One man was true to what is in you and me. He saw that God incarnates himself in man, and evermore goes forth anew to take possession of his world. He said, in this jubilee of sublime emotion, "I am divine. Through me, God acts; through me, speaks. Would you see God, see me; or, see thee, when thou also thinkest as I now think." But what a distortion did his doctrine and memory suffer in the same, in the next, and the following ages! There is no doctrine of the Reason which will bear to be taught by the Understanding. The understanding caught this high chant from the poet's lips, and said, in the next age, "This was Jehovah come down out of heaven. I will kill you,

Source: Ralph Waldo Emerson, *Nature, Addresses, and Lectures* (Boston and Cambridge: James Munroe and Co., 1849), 119–25.

if you say he was a man." The idioms of his language, and the figures of his rhetoric, have usurped the place of his truth; and churches are not built on his principles, but on his tropes. Christianity became a Mythus, as the poetic teaching of Greece and of Egypt, before. He spoke of miracles; for he felt that man's life was a miracle, and all that man doth, and he knew that this daily miracle shines, as the character ascends. But the word Miracle, as pronounced by Christian churches, gives a false impression; it is Monster. It is not one with the blowing clover and the falling rain.

He felt respect for Moses and the prophets; but no unfit tenderness at postponing their initial revelations, to the hour and the man that now is; to the eternal revelation in the heart. Thus was he a true man. Having seen that the law in us is commanding, he would not suffer it to be commanded. Boldly, with hand, and heart, and life, he declared it was God. Thus is he, as I think, the only soul in history who has appreciated the worth of a man.

1. In this point of view we become very sensible of the first defect of historical Christianity. Historical Christianity has fallen into the error that corrupts all attempts to communicate religion. As it appears to us, and as it has appeared for ages, it is not the doctrine of the soul, but an exaggeration of the personal, the positive, the ritual. It has dwelt, it dwells, with noxious exaggeration about the *person* of Jesus. The soul knows no persons. It invites every man to expand to the full circle of the universe, and will have no preferences but those of spontaneous love. But by this eastern monarchy of a Christianity, which indolence and fear have built, the friend of man is made the injurer of man. The manner in which his name is surrounded with expressions, which were once sallies of admiration and love, but are now petrified into official titles, kills all generous sympathy and liking. All who hear me, feel, that the language that describes Christ to Europe and America, is not the style of friendship and enthusiasm to a good and noble heart, but is appropriated and formal,—paints a demigod, as the Orientals or the Greeks would describe Osiris or Apollo. Accept the injurious impositions of our early catechetical instruction, and even honesty and self-denial were but splendid sins, if they did not wear the Christian name. One would rather be

"A pagan, suckled in a creed outworn,"

than to be defrauded of his manly right in coming into nature, and finding not names and places, not land and professions, but even virtue and truth foreclosed and monopolized. You shall not be a man even. You shall not own the world; you shall not dare, and live after the infinite Law that is in you, and in company with the infinite Beauty which heaven and earth reflect to you in all lovely forms; but you must subordinate your nature to Christ's nature; you must accept our interpretations; and take his portrait as the vulgar draw it.

That is always best which gives me to myself. The sublime is excited in me by the great stoical doctrine, Obey thyself. That which shows God in me, fortifies me. That which shows God out of me, makes me a wart and a wen. There is no longer a necessary reason for my being. Already the long shadows of untimely oblivion creep over me, and I shall decease forever.

The divine bards are the friends of my virtue, of my intellect, of my strength. They admonish me, that the gleams which flash across my mind, are not mine, but God's; that they had the like, and were not disobedient to the heavenly vision. So I love them. Noble provocations go out from them, inviting me to resist evil; to subdue the world; and to Be. And thus by his holy thoughts, Jesus serves us, and thus only. To aim to convert a man by miracles, is a profanation of the soul. A true conversion, a true Christ, is now, as always, to be made, by the reception of beautiful sentiments. It is true that a great and rich soul, like his, falling among the simple, does so preponderate, that, as his did, it names the world. The world seems to them to exist for him, and they have not yet drunk so deeply of his sense, as to see that only by coming again to themselves, or to God in themselves, can they grow forevermore. It is a low benefit to give me something; it is a high benefit to enable me to do somewhat of myself. The time is coming when all men will see, that the gift of God to the soul is not a vaunting, overpowering, excluding sanctity, but a sweet, natural goodness, a goodness like thine and mine, and that so invites thine and mine to be and to grow.

The injustice of the vulgar tone of preaching is not less flagrant to Jesus, than to the souls which it profanes. The preachers do not see that they make his gospel not glad, and shear him of the locks of beauty and the attributes of heaven. When I see a majestic Epaminondas, or Washington; when I see among my contemporaries, a true orator, an upright judge, a dear friend; when I vibrate to the melody and fancy of a poem; I see beauty that is to be desired. And so lovely, and with yet more entire consent of my human being, sounds in my ear the severe music of the bards that have sung of the true God in all ages. Now do not degrade the life and dialogues of Christ out of the circle of this charm, by insulation and peculiarity. Let them lie as they befel, alive and warm, part of human life, and of the landscape, and of the cheerful day.

2. The second defect of the traditionary and limited way of using the mind of Christ is a consequence of the first: this, namely; that the Moral Nature,

that Law of laws, whose revelations introduce greatness,—yea, God himself, into the open soul, is not explored as the fountain of the established teaching in society. Men have come to speak of the revelation as somewhat long ago given and done, as if God were dead. The injury to faith throttles the preacher; and the goodliest of institutions becomes an uncertain and inarticulate voice.

It is very certain that it is the effect of conversation with the beauty of the soul, to beget a desire and need to impart to others the same knowledge and love. If utterance is denied, the thought lies like a burden on the man. Always the seer is a sayer. Somehow his dream is told: somehow he publishes it with solemn joy: sometimes with pencil on canvas; sometimes with chisel on stone; sometimes in towers and aisles of granite, his soul's worship is builded; sometimes in anthems of indefinite music; but clearest and most permanent, in words.

The man enamored of this excellency, becomes its priest or poet. The office is coeval with the world. But observe the condition, the spiritual limitation of the office. The spirit only can teach. Not any profane man, not any sensual, not any liar, not any slave can teach, but only he can give, who has; he only can create, who is. The man on whom the soul descends, through whom the soul speaks, alone can teach. Courage, piety, love, wisdom, can teach; and every man can open his door to these angels, and they shall bring him the gift of tongues. But the man who aims to speak as books enable, as synods use, as the fashion guides, and as interest commands, babbles. Let him hush.

---

## Selection 21

---

# The Vicarious Sacrifice

### *Horace Bushnell (1866)*

The first named ground of apprehension is, that the law precept may seem to be loosely held and fall into practical dishonor. Do we then make void the law through faith? God forbid; yea we establish the law.

I turn the question here, as regards the precept of the law, upon the particular word *honor;* partly because it is historical, being a favorite word of Anselm for such uses; and partly because there is no other word so appropriate. Sin

Source: Horace Bushnell, *The Vicarious Sacrifice: Grounded in Principles of Universal Obligation* (New York: Charles Scribners, 1866), 299–310.

dishonors the law, breaks it down, tramples it in customary contempt, raises a feeling of disrespect in mankind strong enough to be itself called the law of this world. Hence the necessity of punishment; which is that self-asserting act of God, in its behalf, by which he invests it with honor. For it must be remembered here, that we are not looking for some scheme of penal substitution, compensation, satisfaction, but are, in fact, discussing the great question how it is that God forgives; or, what is the same, accomplishes the restoration of fallen character? Where it is coming out, that he gets a great part of this power, not by his mere love and suffering patience and divine sympathy in Christ, but also in part by the invigoration of law and its moral impressions. A very small matter it will be in this view, that he manages to just save the law by some judicial compensation—he does infinitely more, he intensifies and deepens the impression of law, to such a degree that it comes out reenacted, as it were, to be fulfilled in a higher key of observance.

To make this very important fact apparent, attention is called to four distinct points of view, in which Christ, by his sacrifice, magnifies, if I should not rather say glorifies, the precept of the law.

I. He restores men to the precept. If there were no instituted law, none but the law before government, there would be no doubt of this. But the instituted law goes by enforcement, and is honored because of the enforcement; how then can it be honored in a loss of the same, that is in forgiveness? Because, I answer, the subject forgiven is restored to all precept; not to the Right or Precept Absolute only, but impliedly to all the statutes of God's instituted government, for the application and the enforced sanction of that. No matter then if the forgiven soul is taken clean by the sanctions, to think only of precept. All the more and not the less does he honor it, that he is brought into a love of it, and of God by whom it is enforced, such that his obedience becomes an inspiration. We may even say that he is released from the law wherein he was held; but we only mean that the righteousness of the law is fulfilled in him, by the free assent of his liberty, outrunning all enforcement. If then Christ restores to such a noble conformity, raising the whole stature of life and quality of being in them that are restored, how can it be said that the precept of the law is made void or put in dishonor? Is it any more dishonored, or made void, in the case of such as are not, and will not be, restored? Has any remission been extended to them? Just contrary to that, they are going to be made responsible in fact and in strict justice, for their contempt and rejection, not of the precept only but of the great mercy tendered them, to help their recovery into it.

On the whole, there appears to be no single point where any loss of honor can be imagined, as far as the precept is concerned. Christ beholds it from the first moment onward, doing nothing and wanting nothing, in all the immense travail of his incarnate ministry and death, but to commend the Righteousness and Beauty of it, and regain lost men to that homage which is at once their own blessedness and its everlasting honor.

II. Christ honors the precept, not only in what he does for our sake, in restoring us to it and forgiving us in it, but quite as much in what he does for its sake, to restore and save it also. For how shall he so magnify the law, as by setting it on high, enthroning it in love, organizing in it a kingdom worthy of its breadth, beneficence, dignity, and all-encompassing order? We often magnify Christ's work as being a work of salvation for men, because it is in this view that it makes an appeal so persuasive to human feeling; but there is nothing he would spurn himself, with a more total disallowance, than the thought of a salvation gotten up for men, one side of the grand, everlasting law, in which God's empire stands. We greatly mistake, if we think that Christ is doing every thing here, as prosecuting a suit before human feeling, and to bring human souls out of trouble; he wants to bring them into righteousness; and that again, not for their sakes only, but a great deal more for righteousness' sake; to heal the elemental war, and settle everlasting order, in that good law which is the inherent principle of order.

What meaning there may be in this ought, henceforth, to be never a secret to our American people. In our four years of dreadful civil war, what immense sacrifices of blood and treasure have we made; refusing to be weakened by sorrow, or shaken by discouragement, or even to be slackened by unexpected years of delay. Failure was prophesied on every hand; compositions were proposed without number. Yet nothing could meet our feeling but to save the integrity of our institutions, and forever establish the broken order of the law. All the stress of our gigantic effort hinged on this and this alone. No composition could be endured, or even thought of, that did not settle us in obedience, and pacify us in the sovereignty of law; and, to the more rational of us, nothing appeared to lay a sufficiently firm basis of order, but the clearance somehow of that which has been the mockery of our principles, and the ferment even, from the first, of our discord. The victory we sighed for, and the salvation we sought, were summed up in the victory and salvation of law. Failing in this every thing would be lost. Succeeding in this all sacrifice was cheap, even that of our first-born.

What now do we see in the sacrifice of Christ, but that he, only in a vastly higher and more grandly heroic devotion of his life, is doing all for the violated honor and broken sovereignty of law. He proposes, indeed, to be a Saviour to men; but the gist of the salvation, both to us and to him, is that heaven's original order is to be restored in us, and made solid and glorious, in the crowning of God's instituted government forever. Everything that we see therefore, in the incarnate life and suffering death, is God magnifying the honors of his law by the stress of his own stupendous sacrifice. Such an amount of feeling, put into the governmental order, commends it to our feeling; and also turns our feeling into awe before it. The law is raised as precept, in this manner, to a new pitch of honor, and the power of impression given to it, by the vicarious sacrifice and more than mortal heroism of Jesus, is the principal cause of that immense progress in moral sensibility and opinion, that distinguishes the Christian populations of the world. What they so much feel and have coming in upon their moral sensibility, in ways so piercing, is the law of duty, glorified by suffering and the visibly divine sacrifice of the cross.

III. Christ adds authority and honor to the law-precept, as being, in his own person, the incarnation of it. In itself, what we call law is impersonal, a cold mandatory of abstraction. Its authority, as such, is the conviction it is able to produce of its own imperative right. An additional honor and authority is given it also, when God reaffirms it, and from the point of his invisible majesty, assumes the maintenance of it. A certain authority is gained for it also by impressive circumstance, when it is delivered from the thundering and smoking mountain top. By the cold intimidation of such a pronouncement, it even becomes appalling; it makes the people quake and shiver. Still the coldness and the stern decretive majesty partly benumb conviction. To have its full authority felt, it must be brought nigh in its true geniality and warmth, as a gift to the higher nature of souls; exactly as it is, when it is incarnated and made personal in Christ, addressing human conviction by his human voice. For Christ is not, as many seem to fancy, a mere half-character of God incarnate, a kind of incarnate weakness in the figure of a love-principle, separated from every thing else in God's greatness, necessary to the tonic vigor of love. Being the incarnation of God, the full round character of God as he is must be included—authority, justice, purity, truth, forgiveness, gentleness, suffering love, all excellence. . . . But these are all inferior and scarcely more than accessory arguments; the principal remains to be added which is this—

IV. The almost inconceivable honor Christ confers on the law precept, in the fact that his incarnation, life, and death upon the cross—all that I have included in his vicarious sacrifice—are the fruit of his own free homage and eternally acknowledged obligation to the law; in one word his deific obedience.

I have spoken of the law before government, the eternal absolute law of right. Under it, and by it, as existing in logical order before God's perfections, even they, as we found reason to believe, have their spring. It was not necessary here to go into any very elaborate argument; for it can not escape the discovery of any one, that if God has moral perfections of any kind, they must have a standard law, and obtain their quality of merit, by their fulfillment of that law. Of course there is no precedence of time in the law, as compared with the date of God's perfections, but there must be a precedence of order, and the law must be obligatory in that precedence. But we come now to a matter which, to most minds, will be more remote and more difficult; viz., to the fact, that God has not only a character everlastingly perfected in right, but that, by the same law, he is held to a suffering goodness for his enemies, even to that particular work in time, which we call the vicarious sacrifice of Christ. Christ was, in this view, under obligation to be the redeemer he was; and fulfilling that obligation, he conferred an honor on the law fulfilled, such as could not be conferred by any stringency of justice laid upon the race itself.

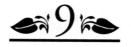

# The Rise of Cults and Deviant Movements

After 1830 few could remain aloof from or be unaware of all that was occurring in the United States. Many of these activities were of a religious nature. In 1840 Ralph Waldo Emerson wrote of America to his Scottish friend Thomas Carlyle, "We are all a little wild here with numberless projects of social reform. Not a reading man but has a draft of a new community in his waistcoat pocket."

Emerson was indulging in hyperbole, but when the groups and movements arising after 1830 are listed—not to mention the enormous vitality among older, orthodox denominations—the ferment and enthusiasm of American religious life becomes apparent. In 1830 the *Book of Mormon* was published and the sect that became the *Church of Jesus Christ of Latter-Day Saints* organized. In 1840 the *Hopedale Community* was founded near Milford, Massachusetts, and in 1841 another experiment in Christian socialism, *Brook Farm*, was begun a few miles from Boston. In 1843 John Humphrey Noyes founded the *Association of Perfectionists* at Putney, Vermont. In the same year William Miller was predicting that the second coming of Christ was to occur at any time, and his *Adventism* was electrifying tens of thousands across the nation. Excitement over the *Millerite movement* had barely subsided before the cult of *Spiritism* swept across the American scene, in 1848. The Fox sisters (Margaret and Katie) of Hydesville, New York, claimed they were disturbed by strange nocturnal rappings in their home. Soon séances were everywhere, Spiritist newspapers flourished, and mediums were advertising their ability to put people in contact with dead relatives, Napoleon, or Julius Caesar. In 1866 Mary Baker Eddy claimed she discovered *Christian Science*, which held that sickness, disease, evil, sin, and death are all errors of mortal mind and are nonexistent. In 1872 Charles Taze Russell founded the *Jehovah's Witnesses*, which taught that the doctrine of the Trinity is "a false, unbiblical doctrine" originated by Satan, and that Christ was in reality the incarnation of Michael the archangel. These are but the most prominent of a long list of nineteenth-century deviant movements.

While definitions vary as to when a religious group can be called a *cult*, certain criteria, or distinguishing marks, are generally found among them. Cults differ from orthodox groups in (1) having an unbiblical doctrine of Christ that reduces him to being less than God; (2) teaching that *they alone* have the way to salvation; (3) frequently having an authoritative book (*The Book of Mormon, Science and Health,* etc.) or translation of the Bible (Jehovah's Witnesses' New World Translation) that supersedes the Bible; (4) often following a magnetic leader who is not only dynamic and mesmerizing but defiantly authoritative, brooking no dissent; (5) using "brainwashing" teaching methods, in which adherents must accept without question whatever the cult leaders tell them.

These are some of the most prominent common features of cults, but differences may outweigh the similarities as old cults fade and new cults proliferate. In America some are completely indigenous, while others, for example the New Age movement, are heavily dependent on oriental thought, such as Hinduism. Some reflect otherworldly pantheism; others are materialistic. Some claim to be the supreme interpreters of the biblical message, asserting that all others are wrong regarding the Bible; some give the Bible no notice. But each of these cults has had a unique appeal for certain segments of American society.

## William Miller's Adventists

Of the groups listed above, the Adventist movement of William Miller (1782–1849) most deserves to be exempted from the category of cult, for the Millerites do not fit into the five criteria for a cult as given. Miller's teachings were those of historic Christianity, with the addition of a literal interpretation of the eschatology of Revelation, Daniel, Ezekiel, and Isaiah.

Miller was born in Massachusetts and raised in New York State, had been a sheriff and farmer, and was converted during a revival in 1816. He then began a study of the Bible that continued for many years, and centered on the biblical prophecies of the latter times and the millennial period of earthly bliss. Interest in prophecy had occupied many scholars from the Puritans on, but most of them had been postmillennialists. The postmillennial view places Christ's Second Coming at the *end* of the millennium. Christians must dedicate themselves to reducing the worldwide influence of evil and spreading good until they inaugurate a thousand-year reign of peace, after which arrives the Second Coming and Last Judgment. Miller reversed this order. As a premillennialist, he believed that evil is escalating and good shrinking throughout the world, and that only the imminent coming of Christ—at the *beginning* of the millennial reign of peace—will put evil down and bring in universal righteousness.

This was revolutionary doctrine at a time when most preachers, including such revivalists as Charles Finney, devoutly taught the postmillennial view. But Miller did something most prophetic scholars avoided: he set the date for Christ's return—sometime between March 1843 and March 1844. Beginning in 1831 he gave lectures on his conclusions, and within a few years he was receiving nationwide publicity. In his lectures he would describe Christ's coming:

> Behold, the heavens grow black with clouds; the sun has veiled himself; the moon, pale and forsaken, hangs in middle air; the hail descends; the seven thunders utter loud their voices; the lightnings send their vivid gleams and sulphurous flames abroad; and the great city of the nations falls to rise no more forever and forever! At this dread moment, look! The clouds have burst asunder; the heavens appear; the great white throne is in sight! Amazement fills the Universe with awe! He comes!—He comes!—Behold the Saviour comes!—Lift up your heads, ye saints—He comes! He comes! He comes![1]

As 1843 approached, apprehension grew, and it has been estimated that hundreds of thousands prepared for the Lord's coming, although most churches and denominations condemned datesetting and the general furor. Tensions mounted, and March 1843 went by with no untoward happenings. Finally, October 22, 1844 passed, the last date set by the movement's leaders. The mass movement collapsed amid disillusionment and feelings of betrayal, only to surface later under new leaders, doctrinal standards, and emphases.

## Joseph Smith and the Mormons

Of all the religious cults in American history the most successful is the Church of Jesus Christ of Latter-Day Saints or Mormons. The story of Joseph Smith (1805–1844) and the Mormons is complex.[2] Smith was born in Vermont to a destitute family who moved to Palmyra, New York, in 1816. Palmyra was in the "Burned-over District," so called because the area had witnessed religious excitements for decades. The Smiths dabbled with different denominations, never permanently affiliating with any. In 1820 Joseph reported having a vision that resulted in a sort of conversion. Selection 22 picks up the story and gives the flavor of the family's interests, telling of Smith's finding "certain keys, by which he could discern things invisible to the natural eye"; also noted is the community's obsession with hunting for buried treasure and silver mines;

and Smith's description of the hill of Cumorah and the golden plates he claimed it contained.

According to Smith, in September 1827 he was commanded by the angel Moroni to take these plates, written in "Egyptian, Chaldiac, Assyric, and Arabic," and translate them with the aid of two stones that had been buried with them. No one else was permitted to examine the plates, and for three years Smith dictated his translation to others as he worked behind a curtain. This "translation," *The Book of Mormon*, was published in 1830 at Palmyra, after Moroni had taken back the plates, still sight unseen. *The Book of Mormon* told the story of the Lamanites and the Nephites, descendants of a lost tribe of Israel, who had migrated to America centuries ago. After his resurrection, Jesus Christ had appeared among them and established the correct order of the church. The Lamanites, who became the American Indians, left the faith and turned on the Nephites in a battle in which all the Nephites were killed except for Mormon and his son Moroni. The records of this tribe were then gathered by Moroni and buried in the hill Cumorah until a true prophet should come along, one who was worthy to bring them to the attention of the world.

On October 30, 1830, Smith and five others met to restore "the Church of Christ in these last days," organizing the Mormon church. The new prophet was invested with powers of direct revelation from God. Eventually new doctrines were added, such as a plurality of gods. In 1831 they took their growing number of followers to Kirtland, Ohio, where a communistic type of community was erected, a temple built, and land purchased. When the Ohio legislature refused to grant a charter to their proposed bank, Smith retaliated by forming an "Anti-Banking Company" which issued $3 bills. During the financial panic of 1837 the bank failed, and lawsuits were brought against the Mormons for violations of the banking laws. Quickly the Mormons fled to Missouri, only to have the populace rise against them. This time they fled to Nauvoo, Illinois, remaining there from 1840 to 1846.

In Nauvoo, Smith had his greatest triumphs. Missionaries were dispatched to England and won many converts who were sent to Nauvoo. Soon the city grew to be the largest in the state, numbering about 14,000. A state charter was granted for a university, which never enrolled a student. A militia was set up, with Smith as general. He became so inflated that he ran for the presidency of the United States in 1844. But in 1843 Smith had confided to his associates that he had received a revelation authorizing the practice of polygamy. When this became known outside of Nauvoo, an incensed populace again rose up, publishing a newspaper to attack Smith for immorality. The Mormon leaders destroyed the presses of the paper, and the state militia came in and arrested Smith and his brother Hyrum, locking them in the jail at Carthage. On June 27, 1844, an infuriated mob stormed the jail and shot the brothers.

A struggle for leadership ensued immediately among Smith's would-be successors. The Mormons split into several groups, with the majority following Brigham Young. He announced his intention to lead them to a place where they would be far from interference, and in July 1847 they reached the Great Salt Lake, where they set up their State of Deseret. Mexico was in control of the area, but in 1848 it came under United States' ownership under the terms of the Mexican Cession. Relations between the Mormons and the United States government were difficult for years, and in 1857 some Mormons massacred a group of settlers bound for California. Polygamy continued for years in Utah, despite the government's prohibition.

## The Burned-Over District

Western New York State spawned an amazing number of movements over a thirty-year period in addition to Mormonism. The area west of the Adirondack and Catskill mountains differed from other newly opened frontiers. Much more than elsewhere, settlers in western New York were inclined to a wide variety of causes and crusades. Enthusiasms and eccentricities reached such an extent that the region has been called a "psychic highway."[3] Some movements in the Burned-over District were respectable, while others were bizarre experiments promoting the perfection of humanity and the coming millennial bliss, unorthodox religious beliefs, and radical new political parties. The religious ultraism of this fascinating area brought Mormonism, the anti-Masonry movement in 1826, the Millerites in 1843, and Spiritism and the perfectionist utopian Oneida Community in 1848.

Perfectionism, the doctrine that people can achieve perfect holiness and freedom from sin, took root in New York at its early settling. Much of the teaching differed little from traditional Methodist ideas stemming from John Wesley. Other contributors to perfectionist philosophies included Charles Finney, Asa Mahan, and the faculty of Oberlin College in Ohio.

John Humphrey Noyes (1811–1886), who was born in Brattleboro, Vermont, was graduated from Dartmouth College in 1830 and underwent a conversion soon after. Deciding for the Congregational ministry, he attended Andover Seminary and Yale Divinity School. Already he was fascinated with ideas of perfection, and he announced that he was sinless in 1834; for this he was ousted from Yale. In 1840 at Putney, Vermont, Noyes drew together a small band of perfectionists and instituted a communism of property. By 1846 he was prop-

A camp meeting at Sing Sing in Upper New York State, August 1859
(*Harper's Weekly*, September 10, 1859)

agating ideas of biblical communism (selection 23), male continence, population control, mutual criticism, and education. Because his followers were equally
yoked in the faith, Noyes reasoned, the practice of primitive Christian communism was acceptable, and this included the marriage relationship. When he
extended his idea of "spiritual union" to renounce conventional marriage in
favor of what he called "complex marriage," outraged citizens pronounced that
this simply meant free love, and threatened violence.

In the face of these threats Noyes moved the community to Oneida, New
York, in 1848. Finding a somewhat more receptive locale, Noyes tried to shield
his followers from too much contact with curious outsiders. Isolation from the
outside world was necessary, he taught, to bring about perfectionism. "Salvation from sin, though possible under the conditions of ordinary society, must
have for its full objective development a reconstructed society," Noyes said.[4] The
commune at Oneida lasted until 1881. But Noyes himself, under intense public
pressure, left the United States in 1876 and lived in Ontario until his death.

## Select Bibliography

Brodie, Fawn M. *No Man Knows My History: The Life of Joseph Smith.* 1945;
    repr. ed., New York: Knopf, 1971.
Cole, Marley. *Jehovah's Witnesses: The New World Society.* New York: Vantage,
    1955.

Flanders, Robert B. *Nauvoo: Kingdom on the Mississippi.* Urbana, Ill.: University of Illinois Press, 1975.

Fornell, Earl W. *The Unhappy Medium: Spiritualism and the Life of Margaret Fox.* Austin: University of Texas Press, 1964.

Holloway, Mark. *Heavens on Earth: Utopian Communities in America, 1680–1880,* rev. ed. New York: Dover, 1966.

Mullen, Robert. *The Latter-Day Saints: The Mormons Yesterday and Today.* Garden City, N.Y.: Doubleday, 1966.

O'Dea, Thomas. *The Mormons.* Chicago: University of Chicago Press, 1957.

# Joseph Smith's Preparation for Mormonism

## *Lucy Smith (1853)*

Shortly after the death of Alvin [Smith, Joseph's brother], a man commenced laboring in the neighborhood, to effect a union of the different churches, in order that all might be agreed, and thus worship God with one heart and with one mind.

This seemed about right to me, and I felt much inclined to join in with them; in fact, the most of the family appeared quite disposed to unite with their numbers; but Joseph, from the first, utterly refused even to attend their meetings, saying, . . . "I can take my Bible, and go into the woods, and learn more in two hours, than you can learn at meeting in two years. . . ."

The shock occasioned by Alvin's death, in a short time passed off, and we resumed our usual avocations. . . . A short time before the house was completed, a man, by the name of Josiah Stoal, came from Chenango county, New York, with the view of getting Joseph to assist him in digging for a silver mine. He came for Joseph on account of having heard that he possessed certain keys, by which he could discern things invisible to the natural eye.

Joseph endeavored to divert him from his vain pursuit, but he was inflexible in his purpose, and offered high wages to those who would dig for him, in search of said mine, and still insisted upon having Joseph to work for him. Accordingly, Joseph and several others, returned with him and commenced digging. After laboring for the old gentleman about a month, without success, Joseph prevailed upon him to cease his operations; and it was from this circumstance of having worked by the month, at digging for a silver mine, that the very prevalent story arose of Joseph's having been a money digger. . . .

Soon after his return, we received intelligence of the arrival of a new agent for the Everson land, of which our farm was a portion. This reminded us of the last payment, which was still due, and which must be made before we could obtain a deed of the place.

Shortly after this, a couple of gentlemen, one of whom was the before-named Stoal, the other a Mr. Knight, came into the neighborhood for the purpose of

Source: Lucy Smith, *Biographical Sketches of Joseph Smith the Prophet* (Liverpool, England: S. W. Richards, 1853), 90–99.

procuring a quantity of either wheat or flour; and we, having sown considerable wheat, made a contract with them, in which we agreed to deliver a certain quantity of flour to them the ensuing fall, for which we were to receive a sufficient amount of money to make the final payment on our farm. This being done, my husband sent Hyrum to Canandaigua to inform the new agent of the fact, namely, that the money should be forthcoming as soon as the twenty-fifth of December 1825. This, the agent said, would answer the purpose, and he agreed to retain the land until that time. . . .

When the time had nearly arrived for the last payment to be made, and when my husband was about starting for Mr. Stoal's and Mr. Knight's, in order to get the money to make the same, Joseph called my husband and myself aside, and said, "I have been very lonely ever since Alvin died, and I have concluded to get married; and if you have no objections to my uniting myself in marriage with Miss Emma Hale, she would be my choice in preference to any other woman I have ever seen." We were pleased with his choice, and . . . requested him to bring her home with him, and live with us. Accordingly he set out with his father for Pennsylvania. . . .

One afternoon my attention was suddenly arrested by a trio of strangers who were just entering. Upon their near approach I found one of these gentlemen to be Mr. Stoddard, the principal carpenter in building the house in which we then lived. . . .

They proceeded to inform my son [Hyrum], that he need put himself to no further trouble with regard to the farm; "for," said they, "we have bought the place, and paid for it, and we now forbid your touching anything on the farm: and we also warn you to leave forthwith, and give possession to the lawful owners." . . .

Hyrum, in a short time, went to an old friend, Dr. Robinson, and related to him the grievous story. Whereupon, the old gentleman sat down, and wrote at some considerable length the character of the family—our industry, and faithful exertions to secure a home, with many commendations calculated to beget confidence in us with respect to business transactions. And, keeping this writing in his own hands, he went through the village, and in an hour procured sixty subscribers. He then sent the same by the hand of Hyrum, to the land agent, who lived in Canandaigua.

On receiving this, the agent was highly enraged. He said the men had told him that Mr. Smith and his son Joseph had run away, and that Hyrum was cutting down the sugar orchard, hauling off the rails, burning them, and doing all manner of mischief to the farm. That, believing this statement, he was induced to sell the place, for which he had given a deed, and received money. . . .

The agent strove . . . to persuade them to retract, and let the land go back into Mr. Smith's hands again. . . . Finally, they agreed; if Hyrum could raise them one thousand dollars, by Saturday at ten o'clock in the evening, they would give up the deed.

It was now Thursday about noon, and Hyrum was at Canandaigua, which was nine miles distant from home, and hither he must ride before he could make the first move towards raising the required amount. He came home with a heavy heart. When he arrived, he found his father, who had returned a short time before him. His father had fortunately found, within fifty miles of home, one of those letters which Hyrum had written. . . .

The anxiety of mind that I suffered that day can more easily be imagined than described. I now looked upon the proceeds of our industry, which smiled around us on every hand, with a kind of yearning attachment that I never before had experienced; and our early losses I did not feel so keenly, for I then realized that we were young, and by making some exertions we might improve our circumstances; besides, I had not felt the inconveniences of poverty as I had since. . . .

[The business of the farm was finally adjusted with the Smiths remaining as tenants. Joseph came back] and remained with us, until the difficulty about the farm came to an issue; he then took leave for Pennsylvania, on the same business as before mentioned, and the next January returned with his wife, in good health and fine spirits.

Not long subsequent to his return, my husband had occasion to send him to Manchester, on business. As he set off early in the day, we expected him home at most by six o'clock in the evening, but . . . he did not get home till the night was far spent. On coming in, he threw himself into a chair, apparently much exhausted. . . .

Presently he smiled, and said in a calm tone, "I have taken the severest chastisement that I have ever had in my life."

My husband, supposing that it was from some of the neighbors, was quite angry, and observed, "I would like to know what business anybody has to find fault with you!"

"Stop, father, stop," said Joseph, "it was the angel of the Lord; as I passed by the hill of Cumorah, where the plates are, the angel met me, and said that I had not been engaged enough in the work of the Lord; that the time had come for the Record to be brought forth; and that I must be up and doing, and set myself about the things which God had commanded me to do. But,

Source: John Humphrey Noyes, *History of American Socialisms* (Philadelphia: J. B. Lippincott Co., 1870), 624–44.

father, give yourself no uneasiness concerning the reprimand which I have received, for I now know the course that I am to pursue, so all will be well."

It was also made known to him at this interview, that he should make another effort to obtain the plates, on the twenty-second of the following Sept., but this he did not mention to us at that time.

---

## Selection 23

# Bible Communism

## *John Humphrey Noyes (1870)*

### Chapter II.—Showing that Marriage is not an institution of the Kingdom of Heaven, and must give place to Communism.

PROPOSITION 5.—In the Kingdom of Heaven, the institution of marriage, which assigns the exclusive possession of one woman to one man, does not exist. Matt. 22:23–30.

6.—In the Kingdom of Heaven the intimate union of life and interest, which in the world is limited to pairs, extends through the whole body of believers; i.e. complex marriage takes the place of simple. John 17:21. . . .

8.—Admitting that the Community principle of the day of Pentecost, in its actual operation at that time, extended only to material goods, yet we affirm that there is no intrinsic difference between property in persons and property in things; and that the same spirit which abolished exclusiveness in regard to money, would abolish, if circumstances allowed full scope to it, exclusiveness in regard to women and children. Paul expressly places property in women and property in goods in the same category, and speaks of them together, as ready to be abolished by the advent of the Kingdom of Heaven. "The time," says he, "is short; it remaineth that they that have wives be as though they had none; and they that buy as though they possessed not; for the fashion of this world passeth away." I Cor. 7:29–31. . . .

10.—The abolishment of exclusiveness is involved in the love-relation required between all believers by the express injunction of Christ and the apostles, and by the whole tenor of the New Testament. "The new commandment is, that we love one another," and that, not by pairs, as in the world, but *en masse*. We are required to love one another fervently. The fashion of the world forbids a man and woman who are otherwise appropriated, to love one another fervently. But if they obey Christ they must do this; and whoever would allow them to do this, and yet would forbid them (on any other ground than that of present expediency), to express their unity, would "strain at a gnat and swallow a camel"; for unity of hearts is as much more important than any external expression of it, as a camel is larger than a gnat. . . .

12.—The abolishment of the marriage system is involved in Paul's doctrine of the end of ordinances. Marriage is one of the "ordinances of the worldly sanctuary." This is proved by the fact that it has no place in the resurrection. Paul expressly limits it to life in the flesh. Rom. 7:2, 3. The assumption, therefore, that believers are dead to the world by the death of Christ (which authorized the abolishment of Jewish ordinances), legitimately makes an end of marriage. Col. 2:20.

13.—The law of marriage is the same in kind with the Jewish law concerning meats and drinks and holy days, of which Paul said that they were "contrary to us, and were taken out of the way, being nailed to the cross." Col. 2:14. The plea in favor of the worldly social system, that it is not arbitrary, but founded in nature, will not bear investigation. All experience testifies (the theory of the novels to the contrary notwithstanding), that sexual love is not naturally restricted to pairs. Second marriages are contrary to the one-love theory, and yet are often the happiest marriages. Men and women find universally (however the fact may be concealed), that their susceptibility to love is not burnt out by one honey-moon, or satisfied by one lover. On the contrary, the secret history of the human heart will bear out the assertion that it is capable of loving any number of times and any number of persons, and that the more it loves the more it can love. This is the law of nature, thrust out of sight and condemned by common consent, and yet secretly known to all.

14.—The law of marriage "worketh wrath." 1. It provokes to secret adultery, actual or of the heart. 2. It ties together unmatched natures. 3. It sunders matched natures. 4. It gives to sexual appetite only a scanty and monotonous allowance, and so produces the natural vices of poverty, contraction of taste and stinginess or jealousy. 5. It makes no provision for the sexual appetite at the very time when that appetite is the strongest. By the custom of the world, marriage, in the average of cases, takes place at about the age of twenty-four; whereas puberty commences at the age of fourteen. For ten years, therefore, and that in the very flush of life, the sexual appetite is starved. This law of society bears hardest on females, because they have less opportunity of choosing their time of marriage than men. This discrepancy between the marriage system and nature, is one of the principal sources of the peculiar diseases of women, of prostitution, masturbation, and licentiousness in general. . . .

17.—The restoration of true relations between the sexes is a matter second in importance only to the reconciliation of man to God. The distinction of male and female is that which makes man the image of God, i.e. the image of the Father and the Son. Gen. 1:27. The relation of male and female was the first social relation. Gen. 2:22. It is therefore the root of all other social relations. The derangement of this relation was the first result of the original breach with God. Gen. 3:7; comp. 2:25. Adam and Eve were, at the beginning, in open, fearless, spiritual fellowship, first with God, and secondly, with each other. Their transgression produced two corresponding alienations, viz., first, an alienation from God, indicated by their fear of meeting him and their hiding themselves among the trees of the garden; and secondly, an alienation from each other, indicated by their shame at their nakedness and their hiding themselves from each other by clothing. These were the two great manifestations of original sin—the only manifestations presented to notice in the record of the apostacy. The first thing then to be done, in an attempt to redeem man and reorganize society, is to bring about reconciliation with God; and the second thing is to bring about a true union of the sexes. In other words, religion is the first subject of interest, and sexual morality the second, in the great enterprise of establishing the Kingdom of Heaven on earth.

The Oneida Community has two hundred and two members, and two affiliated societies, one of forty members at Wallingford, Connecticut, and one of thirty-five members at Willow Place, on a detached part of the Oneida domain. This domain consists of six hundred and sixty-four acres of choice land, and three excellent water-powers. The manufacturing interest here created is valued at over $200,000. The Wallingford domain consists of two hundred and twenty-eight acres, with a water-power, a printing-office and a silk-factory. The three Community families (in all two hundred and seventy-seven persons) are financially and socially a unit.

# 10

# Reformers and New Rights

While a number of the "mainline" Protestant denominations have drifted in a liberal direction over the last century, they did not begin that way. Most of the major denominations—the Methodists, Presbyterians, Baptists, and Congregationalists—built up their rolls during the nineteenth century through aggressive evangelism, using the methods of revivalism. Timothy L. Smith has called attention to this, writing, "Church historians of a later day, anxious to make plain the origins of modern religious outlooks, wrote the history of the great popular sects in such a way as to becloud the memory of evangelism's power. . . . The myth persists that revivalism is but a half-breed child of the Protestant faith, born on the crude frontier, where Christianity was taken captive by the wilderness."[1]

The Second Great Awakening rolled on for an amazing length of years in the eastern cities and in the West, from approximately 1795 to 1840. By then the agitation over the slavery question was absorbing the attention of the entire nation, and revivals declined for a time. Suddenly and with little warning, the Third Great Awakening came upon the scene, to last for only one year, 1858. This massive revival, so much briefer than the Second Awakening, swept through the northern states just before the outbreak of the Civil War with its awful bloodshed.

## A third movement of revivals

The Third Awakening began inconspicuously in Hamilton, Ontario, in October 1857. Since 1850 Dr. Walter Palmer, a physician and layman, and his wife Phoebe had been preaching half of each year in Methodist camp meetings and revival services. Phoebe did most of the speaking and had become a powerful force in Methodism, urging the doctrine of holiness upon her hearers with great effect. She was not only an effective evangelist but was writing a number of influential books—*The Promise of the Father, Faith and Its Effects, Entire Devotion, The Way to Holiness,* and others—all of which went through numerous editions over the years.

From June through October 1857 the Palmers conducted camp meetings in Ontario and Quebec before as many as 5000 listeners. Waiting in Hamilton for a train connection to New York City, they were asked by a Wesleyan pastor to speak at his church. Their message was well received, and 21 people were converted. Postponing their trip to New York, the Palmers remained for several weeks, during which time a revival began, and about 600 people professed faith in Christ. The revival in Hamilton was declared by both Canadian and American newspapers to be a model of dignity and order, with no emotionalism or fanaticism. This was the first instance of an unusual power of conviction in the movement that afterwards swept around the world. The Third Great Awakening had begun.

A section from Palmer's *The Promise of the Father* (selection 24) is presented for several reasons. Not only does she deserve to be included as arguably the most influential American Christian woman of the nineteenth century, but this book also gave an eloquent early presentation of the case for the ministry of women. In addition she was an excellent representative of the holiness tradition, a grass-roots non-Puritan/Princeton movement that provides a different understanding of Christianity in America. The holiness movement has been very influential.

Hearing of the revival in Canada, pastors across the United States gathered in large numbers to pray for the Holy Spirit to empower the churches. On December 1, 1857, 200 clergymen gathered at Pittsburgh to discuss the opportunities for and hindrances to an awakening. The meetings continued for three days in an anxious and solemn manner. Shortly thereafter a similar convention gathered at Cincinnati, and other meetings were convened in a number of cities. Since the Second Awakening had ended twenty years before, many pastors and laypeople desperately wished for another such turning to God in a nation that was writhing in vexation over an impending civil war.

In New York City concern for a revival had prompted a number of people to organize weekly lay prayer meetings during 1857. The first one to become prominent was sponsored by Jeremiah C. Lanphier, a tall, quiet, 48-year-old businessman who began work as an urban missionary for the North Dutch Reformed Church in July 1857. On October 7, 1857, this prayer session began meeting on a daily basis, with large numbers of laypeople attending. In a few days the stock market crashed, prostrating business everywhere. This financial panic shattered complacency and forced multitudes into bankruptcy. The crisis was the catalyst that triggered the awakening, and within six months 10,000 people gathered daily for prayer throughout New York City. City after city followed suit. When the churches of the large cities were filled to capacity, the meetings were moved to theaters.

Everywhere the clergy stepped back and allowed laypeople to lead. What amazed secular reporters and other observers was that there was no objectionable behavior or fanaticism in these great crowds, but a moving and orderly impulse to pray. Very little preaching was done anywhere. In New York, as the financial panic began to recede after five months, the *New York Herald* of March 6, 1858, noted with amusement, "Satan is busy all the morning in Wall Street among the brokers, and all the afternoon and evening the churches are crowded with saints who gambled in the morning." Timothy L. Smith wrote:

> If the awakening dramatized the nearly complete acceptance of revivalism among Baptists, it evoked surprising support from Old School Presbyterians, Episcopalians, and even Unitarians and Universalists. . . . Even more remarkable is the fact that Unitarian churches in New York and Boston united that spring in 'densely crowded' weekly meetings for testimony and prayer. . . . Reports of extensive awakenings in Europe during 1859 seemed to American evangelicals an extension and in some sense a validation of the Spirit's work begun here.[2]

The influence of the awakening was felt everywhere in the nation. Coming on the very eve of the Civil War, with the land being torn apart by controversy and hatreds, the Third Great Awakening was an astounding phenomenon. Calm and impressively orderly, with an enormous emphasis on prayer, a truly ecumenical spirit and no sectarian rivalry, the movement continued to exert powerful influences after the war's outbreak. Estimates of its total number of converts have varied from 500,000 to well over 1 million.[3]

Revivalism tended to depreciate doctrine and play down denominational differences, so that various groups could cooperate in a common task. It was forced to simplify the Christian message, so that it might be intelligible for the unchurched. Also, in its quest for conversions it was impelled to emphasize the part played by human free will in opting for salvation. Both of these characteristics have been seen in the teaching of Charles G. Finney (selection 17). The great evangelist of the 1820s and 1830s had not studied at Yale, yet the influence of the Presbyterian New School and Nathaniel W. Taylor's New Divinity (selection 19) are clearly seen in his thought Finney laid heavy stress upon the human role in the conversion of sinners. He taught that people were only brought to a verdict for Christ as they were moved intellectually, and the evangelist's task was to move them—to so persuade them of their lostness and need that they could not fail to respond. These later versions of Calvinism had come a long way since Jonathan Edwards—if they still could be called Calvinist in any accurate sense.

In addition to the new emphases toward free will and away from radical human depravity, other forces influenced revivalism. The most important of these was the Methodist message of free grace and free will. John Wesley (1703–1791) had modified the Calvinist doctrines of divine sovereignty, electing grace, predestination, and total depravity. Wesley taught that God had canceled the effects of original sin in the sacrifice of Christ. Therefore the atonement was universal in its effects. After Christ's sacrifice was completed, every person had the ability to respond to the benefits of the gospel. Each person is free to answer the call of God, or reject it and race on in disobedience toward destruction. Wesley added to this the concept that, the person who receives the grace of God may then move on to seek the "second blessing" of entire sanctification, which leads to sinlessness and cleanses away remaining sin and depravity. In chapter nine we have noted the similarities of perfectionism to this position of Wesley's.

**CONSTITUTION**
OF THE
**AMERICAN TRACT SOCIETY.**
WITH
ADDRESSES TO CHRISTIANS
RECOMMENDING THE
DISTRIBUTION OF RELIGIOUS TRACTS,
AND
**Anecdotes**
ILLUSTRATING THEIR BENEFICIAL EFFECTS.

—I handed him the *Swearer's Prayer*, and went on my journey.—
See p. 24.

## Christians united for reform

In their desires to keep the Christian message abreast of the times, and to present a united evangelical front for the conversion of America, both revivalistic Calvinists and evangelical Arminians thus came to almost the same formula: a gospel of God's grace that would strongly appeal to every morally responsible person. Then, as with Finney, both Arminians and Calvinists wished to draw each convert into a practical, pragmatic Christianity—to further the Kingdom of God on earth through specific projects and reform efforts. Since this fit the American spirit of activism, human cooperation with the Deity was readily directed toward social reform.

Reform movements had begun early in the century, and had flourished for decades. Among literally dozens of such agencies, the foremost were the "Great Eight Benevolent Societies":

1. The American Board of Commissioners for Foreign Missions, founded in 1810 and headquartered in Boston;
2. the American Education Society, founded in 1815 and located in Boston;
3. the American Bible Society, founded in 1816 and located in New York City;
4. the American Colonization Society, founded in 1816 and located in New York City;
5. the American Sunday School Union, founded in 1817 and located in Philadelphia;
6. the American Tract Society, founded in 1826 and located in New York City;
7. the American Temperance Society, founded in 1826 and located in New York City, and
8. the American Home Missionary Society, founded in 1826 and located in New York City.[4]

Innumerable lesser societies promoted women's rights, prison reform, fought the desecration of the Sabbath, helped reform prostitutes, and a variety of other endeavors. Great amounts of money rolled in to support the work, and the societies became, in the view of one observer, "immense institutions spreading over the country, combining hosts . . . a gigantic religious power, systematized, compact in its organization, with a polity and a government entirely its own." The combined budgets of the fourteen largest societies rivaled the major expenditures of the federal government.[5]

Thoroughly involved in all of these enterprises, and the founder of some of them, was the redoubtable champion of evangelical causes, Lyman Beecher (see p. 77; selection 12). A man of astounding energies, in his hands revivalism became a powerful tool for churches that had been vitiated by liberal notions and weakened by the effects of declining spirituality. Beecher, earlier than did Finney, grasped the vision that revivalism and social reform could be successfully combined. In his view this merger could be the chief means to evangelize and perfect America. Beecher and other like-minded Christians singled out, one by one, areas of social life that needed attention. The heavy consumption of alcohol was one, and until Beecher and others realized its effects, "spirits" were indulged in by all classes of society, including the clergy. Selection 25 gives Beecher's picturesque account of his conscientious reaction when he realized the impression made by slightly-tipsy ministers and the means he immediately took to awaken the nation to the dangers of alcoholism. At the forefront of a number of reform movements for many years, his vision and leadership are indeed impressive.

Much of the impetus for the women's rights movement may be traced to Finney, who encouraged women to enter a number of situations from which they had been excluded. While most Protestants were horrified at any defiance of the Apostle Paul's injunctions against women speaking and praying in "promiscuous assemblies" (gatherings of women and men), Methodists, Free-Will Baptists, and other groups had been allowing it for years. By 1825 Finney was urging women on,[6] with Palmer adding her voice later.

Finney's greatest, most impressive, and dignified revival was in Rochester, New York, from September 1830 through March 1831. Among the great number of professional and business people converted were Joseph Brown and the deputy county clerk, Henry Brewster Stanton. Brown's daughter Antoinette later followed Finney to Oberlin College to study under him, becoming in 1853 the first woman to receive full ordination (Congregational) to the ministry, and going on to become a leader in the women's rights movement. And Stanton married Elizabeth Cady in 1840, not long before she met Philadelphia Quaker preacher Lucretia Mott in London at the World's Anti-Slavery Conference, where American women delegates were refused seats.

Stanton (1815–1902) and Mott (1793–1880) were among women who called the first women's rights convention. It was held on July 19, 1848, in the Wesleyan Methodist Church of Seneca Falls, New York. What happened, along with the "Declaration of Sentiments" adopted, is given in selection 26.

## Select Bibliography

Beecher, Lyman. *The Autobiography of Lyman Beecher*, 2 vols. Edited by Barbara M. Cross. Cambridge, Mass.: Harvard University Press, 1961.

Cole, Charles. *The Social Ideas of the Northern Evangelists, 1826–1860*. New York: Columbia University Press, 1954.

Foster, Charles. *An Errand of Mercy: The Evangelical United Front, 1790–1830*. Chapel Hill, N.C.: University of North Carolina Press, 1960.

Hardesty, Nancy A. *Your Daughters Shall Prophesy; Revivalism and Feminism in the Age of Finney*. Brooklyn, N.Y.: Carlson, 1991.

Hardman, Keith J. *Charles Grandison Finney, 1792–1875: Revivalist and Reformer*. Syracuse, N.Y.: Syracuse University Press, 1987.

Henry, Stuart C. *Unvanquished Puritan: A Portrait of Lyman Beecher.* Grand Rapids: Eerdmans, 1973.

McLoughlin, William G. *Modern Revivalism: Charles Grandison Finney to Billy Graham.* New York: Ronald, 1959.

Marsden, George M. *The Evangelical Mind and the New School Presbyterian Experience.* New Haven, Conn.: Yale University Press, 1970.

Smith, Timothy L. *Revivalism and Social Reform: American Protestantism on the Eve of the Civil War.* Nashville: Abingdon, 1957.

White, Charles E. *The Beauty of Holiness: Phoebe Palmer as Theologian, Revivalist, Feminist, and Humanitarian.* Grand Rapids: Zondervan, 1986.

# The Promise of the Father

## *Phoebe Palmer (1859)*

### Important Question

A question of grave interest is now demanding the attention of all Christians, irrespective of name or sect. Especially does it demand the attention of the Christian ministry, inasmuch as it is believed by many to stand in vital connection with the ultimate triumphs of the cross.

And ere we lay this question before you, Christian reader, let us ask, that you will present yourself, as in the more immediate presence of the Father of Lights, and implore the illumination of the all-gracious Spirit, resolved that you will yield your mind up to the convictions of truth, and in outspoken declaration defend its claims.

The question is this: Has not a gift of power, delegated to the church on the day of Pentecost, been neglected? Or, in other words, has not a marked speciality of the Christian dispensation been comparatively unrecognized and kept out of use?

When the Founder of our holy Christianity was about leaving his disciples, to ascend to his Father, he commanded them to tarry at Jerusalem until endued with power from on high. And of whom was this company of disciples composed? Please turn to the first chapter of the Acts of the Apostles. Here we see that the number assembled in that upper room were about one hundred and twenty. Here were Peter, James, John, Andrew, Philip, Thomas, Bartholomew, Matthew, James the son of Alpheus, and Simon Zelotes, and Judas the brother of James. "These all continued with one accord in prayer and supplication with the women, and Mary, the mother of Jesus, and with his brethren." Here, we see, were both male and female disciples, continuing with one accord in prayer and supplication, in obedience to the command of their risen Lord; they are all here, waiting for the promise of the Father.

And here let us ask, From whence has the doctrine obtained, that women may not open their mouth in supplication and prayer in the presence of their

Source: Phoebe Palmer, *The Promise of the Father* (Philadelphia: 1859), 14–15, 22–24, 34, 45–46, 49–50.

brethren? Surely, those who thus set forth, teach for doctrines the commandments of men. And if the usage of apostolic days reprove those who have thus *publicly* taught, is not a *public* refutation of the error called for? Has not an endowment of power thus been kept back in the church? and will not God require for this? Who that has heard the melting, subduing tones of the female voice, as it has fallen on the ear of man in prayer, but will be penetrated with the force of the fact, that a gift of power has been withheld from the social assemblies of the pious, of serious magnitude?

And now, in the name of the Head of the church, let us ask, Was it designed that these demonstrations of power should cease with the day of Pentecost? If the Spirit of prophecy fell upon God's daughters, alike as upon his sons in that day, and they spake in the midst of that assembled multitude, as the Spirit gave utterance, on what authority do the angels of the churches restrain the use of that gift now? Has the minister of Christ, now reading these lines, never encouraged open female testimony, in the charge which he represents? Let us ask, What account will you render to the Head of the church, for restricting the use of this endowment of power? Who can tell how wonderful the achievements of the cross might have been, if this gift of prophecy, in woman, had continued in use, as in apostolic days? Who can tell but long since the gospel might have been preached to every creature? Evidently this was a *speciality* of the last days, as set forth by the prophecy of Joel. Under the old dispensation, though there was a Miriam, a Deborah, a Huldah, and an Anna, who were prophetesses, the special outpouring of the Spirit upon God's daughters as upon his sons, seems to have been reserved as a characteristic of the last days. This, says Peter, as the wondering multitude beheld these extraordinary endowments of the Spirit, falling alike on all the disciples,—this is that which was spoken by the prophet Joel, "And also upon my servants and upon my handmaidens will I pour out my Spirit.". . .

Says the Rev. Dr. Taft, "If the nature of society, its good and prosperity, in which women are jointly and equally concerned with men, if, in *many cases,* their fitness and capacity for instructors being admitted to be equal to the other sex, be not reasons sufficient to convince the candid reader of woman's teaching and preaching, because of two texts in Paul's Epistles, (1 Cor. xiv. 34; 1 Tim. ii. 12,) let him consult the paraphrase of Locke, where he has proved to a demonstration that the apostle, in these texts, never intended to prohibit women from praying and preaching in the church, provided they were dressed as became women professing godliness, and were qualified for the sacred office. Nor is it likely that he would, in one part of his Epistle, give directions how a woman, as well as a man, should pray and prophesy in public, and presently after, in the very same Epistle, forbid women, endowed with the gifts of prayer and prophecy, from speaking in the church, when, according to his own explication of prophecy, it is 'speaking unto others for edification, exhortation, and comfort.'". . . .

In what does the gift of prophecy consist?

We have remarked that it was not our aim in this volume to set forth the expediency of woman's preaching, technically so called. But the scriptural idea of the terms *preach* and *prophesy* stands so inseparably connected as one and the same thing, that we should find it difficult to get aside from the fact that women did preach, or, in other words, prophesy, in the early ages of Christianity, and have continued to do so down to the present time, to just the degree that the spirit of the Christian dispensation has been recognized. And it is also a significant fact, that to the degree denominations, who have once favored the practice, lose the freshness of their zeal, and as a consequence their primitive simplicity, and, as ancient Israel, yield to a desire to be like surrounding communities, in a corresponding ratio are the labors of females discountenanced.

This is a most suggestive consideration, and if any one reading these pages is disposed to doubt the statement, let him take pains to inquire into the facts in the case. We might specify more than one denomination to which this is particularly applicable. . . .

What would be thought of a Christian minister of the present day who would strenuously enforce as a scriptural requisition that every female member of his charge should adhere to the custom of coming to the house of the Lord veiled or muffled, as enjoined by the apostle Paul, 1 Cor. xi. 4–16? Yet there would be far more consistency in enforcing a scrupulous adherence to this custom, which has become obsolete except in Eastern heathen countries, than in enforcing the doctrine that women shall not pray or prophesy in religious assemblies. "Judge ye yourselves, is it comely that a woman pray unto God *uncovered?*"—that is, unveiled. But it seems not to have entered into the apostle's conceptions that the daughters of the Lord would not obey the impellings of their Spirit-baptized souls, and pray and speak as the Spirit gave utterance. That they would do so he anticipates as a matter of course, and therefore suggests the manner in which they shall be attired in the performance of the duty.

But why do not ministers of the present day enforce as a scriptural doctrine this ancient practice of covering the head in public assemblies, as now practised in Eastern heathen countries? Because the dictates of common sense tell them that it was merely an enjoinment of temporary expediency suggested by the then prevailing custom, and can have no bearing on the present day. But, while justly no account whatever is made of the apostle's admonition in regard to the veiling of the head, another subject, standing in vital connection with the spiritual interest of thousands, is overlooked. Overlooked, did we say? Nay, far worse than this: by the identical passages where Paul so evidently infers that Christian women were expected to obey the constrainings of the divinity within them, and pray or prophesy as the Spirit gave utterance—by these same passages those who would restrain the Spirit's utterances justify their resistance. . . .

What serious errors in faith and practice have resulted from taking isolated passages dissevered from their proper connections to sustain a favorite theory! It is thus that the Universalist would have all men unconditionally saved, inasmuch as the Bible says, "Christ is the Saviour of all men," disconnected with the fact that Christ is only the *special* Saviour of them that believe. The Antinomian may gather his faith from the Bible, inasmuch as the Bible says that "men are saved by faith, and not by works." And the evil doer may take the Bible as a plea for his evil doings, inasmuch as it is said in the Bible, "Let us do evil that good may come." And on the same principle has the passage, "Let your women keep silence in the churches," been wrested from its explanatory connections, and made subservient to the egregious and most harmful error of withstanding the utterances of the Holy Spirit from the lips of women, and thereby averting the attention of the Christian world from an endowment of power ordained by God as a speciality of the last days. And permit us here to say that we are constrained to believe that this is one among the more prominent innovations of the "man of sin"—yes, a relic of Popery, which, before the brightness of Christ's appearing, must be openly abrogated.

The scriptural way of arriving at right Bible conclusions is by comparing scripture with scripture. And had this scriptural mode of interpretation been observed in regard to this subject, a distinguishing characteristic of the last days had not been disregarded, and an endowment of power withheld from the church, which might have resulted in the salvation of thousands.

# The Temperance Movement

## *Lyman Beecher (1864)*

Soon after my arrival at Litchfield I was called to attend the ordination at Plymouth of Mr. Heart, ever after that my very special friend. I loved him as he did me. He said to me one day, "Beecher, if you had made the least effort to govern us young men, you would have had a swarm of bees about you; but, as you have come and mixed among us, you can do with us what you will."

Well, at the ordination at Plymouth, the preparation for our creature comforts, in the sitting-room of Mr. Heart's house, besides food, was a broad sideboard covered with decanters and bottles, and sugar, and pitchers of water. There we found all the various kinds of liquors then in vogue. The drinking was apparently universal. This preparation was made by the society as a matter of course. When the Consociation arrived, they always took something to drink round; also before public services, and always on their return. As they could not all drink at once, they were obliged to stand and wait as people do when they go to mill.

There was a decanter of spirits also on the dinner-table, to help digestion, and gentlemen partook of it through the afternoon and evening as they felt the need, some more and some less; and the sideboard, with the spillings of water, and sugar, and liquor, looked and smelled like the bar of a very active grog-shop. None of the Consociation were drunk; but that there was not, at times, a considerable amount of exhilaration, I can not affirm.

There had been already so much alarm on the subject, that at the General Association at Fairfield in 1811, a committee of three had been appointed to make inquiries and report measures to remedy the evil. A committee was also appointed by the General Association of Massachusetts for the same purpose that same month, and to confer with other bodies.

I was a member of General Association which met in the year following at Sharon, June, 1812, when said committee reported. They said they had attended to the subject committed to their care; that intemperance had been for some time increasing in a most alarming manner; but that, after the most faithful

Source: *Autobiography, Correspondence, etc. of Lyman Beecher, D.D.*, 2 vols. edited by Charles Beecher (New York: Harper and Brothers, 1864), 1:245–52.

and prayerful inquiry, they were obliged to confess they did not perceive that any thing could be done.

The blood started through my heart when I heard this, and I rose instanter, and moved that a committee of three be appointed immediately, to report at this meeting the ways and means of arresting the tide of intemperance.

The committee was named and appointed. I was chairman, and on the following day brought in a report, the most important paper that ever I wrote.

## Abstract of Report

"The General Association of Connecticut, taking into consideration the undue consumption of ardent spirits, the enormous sacrifice of property resulting, the alarming increase of intemperance, the deadly effect on health, intellect, the family, society, civil and religious institutions, and especially in nullifying the means of grace and destroying souls, recommend,

"1. Appropriate discourses on the subject by all ministers of Association.

"2. That District Associations abstain from the use of ardent spirits at ecclesiastical meetings.

"3. That members of Churches abstain from the unlawful vending, or purchase and use of ardent spirits where unlawfully sold; exercise vigilant discipline, and cease to consider the production of ardent spirits a part of hospitable entertainment in social visits.

"4. That parents cease from the ordinary use of ardent spirits in the family, and warn their children of the evils and dangers of intemperance.

"5. That farmers, mechanics, and manufacturers substitute palatable and nutritious drinks, and give additional compensation, if necessary, to those in their employ.

"6. To circulate documents on the subject, especially a sermon by Rev. E. Porter and a pamphlet by Dr. Rush.

"7. To form voluntary associations to aid the civil magistrate in the execution of the law.

"And that these practical measures may not be rendered ineffectual, the Association do most earnestly entreat their brethren in the ministry, the members of our churches, and the persons who lament and desire to check the progress of this evil, that they neither express nor indulge the melancholy apprehension that nothing can be done on this subject; a prediction eminently calculated to paralyze exertion, and become the disastrous cause of its own fulfillment. For what if the reformation of drunkards be hopeless, may we not stand between the living and the dead, and pray and labor with effect to stay the spreading plague? And what if some will perish after all that can be done, shall we make no effort to save any from destruction, because we may not be able to turn away every one from the path of ruin?

"Immense evils, we are persuaded, afflict communities, not because they are incurable, but because they are tolerated; and great good remains often unaccomplished merely because it is not attempted.

"Had a foreign army invaded our land to plunder our property and take away our liberty, should we tamely bow to the yoke and give up without a struggle? If a band of assassins were scattering poison, and filling the land with widows and orphans, would they be suffered, without molestation, to extend from year to year the work of death? If our streets swarmed with venomous reptiles and beasts of prey, would our children be bitten and torn to pieces before our eyes, and no efforts made to expel these deadly intruders? But intemperance is that invading enemy preparing chains for us; intemperance is that band of assassins scattering poison and death; intemperance is that assemblage of reptiles and beasts of prey, destroying in our streets the lambs of the flock before our eyes.

"To conclude, if we make a united exertion and fail of the good intended, nothing will be lost by the exertion; we can but die, and it will be glorious to perish in such an effort. But if, as we confidently expect, it shall please the God of our fathers to give us the victory, we may secure to millions the blessings of the life that now is, and the ceaseless blessings of the life to come."

This report was thoroughly discussed and adopted, and a thousand copies ordered to be printed; and that, too, was before people had learned to do much. It was done with zeal and earnestness, such as I had never seen in a deliberative body before.

All my expectations were more than verified. The next year we reported to the Association that the effect had been most salutary. Ardent spirits were banished from ecclesiastical meetings; ministers had preached on the subject; the churches generally had approved the design; the use of spirits in families and private circles had diminished; the attention of the community had been awakened; the tide of public opinion had turned; farmers and mechanics had begun to disuse spirits; the Legislature had taken action in favor of the enterprise; a society for Reformation of Morals had been established, and ecclesiastical bodies in other states had commenced efforts against the common enemy. The experience of one year had furnished lucid evidence that nothing was impossible to faith.

From that time the movement went on, by correspondence, lectures, preaching, organization, and other means, not only in Connecticut, but marching through New England, and marching through the world. Glory to God! Oh, how it wakes my old heart up to think of it! though hearts never do grow old, do they?

---

## Selection 26

---

# The Seneca Falls Convention

### *Elizabeth Cady Stanton (1881)*

The *Seneca County Courier,* a semi-weekly journal, of July 14, 1848, contained the following startling announcement:

### Seneca Falls Convention

WOMAN'S RIGHTS CONVENTION.—A Convention to discuss the social, civil, and religious condition and rights of woman, will be held in the Wesleyan Chapel, at Seneca Falls, N.Y., on Wednesday and Thursday, the 19th and 20th of July, current; commencing at 10 o'clock A.M. During the first day the meeting will be exclusively for women, who are earnestly invited to attend. The public generally are invited to be present on the second day, when Lucretia Mott, of Philadelphia, and other ladies and gentlemen, will address the convention.

This call, without signature, was issued by Lucretia Mott, Martha C. Wright, Elizabeth Cady Stanton, and Mary Ann McClintock. At this time Mrs. Mott was visiting her sister Mrs. Wright, at Auburn, and attending the Yearly Meeting of Friends in Western New York. Mrs. Stanton, having recently removed from Boston to Seneca Falls, finding the most congenial associations in Quaker families, met Mrs. Mott incidentally for the first time since her residence there. They at once returned to the topic they had so often discussed, walking arm in arm in the streets of London, and Boston, "the propriety of holding a woman's convention." These four ladies, sitting round the tea-table of Richard Hunt, a prominent Friend near Waterloo, decided to put their long-talked-of resolution into action, and before the twilight deepened into night, the call was written, and sent to the *Seneca County Courier.* On Sunday morning they

Source: "The Seneca Falls Convention," in Elizabeth Cady Stanton, *History of Woman Suffrage,* 2 vols. (New York: Fowler and Wells, 1881), 1:67–71.

met in Mrs. McClintock's parlor to write their declaration, resolutions, and to consider subjects for speeches. As the convention was to assemble in three days, the time was short for such productions; but having no experience in the *modus operandi* of getting up conventions, nor in that kind of literature, they were quite innocent of the herculean labors they proposed. . . .

After much delay, one of the circle took up the Declaration of 1776, and read it aloud with much spirit and emphasis, and it was at once decided to adopt the historic document, with some slight changes such as substituting "all men" for "King George." Knowing that women must have more to complain of than men under any circumstances possibly could, and seeing the Fathers had eighteen grievances, a protracted search was made through statute books, church usages, and the customs of society to find that exact number. Several well-disposed men assisted in collecting the grievances, until, with the announcement of the eighteenth, the women felt they had enough to go before the world with a good case. One youthful lord remarked, "Your grievances must be grievous indeed, when you are obliged to go to books in order to find them out."

The eventful day dawned at last, and crowds in carriages and on foot, wended their way to the Wesleyan church. When those having charge of the Declaration, the resolutions, and several volumes of the Statutes of New York arrived on the scene, lo! the door was locked. However, an embryo Professor of Yale College was lifted through an open window to unbar the door; that done, the church was quickly filled. It had been decided to have no men present, but as they were already on the spot, and as the women who must take the responsibility of organizing the meeting, and leading the discussions, shrank from doing either, it was decided, in a hasty council round the altar, that this was an occasion when men might make themselves pre-eminently useful. It was agreed they should remain, and take the laboring oar through the Convention.

James Mott, tall and dignified, in Quaker costume, was called to the chair; Mary McClintock appointed Secretary, Frederick Douglass, Samuel Tillman, Ansel Bascom, E. W. Capron, and Thomas McClintock took part throughout in the discussions. Lucretia Mott, accustomed to public speaking in the Society of Friends, stated the objects of the Convention, and in taking a survey of the degraded condition of woman the world over, showed the importance of inaugurating some movement for her education and elevation. Elizabeth and Mary McClintock, and Mrs. Stanton, each read a well-written speech; Martha Wright read some satirical articles she had published in the daily papers answering the diatribes on woman's sphere. Ansel Bascom, who had been a member of the Constitutional Convention recently held in Albany, spoke at length on the property bill for married women, just passed the Leg-

islature, and the discussion on woman's rights in that Convention. Samuel
Tillman, a young student of law, read a series of the most exasperating statutes
for women, from English and American jurists, all reflecting the *tender mer-
cies* of men toward their wives, in taking care of their property and protect-
ing them in their civil rights.

The Declaration having been freely discussed by many present, was re-read
by Mrs. Stanton, and with some slight amendments adopted.

## Declaration of Sentiments

When, in the course of human events, it becomes necessary for one portion
of the family of man to assume among the people of the earth a position different from that which they have hitherto occupied, but one to which the laws
of nature and of nature's God entitle them, a decent respect to the opinions
of mankind requires that they should declare the causes that impel them to
such a course.

We hold these truths to be self-evident: that all men and women are created equal; that they are endowed by their Creator with certain inalienable
rights; that among these are life, liberty, and the pursuit of happiness; that to
secure these rights governments are instituted, deriving their just powers from
the consent of the governed. Whenever any form of government becomes
destructive of these ends, it is the right of those who suffer from it to refuse
allegiance to it, and to insist upon the institution of a new government, laying
its foundation on such principles, and organizing its powers in such form, as
to them shall seem most likely to effect their safety and happiness. Prudence,
indeed, will dictate that governments long established should not be changed
for light and transient causes; and accordingly all experience hath shown that
mankind are more disposed to suffer, while evils are sufferable, than to right
themselves by abolishing the forms to which they were accustomed. But when
a long train of abuses and usurpations, pursuing invariably the same object
evinces a design to reduce them under absolute despotism, it is their duty to
throw off such government, and to provide new guards for their future security. Such has been the patient sufferance of the women under this government, and such is now the necessity which constrains them to demand the
equal station to which they are entitled.

The history of mankind is a history of repeated injuries and usurpations on
the part of man toward woman, having in direct object the establishment of
an absolute tyranny over her. To prove this, let facts be submitted to a candid
world.

He has never permitted her to exercise her inalienable right to the elective franchise.

He has compelled her to submit to laws, in the formation of which she had no voice.

He has withheld from her rights which are given to the most ignorant and degraded men—both natives and foreigners.

Having deprived her of this first right of a citizen, the elective franchise, thereby leaving her without representation in the halls of legislation, he has oppressed her on all sides.

He has made her, if married, in the eye of the law, civilly dead.

He has taken from her all right in property, even to the wages she earns.

He has made her, morally, an irresponsible being, as she can commit many crimes with impunity, provided they be done in the presence of her husband. In the covenant of marriage, she is compelled to promise obedience to her husband, he becoming, to all intents and purposes, her master—the law giving him power to deprive her of her liberty, and to administer chastisement.

He has so framed the laws of divorce, as to what shall be the proper causes, and in case of separation, to whom the guardianship of the children shall be given, as to be wholly regardless of the happiness of women—the law, in all cases, going upon a false supposition of the supremacy of man, and giving all power into his hands.

After depriving her of all rights as a married woman, if single, and the owner of property, he has taxed her to support a government which recognizes her only when her property can be made profitable to it.

He has monopolized nearly all the profitable employments, and from those she is permitted to follow, she receives but a scanty remuneration. He closes against her all the avenues to wealth and distinction which he considers most honorable to himself. As a teacher of theology, medicine, or law, she is not known.

He has denied her the facilities for obtaining a thorough education, all colleges being closed against her.

He allows her in Church, as well as State, but a subordinate position, claiming Apostolic authority for her exclusion from the ministry, and, with some exceptions, from any public participation in the affairs of the Church.

He has created a false public sentiment by giving to the world a different code of morals for men and women, by which moral delinquencies which exclude women from society, are not only tolerated, but deemed of little account in man.

He has usurped the prerogative of Jehovah himself, claiming it as his right to assign for her a sphere of action, when that belongs to her conscience and to her God.

He has endeavored, in every way that he could, to destroy her confidence in her own powers, to lesson her self-respect, and to make her willing to lead a dependent and abject life.

Now, in view of this entire disfranchisement of one-half the people of this country, their social and religious degradation—in view of the unjust laws above mentioned, and because women do feel themselves aggrieved, oppressed, and fraudulently deprived of their most sacred rights, we insist that they have immediate admission to all the rights and privileges which belong to them as citizens of the United States.

In entering upon the great work before us, we anticipate no small amount of misconception, misrepresentation, and ridicule; but we shall use every instrumentality within our power to effect our object. We shall employ agents, circulate tracts, petition the State and National legislatures, and endeavor to enlist the pulpit and the press in our behalf. We hope this Convention will be followed by a series of Conventions embracing every part of the country.

# 11

# The Growth of Roman Catholicism

The establishment of Roman Catholicism was an important facet of the Spanish conquest of Latin America. The task of converting the native populations of Central and South America was, for the most part, undertaken by monastic orders, mainly Jesuits, Dominicans, and Franciscans, with the support of the government of Spain. By 1550 Franciscans had begun work in Argentina, Peru, Venezuela, and Mexico, and by 1600 they had set up communities in what is today Texas and New Mexico. An entire chain of missions was developed in California by 1770, and that enterprise continued for half a century.

The Dominicans began work in Mexico in 1526, and within a few years they were active in Peru, Colombia, and Venezuela. The Jesuits conducted even more far-flung activities, beginning in 1549 in Brazil and continuing within a few years in Colombia, Peru, Mexico, Ecuador, Bolivia, Chile, and Paraguay. In 1551 universities were founded in Mexico City and Lima.

In Canada the Jesuits again led in the work. The story of their sacrifices and endurance of dangers and hardship is inspiring. Isaac Jogues suffered terribly in his work among the warring Mohawk and Iroquois tribes and finally was martyred by them in 1646. In 1673 a Jesuit missionary, Jacques Marquette, discovered the Mississippi River. Thereafter, a series of mission stations was established through the Mississippi Valley as far south as Louisiana, but these did not prove to be permanent. While the growth of Catholicism in Latin America was through the conversion of the natives, in Canada its growth was furthered by immigration, largely from France. The most aggressive leader in this was the first bishop of Quebec, Francois de Laval (1623–1708).

In what was to become the United States, the most important early settlement of Roman Catholicism was in Maryland. In 1632 a Roman Catholic,

George Calvert, Lord Baltimore (1580?–1632), was granted the proprietary ownership of Maryland by King Charles I. Eager to set up a place of refuge and religious toleration under the sovereignty of Great Britain for his fellow Catholics, Calvert had high hopes for the colony, but he died before the royal charter could be granted. Cecilius Calvert, Lord Baltimore's oldest son (1605–1675), inherited the title, and Charles I delivered the Maryland charter to him. As eager as his father had been to provide toleration, the second Lord Baltimore allowed religious freedom to all Christians who settled in Maryland, and it was well he did, for Protestants outnumbered Catholics from the beginning.

On April 21, 1649, the Maryland Assembly passed its famous *Act Concerning Religion*, which has frequently been hailed as one of the great advances in the history of religious toleration. Certainly it was advanced for its time, but it allowed toleration only for Christians, and it decreed the death penalty for those who denied the deity of Jesus Christ, the Trinity, or the unity of the Godhead. The basic thrust of the act is in its concluding article:

> And whereas the inforceing of the conscience in matters of Religion hath frequently fallen out to be of dangerous Consequence in those commonwealthes where it hath been practised . . . Be it Therefore . . . enacted . . . that noe person or persons whatsoever within this Province . . . professing to believe in Jesus Christ, shall from henceforth bee any waies troubled, Molested or discountenanced for or in respect of his or her religion nor in the free exercise thereof within this Province.[1]

By no means did this fend off trouble for Lord Baltimore or for Maryland over the succeeding decades, and finally, in 1691 when William III came to the throne, he made Maryland a royal colony. In 1692 the Church of England was established by law, although the population was by this time diverse, with many Presbyterians, Quakers, and Baptists. In the years that followed the fortunes of Catholics in America were closely tied to events concerning their church in Europe, and there were many serious problems.

## Creating an American church

John Carroll (1735–1815), destined to become the first Roman Catholic bishop in America and the first archbishop of Baltimore, spent his boyhood at Rock Creek, Maryland, the family estate, and at age fourteen he was sent to a Jesuit school in Flanders, France. In 1753 he entered the Jesuit novitiate, at the time when the Society of Jesus was seeing much persecution in France and Portugal. In August 1773 the Pope dissolved the Jesuits. This, combined with the beginning of the American Revolution, had dire consequences for American Catholics. The Jesuits were the only stable group of Catholic clergy in the new United States, and now they were without ecclesiastical support except for that of the London vicar apostolic.

Carroll came home to Maryland in 1774 to find the Catholic church, and particularly the Jesuits, in a sorry state. Consequently, he formulated a plan that later would bear fruit as Georgetown College (now Georgetown University) and St. Mary's Seminary. Leaders at the Vatican realized she needed an authority in the newly formed nation, and after some delicate negotiations, Carroll himself was appointed prefect apostolic on June 9, 1784.

In this office all of Carroll's abilities were needed to confront a number of problems. One of the greatest was *trusteeism*, an attitude in which congregations contended that, through their trustees, they held the right to administer their own affairs. This desire for congregational rule extended even to calling the pastor of their choice as did Protestant churches. This custom plagued the Roman church for decades. Roman Catholic laymen had so long been accustomed to conducting their own parochial affairs that they refused to relinquish it. They wished more freedom in America from the tightly hierarchical government of the European church. The first trustee incident occurred in New York City, where Carroll had appointed Maurice Whelan, a priest who was a poor preacher. In 1785 Andrew Nugent, who possessed excellent oratorical gifts, arrived, and a large faction in the congregation wished to oust Whelan and install Nugent. The trustees, who were in charge of the property and strongly pro-Nugent, refused to pay Whelan's salary. Carroll asserted that Father Nugent had no grounds for his invasion of the church, nor did the trustees have any right to ask for Father Whelan's dismissal. But Whelan gave up the struggle and fled to Canada, leaving Nugent in charge of the congregation. Later the congregation divided over Nugent. When Carroll suspended him Nugent refused to leave. The odorous matter finally had to be settled in the civil court.

The Vatican now realized that episcopal powers were desperately needed to avoid schism, and American priests were granted the right to elect a bishop. They met at Whitemarsh, Maryland, and selected Carroll, who sailed for London and was consecrated bishop of Baltimore on August 15, 1790. Carroll faced monumental challenges, which threatened the very future of the church. One of the most pressing, along with the continuing problem of trusteeism, was the great shortage of clergy, a difficulty with which Protestant groups had struggled since the first settlements in America. After the Revolution it was almost impossible to get English priests to work in the United States. Only when Irish priests came to America in the early nineteenth century did the shortage ease.

In 1791 Carroll called a national synod, the first occasion for Catholic clergy to convene and discuss their needs. That year Carroll also realized his fondest dream, the founding of Georgetown College, which meant that native clergy would no longer have to risk the long ocean voyage to Europe to obtain a sufficient education. St. Mary's Seminary was also initiated in that year with a staff of Sulpician priests.

On the matter of trusteeism see selection 27. This document was sent to the trustees of St. Mary's Church by the coadjutor bishop of Philadelphia, Francis Patrick Kenrick (1796–1863). In 1831 a situation existed there similar to the 1785 incident in New York City. The trustees of St. Mary's had engaged William Hogan as their priest in 1819. The next year Henry Conwell arrived from Ireland as bishop of Philadelphia. Conwell tried to assert his authority over Hogan and the trustees to no avail, and the congregation was bitterly divided. Ecclesiastical and civil trials could not end the dispute, which dragged on until Kenrick was appointed coadjutor to Conwell in 1830. A month after this pastoral address was sent the trustees gave in to the episcopal demands.

By 1820 two new dioceses had been erected, at Charleston and Richmond, and such important leaders as John England (1786–1842), bishop of Charleston, and John Hughes (1797–1864), bishop and later archbishop of New York, came to the fore. Meanwhile much was happening to the church in Europe, and American Catholics had to contend with that as well as their own problems. The complex world situation is beyond the scope of this text and partly stemmed from reactions to the French Revolution. This came as an enormous shock to the Holy See: France, a bastion of Catholicism, had defected to atheism! As anti-clericalism ran rampant throughout Europe, church officials became defensive.

## Retrenchment under Pius IX

Possibly no pontificate in history saw more crucial developments in Roman Catholicism than that of Pope Pius IX (1792–1878), who governed the church from 1846 to 1878. This period was marked by the political unification of Italy and Germany, popular revolutions, and the rise of the evolutionary theory. When he began his rule Pius had the reputation of being a liberal, but events soon changed him into a reactionary who believed that vital beliefs were in danger of being swept away by highly questionable fads and notions. Most urgent, Pius believed, was increased enforcement of papal authority and control. In 1854, in line with this, he proclaimed the *dogma of the Immaculate Conception*, a teaching that, from the moment of her creation, the Virgin Mary was "immune from all taint of original sin." Pius proclaimed this dogma on his own authority, although he did consult the bishops of the church.

Then in 1864 Pius issued the famous *Syllabus of Errors,* along with the bull *Quanta Cura.* In it were listed eighty errors of modern thought. This was a major event, because Pius placed the entire authority of the Roman church and the Papacy squarely against a great number of liberalizing tendencies, provoking a headlong confrontation. Among ideas condemned were:

pantheism;
rationalism;
latitudinarianism;
universalism;
indifferentism;
belief that Protestantism is acceptable to God as a variety of Christianity;
the permission of socialism, communism, secret societies, and Bible
    societies;
separation of church and state, and
state administration of marriage and divorce.

Immediately Pius was charged with taking the church a giant step back into medieval times. Whatever truth there might have been to that, the *Syllabus* brought great concern to the hierarchy in the United States, since it took stances that were decidedly unpopular (if not outrageous) to Americans. Not only did it bring much embarrassment to American Catholics, but it served to lessen what prestige the church had gained through great effort. While it is not an American document, it had such effect on the Catholic church in America that it is included as selection 28.

Six years later, in 1870, Pius called *Vatican Council I,* bringing together bishops from around the world. This was the first general council of the church since the Council of Trent, 300 years before. In line with Pius's entire program of gaining increased authority, the principal question before the bishops was that of papal infallibility (the pope does not need the concurrence of the bishops when he speaks *ex cathedra* on matters of faith). This was highly controversial, and opposition was led by Johann Duhlinger, who later began the Old Catholic movement. But when the vote came, only two negative votes were cast. Rome had come a long way under Pius IX.

## Select Bibliography

Aretin, Karl Otmar Freiherr von. *The Papacy and the Modern World,* translated by R. Hill. New York: McGraw-Hill, 1970.

Ellis, John T. *The Life of James Cardinal Gibbons, Archbishop of Baltimore, 1834–1921,* edited by Francis L. Broderick. Milwaukee: Bruce, 1952.

Fülöp-Miller, Rene. *The Jesuits: A History of the Society of Jesus,* translated by F. S. Flint and D. F. Tait. New York: Capricorn, 1963.

Grant, Dorothy F. *John England, American Christopher.* Milwaukee: Bruce, 1949.

Hennesey, James J. *American Catholics: A History of the Roman Catholic Community in the United States.* New York: Oxford University Press, 1981.

Leckie, Robert. *American and Catholic.* Garden City, N.Y.: Doubleday, 1970.

Melville, Annabelle M. *John Carroll of Baltimore: Founder of the American Catholic Hierarchy.* New York: Scribner, 1955.

# On the Problem of Trusteeism

## *Bishop Francis Patrick Kenrick (1831)*

Beloved Children in Christ:

With much anguish of heart, we have, through the deepest sense of duty, ordered the cessation from all sacred functions in the Church and Cemeteries of St. Mary's, under penalty of the Ecclesiastical censure of suspension, to be incurred by any clergyman attempting the exercise of any such function. On the cause which led to the adoption of this painful measure, you are already apprised; yet we deem it expedient to state the events that led to it, clearly and distinctly, lest any amongst you should imagine that we had in any degree ceased to cherish that tender affection and zeal for your happiness and salvation, which from our first coming amongst you, we invariably manifested. Though discharging the duties of the sublime office originally committed to the Apostles of Christ, we became little ones in the midst of you, as a nurse should cherish her children. So desirous of you, we would gladly have imparted to you not only the gospel of God, but also our own souls, because you were become most dear to us.

At an early period after we had made the Episcopal visitation of the Diocese, and promulgated the Jubilee throughout the Churches of the city, namely, on the 27th day of December last, we resolved to devote ourselves to the discharge of the pastoral duties amongst you, and we officially communicated to the Board of Trustees our determination, which sprang only from the sincerest zeal for your spiritual welfare. To our astonishment and affliction the Lay-Trustees made the communication a matter of deliberation, instead of simply recording it on their books, and even expressed to us their dissatisfaction, though the Charter of Incorporation gives them no right whatever of interference under any shape or form in pastoral appointments, and though the discipline of the Catholic Church does not allow such interference. Having complained in a solemn and paternal manner, nowise unworthy the sanctity of the Pulpit, or the meekness of the Prelacy, of this attempt to impede the conscientious exercise of our Episcopal authority, we received from the Lay-Trustees

Source: Joseph L. J. Kirlin, *Catholicity in Philadelphia: From the Earliest Missionaries down to the Present Time* (Philadelphia: J. J. McVey and Co., 1909), 270–73.

a letter dated the 12th of January, wherein, in terms not usually employed by the faithful to the Bishops of the Church, they expressed their determination to persevere in their resistance. We patiently bore their opposition, in the hope that our untiring efforts for the instruction and sanctification of our flock would convince them of the justice of our views, and induce them spontaneously to desist from a course directly opposed to the principles of Church government, and the provisions of the Charter; and we carefully abstained from all attempts to influence the election, avowing nevertheless publicly in our pastoral address our unchangeable resolution to maintain, at every risk and sacrifice, the spiritual rights with whose guardianship we have been entrusted. More than three months having passed, and the Lay-Trustees after their re-election having proved their determination to persist in disregarding our corporate rights as Chief Pastor, by assembling a Board without our participation, though the Charter declares the three Pastors of St. Mary's Members of the Board by their office, we could no longer tolerate this violation of our chartered rights which implied manifestly the denial of our Pastoral office. We therefore in a Circular Letter of the 12th of April, apprised the Pewholders of the illegal course of the Lay-Trustees, and of the penalty decreed by the Provincial Council and Apostolic See against such interference in Pastoral Appointments. On the 15th we received a letter signed by seven of their number, the other having refused to persevere with them in their resistance to the Episcopal authority. In this communication they denied having assumed or asserted the right of choosing their own Pastors; but they did not venture to deny that they had indirectly, (as we had charged them in our Circular) asserted and assumed it, by rejecting the Pastors duly appointed, and especially by violating our corporate rights as chief Pastor. We called on them for a formal and explicit disclaimer of all right of interfering, directly or indirectly, in the appointment, rejection, or dismissal of Pastors, and for a pledge that they would henceforward act according to the provisions of the Charter; but they explicitly declined that disclaimer and pledge, and six of them merely offered to subscribe a memorandum declaring that they agreed to recognize us, and the Rev. Jeremiah Keilly, as clerical members of the Board of Trustees. Such an agreement, so far from being a practical proof of their adherence to the Catholic principles of church government, and of their respect for the provisions of the charter, was a measure calculated to confirm and establish the assumed right of agreeing to or dissenting from the Episcopal appointments. The letter which accompanied the memorandum contained still further evidence, that the Lay-Trustees claimed and attempted to exercise in our regard this power, since they grounded their assent to our future exercise of the pastoral office, on the actual want of another

Pastor; thereby intimating, that though we had since the 27th of December declared our determination to act thenceforward as chief pastor of St. Mary's, and though we had since that time constantly performed all the duties of that office, yet we were not in reality chief pastor hitherto, because the Lay-Trustees had withheld their assent and approbation.

Under such circumstances we could not consistently with our attachment to Catholic principles and the rights of our office, recall the order for the cessation from sacred functions in St. Mary's Church and Cemeteries, which we had on the preceding evening issued, when the receipt of the letter of the seven Trustees had convinced us of their determination to persevere in eluding Episcopal authority. We did indeed abstain from issuing the more solemn sentence of Interdict, which the provincial Council authorizes us to pronounce, though we well knew that the evil which called for this severity was not of recent growth, but had originated and been matured in times of schism and confusion, and had long since defied every mild remedy.

We still hope that the speedy acknowledgment of the Catholic principles of church government, may enable us not only to abstain from any more painful exercise of authority, but even to restore to our beloved children in Christ, the consolation of worshipping in the splendid edifice in which you and your fathers worshipped, and which your and their generous piety erected, and the legislative authority of this State secured for the exercise of the Roman Catholic religion. We willingly persuade ourselves, that those who have hitherto resisted the conscientious and mild exercise of Episcopal authority, acted under misconception; and we indulge the hope, that they will soon render us that rational and Christian obedience and subjection, which the Apostle requires of the faithful to the Prelates of the Church, whom the Holy Ghost has placed Bishops to rule the Church of God purchased with His blood. We shall hail with joy and thanksgiving to God, their return to duty, and endeavor by all the exhibitions of paternal tenderness and affection, to obliterate from their minds, and from yours, the remembrance of these days of affliction, wherein the Church sits solitary that was full of people.

May the God of peace crush Satan speedily under your feet. The grace of our Lord Jesus Christ be with you.

Given at Philadelphia, this 22nd day of April, 1831, in the first year of our Episcopacy.

Francis Patrick,
*Bishop of Arath, and Coadjutor of Phila.*

By Order John Hughes, *Sec'y.*

# The Syllabus of Errors

## Pope Pius IX (1864)

### V. Errors Concerning the Church and Her Rights

19. The Church is not a true and perfect Society, entirely free; nor is she endowed with proper and perpetual rights of her own, conferred upon her by her Divine Founder; but it appertains to the civil power to define what are the rights of the Church, and the limits within which she may exercise those rights.

20. The ecclesiastical power ought not to exercise its authority without the permission and assent of the Civil Government.

21. The Church has not the power of defining dogmatically that the religion of the Catholic Church is the only true religion.

22. The obligation by which Catholic teachers and authors are strictly bound, is confined to those things only which are proposed to universal belief as dogmas of Faith by the infallible judgment of the Church.

23. Roman Pontiffs and Œcumenical Councils have wandered outside the limits of their powers, have usurped the rights of princes, and have even erred in defining matters of faith and morals.

24. The Church has not the power of using force, nor has she any temporal power, direct or indirect.

25. Beside the power inherent in the Episcopate, other temporal power has been attributed to it by the civil authority, granted either expressly or tacitly, which on that account is revocable by the civil authority whenever it thinks fit.

26. The Church has no innate and legitimate right of acquiring and possessing property.

27. The sacred ministers of the Church and the Roman Pontiff are to be absolutely excluded from every charge and dominion over temporal affairs.

28. It is not lawful for bishops to publish even Letters Apostolic without the permission of Government.

Source: *The Syllabus for the People: A Review of the Propositions Condemned by His Holiness Pope Pius IX with Text of the Condemned List* (New York: Catholic Publishing Society, 1875), 13–15, 19–20, 22–23.

29. Favours granted by the Roman Pontiff ought to be considered null, unless they have been sought for through the civil government.

30. The immunity of the Church and of ecclesiastical persons derived its origin from civil law.

31. The ecclesiastical Forum or tribunal for the temporal causes, whether civil or criminal, of clerics, ought by all means to be abolished, even without consulting and against the protest of, the Holy See.

32. The personal immunity by which clerics are exonerated from Military Conscription and service in the Army may be abolished without violation either of natural right or of equity. Its abolition is called for by civil progress, especially in a society framed on the model of a liberal government.

33. It does not appertain exclusively to the power of ecclesiastical jurisdiction by right, proper and innate, to direct the teaching of theological questions.

34. The teaching of those who compare the Sovereign Pontiff to a Prince, free, and acting in the universal Church, is a doctrine which prevailed in the middle ages.

Pius IX (Billy Graham Center Museum, Wheaton, Ill.)

35. There is nothing to prevent the decree of a General Council, or the act of all peoples, from transferring the Supreme Pontificate from the Bishop and City of Rome to another bishop and another city.

36. The definition of a National Council does not admit of any subsequent discussion, and the civil authority can assume this principle as the basis of its acts.

37. National Churches, withdrawn from the authority of the Roman Pontiff and altogether separated, can be established.

38. The Roman Pontiffs have, by their too arbitrary conduct, contributed to the division of the Church into Eastern and Western.

## VII. Errors Concerning Natural and Christian Ethics

56. Moral laws do not stand in need of the Divine sanction, and it is not at all necessary that human laws should be made conformable to the laws of nature, and receive their power of binding from God.

57. The science of philosophical things and morals, and also civil laws, may and ought to keep aloof from Divine and ecclesiastical authority.

58. No other forces are to be recognized except those which reside in matter, and all the rectitude and excellence of morality ought to be placed in the accumulation and increase of riches by every possible means, and the gratification of pleasure.

59. Right consists in the material fact. All human duties are an empty word, and all human facts have the force of right.

60. Authority is nothing else but numbers and the sum total of material forces.

61. The injustice of an act when successful, inflicts no injury upon the sanctity of right.

62. The principle of non-intervention, as it is called, ought to be proclaimed and observed.

63. It is lawful to refuse obedience to legitimate princes, and even to rebel against them.

64. The violation of any solemn oath, as well as any wicked and flagitious action repugnant to the eternal law, is not only not blameable, but is altogether lawful and worthy of the highest praise, when done through love of country.

## X. Errors Having Reference to Modern Liberalism

77. In the present day it is no longer expedient that the Catholic religion should be held as the only religion of the State, to the exclusion of all other forms of worship.

78. Hence it has been wisely provided by law, in some Catholic countries, that persons coming to reside therein shall enjoy the public exercise of their own peculiar worship.

79. Moreover it is false that the civil liberty of every form of worship, and the full power, given to all, of overtly and publicly manifesting any opinions whatsoever and thoughts, conduce more easily to corrupt the morals and minds of the people, and to propagate the pest of indifferentism.

80. The Roman Pontiff can, and ought, to reconcile himself, and come to terms with progress, liberalism, and modern civilization.

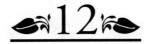

# The Agonizing Question of Slavery

While some contemporary accounts of American history give little or no notice of the part played by the churches, in many situations they played a large role indeed, and nowhere is this better shown than in the movement to free the slaves. Christians of all denominations took both sides of the issue, but on balance the Christian faith did more than anything else to sensitize the nation to the plight of the black race.

In 1619—a fateful date in American history—what was probably a Dutch warship appeared off Jamestown, Virginia, and sent ashore for sale about twenty Africans. Black slavery probably would have been introduced in a few years" time anyway, but this was the ill-omened beginning. During the seventeenth century slaves were not brought to the New World in large numbers. But in 1793 Eli Whitney invented the cotton gin and thereby made the raising of cotton highly profitable. The immediate insatiable demand for cotton caused Southern slavery, which had been dying out, to become essential.

## The early anti-slavery impulse

As the horrors of the American slave system became known, Christians were the first to show concern. We have already noted the distress of George White-field over the condition of slaves (selection 8), and the efforts of John Wool-man against the slave trade (selection 9). Sporadic concern began to turn to concerted action when the Quaker Anthony Benezet led the Society of Friends to expel its slaveholding members in 1776. In 1775 a group of Philadelphia Quakers organized the country's, and possibly the world's, first abolitionist organization. John Wesley adopted Benezet's ideas, and those attending the

One early setting where blacks and whites could mingle was at camp meetings, such as this Methodist gathering in Queen Anne's County Maryland.

Christmas Conference of 1784, from which American Methodism dates its formal origins, took steps to exclude owners or traders of slaves from membership. During the period of the Revolutionary War the Baptists also took similar steps. More positive measures were modeled by Samuel Hopkins (1721–1803), the eminent theologian of Newport, Rhode Island. In 1769 Hopkins persuaded his slave-holding and trading church members to go on record against human bondage. He suggested that some blacks should be educated and sent back to their native lands as teachers and pastors, to make some slight compensation for the evil and misery of the slave trade.

In 1800 the Virginia legislature asked Governor James Monroe to correspond with President Thomas Jefferson regarding the purchase of land overseas to colonize free blacks. In 1816 the American Society for Colonizing the Free People of Color in the United States was organized, and in April 1818 Samuel J. Mills, Jr., selected Liberia as an ideal site where blacks might colonize. While the society was able to accomplish little to free blacks, it nurtured a number of men who became leaders in the fight for emancipation in years to come: Arthur and Lewis Tappan, Benjamin Lundy, Gerrit Smith, James G. Birney, Theodore D. Weld, Elizur Wright, and others.

By 1830 a great shift with far-reaching effects had occurred in the nation's regard for slavery. Some of this was set off when William Lloyd Garrison (1805–1879), a man of meager education and explosive temperament, was recruited to the abolitionist cause. In 1829 Garrison was editing a small Baptist temperance journal. Benjamin Lundy (1789–1839), a New Jersey Quaker, asked Garrison to assist him with his paper, the *Genius of Universal Emancipation,* published in Baltimore.

In the summer of 1830 Garrison accused a shipmaster of "domestic piracy" for transporting slaves to a new plantation in Louisiana for their owner. Showing his violent tendencies, he raged in Lundy's paper, "Francis Todd . . . should be sentenced to solitary confinement for life!" He and all who transport slaves "are the enemies of their own species—highway robbers and murders; and their final doom will be, unless they speedily repent, to occupy the lowest depths of perdition." For this Garrison was jailed in Baltimore on a charge of libel.

Word of this reached Arthur Tappan (1786–1865), a dedicated, generous Christian merchant in New York City, who, with his brother Lewis (1788–1873), was financing a number of benevolent causes. Although the two were strangers, Tappan sent money to release Garrison on bail. Garrison issued the first number of his own paper, the *Liberator,* in Boston on January 1, 1831, financed by the Tappans and other Christian philanthropists. The paper was thoroughly militant, demanding the immediate freedom, without compensation to owners, "of our slave population." Unfortunately, Garrison had no practical plan or interest in the many political, economic, and social difficulties involved in emancipating the millions of slaves in the United States. As Gilbert Barnes says, "His ardent, suggestible imagination seized upon the abstract absolutes of the radical pamphleteers of immediate abolition, and he made them his own."[1]

Garrison was a master of quotable invective, and his unbridled vehemence in the pages of the *Liberator* lashed out with increasing intensity over the years at any hesitation in the movement toward emancipation. At first he welcomed the support of the churches; later, when he found they did not possess his hyper-radical approach, he cast them off. In the spring of 1837, Garrison came under the influence of one who had already rebelled against the churches, John Humphrey Noyes (selection 23). Garrison eschewed Noyes' ideas of Christian perfectionism and spiritual wifery, but he added to his own inclinations the reformer's pugnacious pacifism, antipatriotism, anti-institutionalism, and high-sounding logical absolutes. In the June 30, 1837, issue of the *Liberator* he adopted Noyes' statement, "My hope of the Millennium begins where Dr. Beecher's expires—viz., AT THE OVERTHROW OF THIS NATION."[2]

Because the Congregationalists of both Massachusetts and Connecticut had prohibited abolitionists from speaking from their pulpits in 1836, Garrison dredged the language for epithets adequate to excoriate them and other denominations. Those pastors stood "at the head of the most implacable foes of God and man," toward whom "the most intense abhorrence should fill the breast of every disciple of Christ." The Methodists were as bad: "a cage of unclean birds and a synagogue of Satan." As he flailed away at the "black-hearted clergy" who would not immediately support his schemes, Garrison eventually concluded that the churches themselves restricted the soaring aspirations of humanity. In one final burst of denunciation, Garrison "renounced all allegiance to his country and had nominated Jesus Christ to the Presidency of the United States and the World."[3] Such was this man. Before sentiments like these, the Tappan brothers and many of the more moderate abolitionists stood appalled.[4]

## A divided church and nation

Garrison's vitriolic attacks on everything and everyone were symptomatic of the incredibly intense feelings of that era and the splits and divisions between various wings of the abolitionist movement. Abolitionists held different positions on immediate emancipation or "gradualism," on colonization and on "amalgamation," a nineteenth-century euphemism for the social mingling of blacks and whites. Multitudes who were eager for abolition still opposed whites and blacks being thrown together in society.

The conflict became so rabid that it caused division in several Protestant churches. In the South, especially the border states, anti-slavery societies organized after 1820 often put their adherents in great danger from enraged slave-holders. The address against slavery by the Presbyterian Synod of Kentucky (selection 29) was one of the last strong statements by a southern denomination as the pressures mounted. One of the most vehement defenders of slavery was the well-known James Henley Thornwell (1812–1862), a professor and later president of Presbyterian Theological Seminary at Columbia, South Carolina. The arguments of most of these defenders of slavery centered in the assertion that Scripture did not condemn it. This attempt was not, of course, persuasive in the view of the northern abolitionists.

John England (1786–1842), bishop of the Charleston Diocese of the Roman Catholic Church, in 1840 defended slavery on biblical grounds, contending that the pope had condemned the slave trade, but had not spoken against domestic slavery (selection 30). In a series of *Letters* England showed that the Roman Church had, over the centuries, sanctioned the institution of slavery. While he personally disliked slavery, England said, "I also see the impossibility of now abolishing it here. When it can and ought to be abolished is a question for the legislature and not for me."

Perhaps the most energetic Christian abolitionist was Theodore Dwight Weld (1803–1895), who was associated with the Tappan brothers in founding Lane Seminary in Cincinnati. In 1839 Weld published *Slavery As It Is,* a vivid account of Southern slavery that had great effect on the reading public.

One of Lyman Beecher's daughters, Harriet (1811–1896), who married Lane Seminary professor Calvin E. Stowe in 1836, was so influenced by *Slavery As It Is* that she slept with it under her pillow, "till its facts crystallized into Uncle Tom."[5] In 1852 Harriet Beecher Stowe published *Uncle Tom's Cabin,* which one critic has called "perhaps the most influential novel ever published . . . a verbal earthquake, an ink-and-paper tidal wave."[6] The author was convinced that it was really God who had written the book. Its searing portrayals of Simon Legree, Sambo, Eliza, Uncle Tom and the other characters so burned themselves into the national consciousness that they are with us still. Selection 31 conveys a sample of the book's power.

While this book and representatives of both sides argued and drove sincere people into deepening hatreds for each other, the nation marched inexorably toward civil war.

## Select Bibliography

Barnes, Gilbert H. *The Antislavery Impulse, 1830–1844.* New York: Harcourt, Brace and World, 1964.

Dumond, Dwight L. *Antislavery Origins of the Civil War in the United States.* 1939; repr., Westport, Conn.: Greenwood, 1980.

Filler, Louis. *The Crusade Against Slavery, 1830–1860.* New York: Harper and Row, 1960.

Lesick, Lawrence T. *The Lane Rebels: Evangelicalism and Antislavery in Antebellum America.* Metuchen, N.J.: Scarecrow, 1980.

Muelder, Hermann R. *Fighters for Freedom.* New York: Columbia University Press, 1959.

Sernett, Milton C. *Abolition's Axe: Beriah Green, Oneida Institute, and the Black Freedom Struggle.* Syracuse, N.Y.: Syracuse University Press, 1986.

_____. *Black Religion and American Evangelicalism: White Protestants, Plantation Missions, and the Flowering of Negro Christianity, 1787–1865.* Metuchen, N.J.: Scarecrow, 1975.

Wyatt-Brown, Bertram. *Lewis Tappan and the Evangelical War Against Slavery.* New York: Atheneum, 1971.

# A Condemnation of the Institution of Slavery

## *The Presbyterian Synod of Kentucky (1835)*

We have exhibited fairly, but briefly, the nature and effects of slavery. For the truth of our facts, we refer to your own observations; for the correctness of our reasoning, we appeal to your judgments and consciences. What, then, must we conclude? Is slavery a system which Christians should sanction or even tolerate, if their efforts can avail to abolish it? The reply is often made, *"God's word sanctions slavery, it cannot therefore be sinful. It cannot be our duty to relinquish our power over our slaves, or the Bible would have enjoined it upon us to do so."* We will not attempt to elaborate argument against this plea for slavery—it needs no such answer. A few observations will suffice to show its utter fallacy. . . .

It has sometimes been said, that the "New Testament does not condemn slaveholding in express terms." And the practice has been advocated, because it has not been denounced. If this assertion were true, and if the Bible only *virtually* denounced it, it would be a sin. No man can righteously continue a practice which God disapproves of, no matter in what form the disapproval is expressed. But the assertion is not true. THE NEW TESTAMENT DOES CONDEMN SLAVEHOLDING, AS PRACTISED AMONG US, IN THE MOST EXPLICIT TERMS FURNISHED BY THE LANGUAGE IN WHICH THE INSPIRED PEN MEN WROTE. If a physician, after a minute examination, should tell a patient that his every limb and organ was diseased— if he should enumerate the various parts of his bodily system, the arms, the legs, the head, the stomach, the bowels, &c., and should say of each one of these parts distinctly that it was unsound; could the man depart and say, "After all, I am not diseased, for the physician has not said, in *express terms,* that my *body* is unsound?" Has he not received a more clear and express declaration of his entirely diseased condition, than if he had been told, in merely general terms, that his *body* was unsound? Thus has God condemned slavery. He has specified the parts which compose it, and denounced them, one by one, in the most ample and unequivocal form. In the English language we have the term

Source: Theodore D. Weld, *The Bible Against Slavery* (Pittsburgh: D. Appleby and Co., 1864), 149–54. From the minutes of the Synod of Kentucky, Presbyterian Church in the U.S.A., 1835.

*servant,* which we apply indiscriminately both to those held in voluntary subjection to another, and to those whose subjection is involuntary. We have also the term *slave,* which is applicable exclusively to those held in involuntary subjection. The Greek language had a word corresponding exactly in signification with our word servant; but it had none that answered precisely to our term slave.* How then was an apostle, writing in Greek, to condemn *our slavery?* Could it be done in the way in which some seem to think it must be done, before they will be convinced of its sinfulness? How can we expect to find in Scripture the words "slavery is sinful"? when the language in which it is written contained no term which expressed the meaning of our word slavery? Would the advocates of slavery wish us to show that the apostles declare it to be unchristian to hold servants (*douloi*)? This would have been denouncing, as criminal, practices far different from slaveholding. But inspiration taught the holy pen men the only correct and efficacious method of conveying their condemnation of this unchristian system. They pronounce of each one of those several things which constitute slavery, that it is sinful—thus clearly and forever denouncing the system, wherever it might appear, and whatever name it might assume. . . .

Had they used such language as this, "slavery is sinful," some modern apologists for the system might have alleged that our slavery was not such as existed among the Greeks—that slavery here was a different thing from that which the apostles denounced. But the course they pursued leaves no room for such a subterfuge. We have received the command, "Love thy neighbor as thyself," and we are conscious that we are violating the whole spirit as well as letter of this precept, when, for our own trifling pecuniary gain, we keep a whole race sunk in ignorance and pain. We are commanded to give our servants "that which is just and equal," and no sophistry can persuade us that we fulfil this towards those whom we deprive of the reward of their labor. We know that the idea of a bondman receiving a just and equal remuneration for his labor, never enters the minds of slaveholders. The precepts against fraud, oppression, pride, and cruelty, all cut directly through the heart of the slave system. Look back at the *constituents* and *the effects* of slavery, and ask yourself, "Is not every one of these things directly at variance with the plainest commands of the

---

* The words *oiketos, andrapodon,* are those which most nearly correspond, in the idea which they present, with our word slave. But oiketos properly signifies a *domestic;* and andrapodon, *one taken and enslaved in war.* The inspired writers could not have denounced *our sort of slavery* by using either of these words. If they had forbidden us to hold oiketal, they would have forbidden us the use of all domestics—if they had forbidden us to hold andrapoda, they might have been interpreted as forbidding our use only of *such slaves as have been taken and enslaved in war.*

gospel?" The maintenance of this system breaks not one law of the Lord, or two laws—it violates the whole code—it leaves scarcely one precept unbroken. And will any one, then, contend that slavery is not reprobated by God, and that he may participate in the system, and assist in its perpetuation, without deep criminality? Forbid it, conscience—forbid it, common sense! Gaming, horse-racing, gladiatorial shows in which men were hired to butcher each other, the selling of children by their parents, which was often practised in ancient days—all these things are condemned by the Scriptures, not by name, but (as slavery is condemned) by denouncing those crimes of which these acts are modifications and illustrations. . . .

It is often urged that our slaves are better off than our free negroes. If mankind had considered this plea for continuing to hold slaves a valid one, the whole world would have been still in slavery—for all nations have been at one time or other in some kind of slavery—and all despots urged this plea against their emancipation. Besides, no man ought to urge this as his reason for retaining his bondmen, unless he feels conscious that it is his real motive. And we willingly appeal to every man's conscience to say whether his own imagined interest is not his real motive for refusing to adopt any efficient measures for changing the condition of his servants. That our negroes, if emancipated, will be worse off, is, we feel, but the specious pretext for lulling our own pangs of conscience, and answering the argument of the philanthropist. None of us believe that God has so created a whole race, that it is better for them to remain in perpetual bondage. One mode of emancipation may be preferable to another—but any mode is preferable to the perpetuation, through generations to come, of a degrading bondage. History, with a hundred tongues, testifies that, as a general rule, to emancipate is to elevate. And it is vain for any man to argue against such a general law of nature by adducing the occasional departures, which have fallen under his own personal observation. We plant ourselves down on the broad and acknowledged principle, that God created all men capable of freedom—if, then, they have become unfit for this condition, it is by our fault they have become so; and our exertions, if we are willing to do our duty, can easily restore to them that fitness of which we have deprived them.

As the conclusion of all that has been advanced, we assert it to be the unquestionable duty of every Christian, to use vigorous and immediate measures for the destruction of the whole system, and for the removal of all its unhappy effects. Both these objects should be contemplated in his efforts.

# On the Subject of Domestic Slavery

## *Bishop John England (1844)*

In the New Testament we find instances of pious and good men having slaves, and in no case do we find the Saviour imputing it to them as a crime, or requiring their servants' emancipation.—In chap. viii, of St. Matthew, we read of a centurion, who addressing the Lord Jesus, said, v. 9, "For I also am a man under authority, having soldiers under me, and I say to this man, go, and he goeth: and to another, come, and he cometh: and to my servant, do this and he doth it." v. 10. "And Jesus hearing this wondered, and said to those that followed him: Amen, I say to you, I have not found so great faith in Israel." v. 13. "And Jesus said to the centurion, go, and as thou hast believed, so be it done to thee. And the servant was healed at the same hour." St. Luke, in ch. vii, relates also the testimony which the ancients of Israel gave of this stranger's virtue, and how he loved their nation, and built a synagogue for them.

In many of his parables, the Saviour describes the master and his servants in a variety of ways, without any condemnation or censure of slavery. In Luke xvii, he describes the usual mode of acting towards slaves as the very basis upon which he teaches one of the most useful lessons of Christian virtue, v. 7. "But which of you having a servant ploughing or feeding cattle, will say to him, when he is come from the field, immediately, go sit down." 8. "And will not rather say to him, make ready my supper, and gird thyself, and serve me while I eat and drink, and afterwards, thou shalt eat and drink?" 9. "Doth he thank that servant because he did the things that were commanded him?" 10. "I think not. So you also, when you shall have done all the things that are commanded you, say: we are unprofitable servants, we have done that which we ought to do."

After the promulgation of the Christian religion by the apostles, the slave was not told by them that he was in a state of unchristian durance. 1 Cor. vii, 20. "Let every man abide in the same calling in which he was called." 21. "Art thou called being a bond-man? Care not for it; but if thou mayest be made free, use it rather." 22. "For he that is called in the Lord, being a bond-man, is the free-man of the Lord. Likewise he that is called being free, is the bond-man

Source: John England, *Letters of the Late Bishop England to the Hon. John Forsyth, on the Subject of Domestic Slavery* (Baltimore: J. Murphy, 1844), 34–39.

of Christ." 23. "You are bought with a price, be not made the bond-slaves of men." 24. "Brethren, let every man, wherein he was called, therein abide with God." Thus a man by becoming a Christian was not either made free nor told that he was free, but he was advised, if he could lawfully procure his freedom, to prefer it to slavery. The 23d verse has exactly that meaning which we find expressed also in chap. vi, v. 20. "For you are bought with a great price, glorify and bear God in your body," which is addressed to the free as well as to the slave: all are the servants of God, and should not be drawn from his service by the devices of men, but should "walk worthy of the vocation in which they are called." Eph. iv, i. and the price by which their souls, (not their bodies) were redeemed, is also described by St. Peter I, c. i, 10. "Knowing that you were not redeemed with corruptible gold or silver from your vain conversation of the tradition of your fathers." 19. "But with the precious blood of Christ, as of a lamb unspotted and undefiled."—That it was a spiritual redemption and a spiritual service, St. Paul again shows, Heb. ix, 14. "How much more shall the blood of Christ, who through the Holy Ghost, offered himself without spot to God, cleanse our conscience from dead works to serve the living God?" It is then a spiritual equality as was before remarked, in the words of St. Paul, 1 Cor. xii, 13. "For in one spirit we are baptized into one body, whether Jews or Gentiles, whether bond or free." And in the same chapter he expatiates to show that though all members of the one mystical body, their places, their duties, their gifts are various and different. And in his epistle to the Galatians, chap. iv, he exhibits the great truth which he desires to inculcate by an illustration taken from the institutions of slavery, and without a single expression of their censure.

Nor did the apostles consider the Christian master obliged to liberate his Christian servant. St. Paul in his epistle to Philemon acknowledges the right of the master to the services of his slave for whom however he asks, as a special favor, pardon for having deserted his owner. 10. "I beseech thee for my son Onesimus whom I have begotten in my chains." 11. "Who was heretofore unprofitable to thee, but now profitable both to thee and to thee [sic]." 12. "Whom I have sent back to thee. And do thou receive him as my own bowels." Thus a runaway slave still belonged to his master, and though having become a Christian, so far from being thereby liberated from service, he was bound to return thereto and submit himself to his owner. . . .

Again it is manifest from the Epistle of St. Paul to Timothy that the title of the master continued good to his slave though both should be Christians, c. vii. "Whosoever are servants under the yoke, let them count their masters worthy of all honor, lest the name and doctrine of the Lord be blasphemed." 2.

"But they who have believing masters, let them not despise them because they are brethren, but serve them the rather, because they are faithful and beloved, who are partakers of the benefit. These things exhort and teach." And in the subsequent part he declares the contrary teaching to be against the sound words of Jesus Christ, and to spring from ignorant pride. . . .

It will now fully establish what will be necessary to perfect the view which I desire to give, if I can show that masters who were Christians were not required to emancipate their slaves, but had pointed out the duties which they were bound as masters to perform, because this will show under the Christian dispensation the legal, moral and religious existence of slave and master.

The apostle, as we have previously seen, 1 *Tim.* vi, 2, wrote of slaves who had believing or Christian masters. The inspired penman did not address his instructions and exhortations to masters who were not of the household of the Faith. 1 *Cor.* v, 12. "For what have I to do, to judge them that are without?" 13. "For them that are without, God will judge; take away the evil one from amongst yourselves." Thus when he addresses masters; they are Christian masters. *Ephes.* vi, 9. "And you, masters, do the same things to them (servants) forbearing threatenings, knowing that the Lord both of them and you is in heaven: and there is no respect of persons with him,"—and again, *Colos.* iv, i, "Masters do to your servants that which is just and equal: knowing that you also have a master in heaven."

We have then in the teaching of the apostles nothing which contradicts the law of Moses, but we have much which corrects the cruelty of the Pagan practice. The exhibition which is presented to us is one of a cheering and of an elevated character. It is true that the state of slavery is continued under the legal sanction, but the slave is taught from the most powerful motives to be faithful, patient, obedient and contented, and the master is taught that though despotism may pass unpunished on earth it will be examined into at the bar of heaven: and though the slave owes him bodily service, yet that the soul of this drudge, having been purchased at the same price as his own, and sanctified by the same law of regeneration, he who is his slave according to the flesh, is his brother according to the spirit.—His humanity, his charity, his affection are enlisted and interested, and he feels that his own father is also, the father of his slave, hence though the servant must readily and cheerfully pay him homage and perform his behests on earth, yet, they may be on an equality in heaven. . . .

To the Christian slave was exhibited the humiliation of an incarnate God, the suffering of an unoffending victim, the invitation of this model of perfection to that meekness, that humility, that peaceful spirit, that charity and forgiveness of injuries which constitute the glorious beatitudes. He was shown the advantage of suffering, the reward of patience, and the narrow road along whose rugged ascents he was to bear the cross, walking in the footsteps of his Saviour. The curtains which divide both worlds were raised as he advanced, and he beheld Lazarus in the bosom of Abraham, whilst the rich man vainly cried to have this once miserable beggar allowed to dip the tip of his finger in water and touch it to his tongue, for he was tormented in that flame.

Thus, sir, did the legislator of Christianity, whilst he admitted the legality of slavery, render the master merciful, and the slave faithful, obedient and religious, looking for his freedom in that region, where alone true and lasting enjoyment can be found.

---

## Selection 31

---

# Uncle Tom's Cabin

## *Harriet Beecher Stowe (1852)*

THE cabin of Uncle Tom was a small log building close adjoining to "the house," as the negro *par excellence* designates his master's dwelling. . . .

Let us enter the dwelling. . . . Two empty casks had been rolled into the cabin, and being secured from rolling by stones on each side, boards were laid across them, which arrangement, together with the turning down of certain tubs and pails, and the disposing of the rickety chairs, at last completed the preparation.

"Mas'r George is such a beautiful reader, now, I know he'll stay to read for us," said Aunt Chloe; "'pears like 't will be so much more interestin'."

George very readily consented, for your boy is always ready for anything that makes him of importance.

The room was soon filled with a motley assemblage, from the old gray-headed patriarch of eighty, to the young girl and lad of fifteen. . . .

After a while the singing commenced, to the evident delight of all present. Not even all the disadvantages of nasal intonation could prevent the effect of the naturally fine voices, in airs at once wild and spirited. The words were sometimes the well-known and common hymns sung in the churches

Source: Harriet B. Stowe, *Uncle Tom's Cabin; Or, Life Among the Lowly,* 2 vols. (Boston: Houghton, Mifflin, 1896), 1:26–39, *passim;* 2:161–78, *passim.*

about, and sometimes of a wilder, more indefinite character, picked up at camp meetings.

The chorus of one of them, which ran as follows, was sung with great energy and unction:—

> "Die on the field of battle,
>     Die on the field of battle,
>         Glory in my soul."

Another special favorite had oft repeated the words,—

> "Oh, I'm going to glory,—won't you come along with me?
> "Don't you see the angels beck'ning, and a-calling me away?
> Don't you see the golden city and the everlasting day?"

There were others, which made incessant mention of "Jordan's banks," and "Canaan's fields," and the "New Jerusalem;" for the negro mind, impassioned and imaginative, always attaches itself to hymns and expressions of a vivid and pictorial nature; and, as they sung, some laughed, and some cried, and some clapped hands, or shook hands rejoicingly with each other, as if they had fairly gained the other side of the river.

Various exhortations, or relations of experience, followed, and intermingled with the singing. One old gray-headed woman long past work, but much revered as a sort of chronicle of the past, rose, and, leaning on her staff, said,—

"Well, chil'en!—well, I'm mighty glad to hear ye all and see ye all once more, 'cause I don't know when I'll be gone to glory; but I've done got ready, chil'en; 'pears like I'd got my little bundle all tied up, and my bonnet on, jest a-waitin' for the stage to come along to take me home; sometimes, in the night, I think I hear the wheels a-rattlin', and I'm lookin' out all the time; now, you jest be ready too, for I tell ye all, chil'en," she said, striking her staff hard on the floor, "dat ar *glory* is a mighty thing! It's a mighty thing! It's a mighty thing, chil'en,—you dunno nothing about it,—it's *wonderful*." And the old creature sat down, with streaming tears, as wholly overcome, while the whole circle struck up,—

> "O Canaan, bright Canaan,
>     I'm bound for the land of Canaan."

Mas'r George, by request, read the last chapters of Revelation, often interrupted by such exclamations as "The *sakes* now!" "Only hear that!" "Jest think on 't!" "Is all that a-comin' sure enough?" . . .

Uncle Tom was a sort of patriarch in religious matters, in the neighborhood. Having, naturally, an organization in which the *morale* was strongly predominant, together with a greater breadth and cultivation of mind than obtained among his companions, he was looked up to with great respect, as a sort of minister among them; and the simple, hearty, sincere style of his exhortations might have edified even better educated persons. But it was in prayer that he especially excelled. Nothing could exceed the touching simplicity, the childlike earnestness of his prayer, enriched with the language of Scripture, which seemed so entirely to have wrought itself into his being as to have become a part of himself, and to drop from his lips unconsciously; in the language of a pious old negro, he "prayed right up." And so much did his prayer always work on the devotional feelings of his audiences, that there seemed often a danger that it would be lost altogether in the abundance of the responses which broke out everywhere around him. . . .

The solemn light of dawn—the angelic glory of the morning star—had looked in through the rude window of the shed where Tom was lying; and, as if descending on that star-beam, came the solemn words, "I am the root and offspring of David, and the bright and morning star." The mysterious warnings and intimations of Cassy, so far from discouraging his soul, in the end had aroused it as with a heavenly call. He did not know but that the day of his death was dawning in the sky; and his heart throbbed with solemn throes of joy and desire, as he thought that the wondrous *all*, of which he had often pondered,—the great white throne, with its ever radiant rainbow; the white-robed multitude, with voices as many waters; the crowns, the palms, the harps,— might all break upon his vision before that sun should set again. And, therefore, without shuddering or trembling, he heard the voice of his persecutor, as he drew near.

"Well, my boy," said [Simon] Legree, with a contemptuous kick, "how do you find yourself? Didn't I tell yer I could larn yer a thing or two? How do yer like it,—eh? How did yer whaling agree with yer, Tom? Ain't quite so crank as ye was last night. Ye couldn't treat a poor sinner, now, to a bit of a sermon, could ye,—eh?"

Tom answered nothing.

"Get up, you beast!" said Legree, kicking him again.

This was a difficult matter for one so bruised and faint; and, as Tom made efforts to do so, Legree laughed brutally.

"What makes ye so spry this morning, Tom? Cotched cold, maybe, last night."

Tom by this time had gained his feet, and was confronting his master with a steady, unmoved front.

"The devil, you can!" said Legree, looking him over. "I believe you haven't got enough yet. Now, Tom, get right down on yer knees and beg my pardon, for yer shines last night."

Tom did not move.

"Down, you dog!" said Legree, striking him with his riding-whip.

"Mas'r Legree," said Tom, "I can't do it. I did only what I thought was right. I shall do just so again, if ever the time comes. I never will do a cruel thing, come what may." . . .

"Hark ye!" [Legree] said to Tom; "I won't deal with ye now because business is pressing, and I want all my hands; but I *never* forget. I'll score it against ye, and some time I'll have my pay out o' yer old black hide,—mind ye!"

Legree turned and went out.

"There you go," said Cassy, looking darkly after him; "your reckoning's to come yet!—My poor fellow, how are you?"

"The Lord God hath sent his angel, and shut the lion's mouth for this time," said Tom.

"For this time, to be sure," said Cassy; "but now you've got his ill will upon you, to follow you day in, day out, hanging like a dog on your throat,—sucking your blood, bleeding away your life, drop by drop. I know the man." . . .

Those who have been familiar with the religious histories of the slave population know that relations like what we have narrated are very common among them. We have heard some from their own lips, of a very touching and affecting character. The psychologist tells us of a state, in which the affections and images of the mind become so dominant and overpowering, that they press into their service the outward senses, and make them give tangible shape to the inward imagining. Who shall measure what an all-pervading Spirit may do with these capabilities of our mortality, or the ways in which he may encourage the desponding souls of the desolate? If the poor forgotten slave believes that Jesus hath appeared and spoken to him, who shall contradict him? Did He not say that his mission, in all ages, was to bind up the broken-hearted, and set at liberty them that are bruised?

When the dim gray of dawn woke the slumberers to go forth to the field, there was among those tattered and shivering wretches one who walked with an exultant tread; for firmer than the ground he trod on was his strong faith in almighty, eternal love. Ah, Legree, try all your forces now! Utmost agony, woe, degradation, want, and loss of all things shall only hasten on the process by which he shall be made a king and a priest unto God!

From this time an inviolable sphere of peace encompassed the lowly heart of the oppressed one,—an ever-present Saviour hallowed it as a temple. Past now the bleeding of earthly regrets; past its fluctuations of hope, and fear, and desire; the human will, bent, and bleeding, and struggling long, was now entirely merged in the Divine. So short now seemed the remaining voyage of life,—so near, so vivid, seemed eternal blessedness,—that life's uttermost woes fell from him unharming.

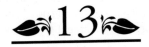

# The Debate Between Science and Religion

Toward the end of the nineteenth century Andrew D. White published his two-volume *History of the Warfare Between Science and Theology*. The thrust of this work is that science's "warfare" is not so much with religion as it is with theology, or with religious doctrine and dogma. Reflecting the confidence of his time in the unassailable accuracy of science, White expressed his conviction that such warfare was fatuous and useless. Religion was, to him, largely an obstruction in the way of science and truth. Although the furor over evolution was then raging, White was convinced that his conclusion was the correct one. Religion, or theology, should stand aside and stop trying to impede progress.

Whatever we may think of that conclusion, there can be no doubt that the warfare has been a long one that does not show signs of abatement. It is also certain that science has become somewhat chastened in making truth claims (as it was not in White's day). Also, after nuclear holocaust, vastly more destructive weapons, ozone depletion, acid rain, the greenhouse effect, and a hundred other byproducts of scientific progress, few thinkers are so convinced that science is an unmixed blessing.

For the five centuries since the beginning of the Renaissance the war has proceeded, with each century having a different focus. In the seventeenth it was in the area of astronomy; in the eighteenth, geology and mathematics, and in the nineteenth, biology and geology. During the twentieth century religion has found itself most often at odds with the social sciences and physics.

In the United States, with its staunch Protestantism, the controversies made little impact until the middle of the nineteenth century. Controversy first erupted in the field of geology. Ever since the Irish archbishop James Ussher

(1581–1656) computed the chronologies of chapters five and eleven of Genesis and stated that God created the universe in 4004 B.C. the matter had seemed settled for most people, even non-Christians. There seemed to be little or no evidence to the contrary. Then in 1788 James Hutton (1726–1797) of Edinburgh wrote *Theory of the Earth,* which introduced the *new geology,* and opened the question for debate. During the first decades of the nineteenth century the German philosopher Georg W. F. Hegel (1770–1831) spun out his dynamic dialectical process with its reconciling of opposites. This type of Hegelian thinking had an enormous effect on all intellectual areas, including science, for the rest of the century. Sir Charles Lyell published *Principles of Geology* (1830–1832), which questioned a recent creation because of the fossils preserved in rocks, and suggested a long developmental period.

## The Darwinian debate

While the French naturalist Jean Baptiste de Lamarck (1744–1829) announced a theory of biological evolution in 1801, it was not popularized until 1859 when Charles Darwin (1809–1882) published *On the Origin of Species by Means of Natural Selection.* The Civil War prevented American scholars from giving much attention to this work immediately but it was fiercely discussed after the war. Then Darwin's *The Descent of Man* appeared in 1871 to fit human origins into the same hypothesis in an incisive way. While *On the Origin of Species* allowed religious people to overlook some of its implications, *The Descent of Man* frontally challenged the divine creation of humanity. There were few who did not comprehend that the statements of the Bible were being attacked, and that this was a foreboding of much to come. The supernatural inspiration and authority of the Bible, so important to most Protestants, had never been so widely challenged; this was an attack that could not be ignored.

In Christian circles, the warfare over *Darwinism* brought sharp divisions between those who rejected and those who accepted it. In the next decades, as evolutionary thinking influenced the study of literature, the critical study of the Bible became another bitter debate. In each case many felt that the new approaches could be reconciled with the Christian faith in one way or another, while many more reacted with chagrin and apprehension, certain that these were inroads of secularism that were inherently contradictory, dangerous, and vicious to the holy citadel of divine authority. Within the churches everyone took a position; neutrality was virtually impossible.

Darwin had sent a copy of *On the Origin of Species* to America's most distinguished biologist, glacial theorist, and paleontologist, the Harvard professor Louis Agassiz, hoping to find support there. Instead of accepting the new hypothesis, Agassiz repeated his adherence to the French biologist Georges Cuvier's position and supported *special creationism* as explaining the existence of fossils and the distribution of species. For this Agassiz was upheld as the exponent of true science by the antievolutionists, and despite his eminence in the field, he was attacked by others.

Within a few years, those within the churches who were appalled by Darwinism found another champion in Charles Hodge (1797–1878), the distinguished professor of theology at Princeton Theological Seminary. Hodge taught over 3000 students during his fifty-year teaching career. In addition, he stood as the recognized leader of Old School Presbyterianism against the New School theology of Albert Barnes, Henry B. Smith, and Charles G. Finney. When Hodge published *What Is Darwinism?* (selection 32) in 1874 it was widely regarded as the definitive orthodox repudiation and overview of the entire matter.

Given his simplistic devotion to science, White, the defender of evolution mentioned above, would have found Hodge's position incomprehensible. Hodge was no obscurantist. He did not fear nor reject all advances made in the name of science; most he welcomed as human discoveries of divine wonders. But he did question whether scientific people were without presuppositions and as open to new truth as they claimed. He also pointed out that scientists, like religionists, were hardly unified. They, and their theories, frequently disagreed violently with each other. Rather, Hodge stood for those Christians who held to the legitimacy of their own pursuit of truth and who were staunchly confident that Biblical truth had withstood the tests of time and abundantly proved itself. Scripture was not to be replaced by each passing fad. Only new-found scientific facts (not unproven or unprovable hypotheses) could be adjuncts to the revealed record, and they could never be contradictory to it. Therefore, in light of the rapid modifications in scientific theory and the likelihood of many more changes to come, Hodge and others were not about to confer either omniscience or infallibility on science. While Hodge used a number of arguments, one of his most basic was that other kinds of evidence were as valid, reliable, and important as the empirical.

## The attempt to accommodate

In *What Is Darwinism?* Hodge demonstrated a mastery of the scientific aspects of Darwin's theory greater than that of Lyman Abbott in his autobiographical work, *Reminiscences* (selection 33). Abbott (1835–1922) did not advocate science over religion, but rather tried to reconcile the two, as did many in his day. The successor in 1890 to Henry Ward Beecher at the influential Plymouth Congregational Church in Brooklyn, Abbott was a bold exponent of evolutionary theory. In *The Evolution of Christianity* (1892), Abbott tried to demonstrate that "in the spiritual, as in the physical, God is the secret and source of light." He went on to speak of the evolution of the church, the Bible, the soul, and Christian society. Since biological evolution was true, Christian theism must be reinterpreted to accord with the new facts. Everything is evolving. Jesus has come from God to show us what we may become; "What Jesus was, humanity is becoming." He accepted completely what John Fiske had proclaimed for years: "Evolution is God's way of doing things." Fiske (1842–1902) was a prolific apologist for Darwinian science and Herbert Spencer's evolution-based social science theories.

Abbott tried to do what White advocated—modify Christianity's stance to accommodate it to new theories. Others, including Hodge, said Abbott and those like him were reconciling nothing. To them, Abbott was asking the Christian faith to collapse before any new drift of thinking that seemed to go against established doctrine, which they believed to be divinely revealed and not susceptible to modification. A fundamental divergence of viewpoint separated Hodge and Abbott. Abbott saw no problem with constant change, whether in nature or divine truth, believing that, as the universe is becoming something different from what it has been, so God created and works through these processes, overseeing and using them in his purposes. To Hodge the universe may be changing, but that does not suggest that God's truth is relative and changing.

## Select Bibliography

Barbour, Ian G. *Issues in Science and Religion*. New York: Harper and Row, 1971.

Brown, Ira V. *Lyman Abbott, Christian Evolutionist: A Study in Religious Liberalism*. 1953; repr., Westport, Conn.: Greenwood, 1970.

Greene, John C. *Darwin and the Modern World-View*. Baton Rouge: Louisiana State University Press, 1973.

_____. *The Death of Adam: Evolution and Its Impact on Western Thought*. Ames, Iowa: Iowa State University Press, 1959.

Hatch, Nathan O., and Mark A. Noll, eds. *The Bible in America: Essays in Cultural History*. New York: Oxford University Press, 1982.

Kennedy, Gail, ed. *Evolution and Religion: The Conflict between Science and Theology in Modern America*. Boston: Heath, 1957.

White, Edward A. *Science and Religion in American Thought: The Impact of Naturalism*. Stanford, Calif.: Stanford University Press, 1952.

# The Incompatibility of Evolution with Theology

## Charles Hodge (1874)

[German Darwinian zoologist Ernst] Haeckel says that Darwin's theory of evolution leads inevitably to Atheism and Materialism. In this we think he is correct. But we have nothing to do with Haeckel's logic or with our own. We make no charge against Mr. Darwin. We cite Haeckel merely as a witness to the fact that Darwinism involves the denial of final causes; that it excludes all intelligent design in the production of the organs of plants and animals, and even in the production of the soul and body of man. This first of German naturalists would occupy a strange position in the sight of all Europe, if, after lauding a book to the skies because it teaches a certain doctrine, it should turn out that the book taught no such doctrine at all. . . .

It is inevitable that minds addicted to scientific investigation should receive a strong bias to undervalue any other kind of evidence except that of the senses, *i.e.*, scientific evidence. We have seen that those who give themselves up to this tendency come to deny God, to deny mind, to deny even self. It is true that the great majority of men, scientific as well as others, are so much under the control of the laws of their nature, that they cannot go to this extreme. The tendency, however, of a mind addicted to the consideration of one kind of evidence, to become more or less insensible to other kinds of proof, is undeniable. . . .

A second cause of the alienation between science and religion, is the failure to make the due distinction between facts and the explanation of those facts, or the theories deduced from them. No sound minded man disputes any scientific fact. Religious men believe with Agassiz that facts are sacred. They are revelations from God. Christians sacrifice to them, when duly authenticated, their most cherished convictions. That the earth moves, no religious man doubts. When Galileo made that great discovery, the Church was right in not yielding at once to the evidence of an experiment which it did not understand.

Source: Charles Hodge, *What Is Darwinism?* (New York: Scribner, Armstrong, and Co., 1874), 95, 129–36, 141–46, 151–52, 173–74.

But when the fact was clearly established, no man sets up his interpretation of the Bible in opposition to it. Religious men admit all the facts connected with our solar system; all the facts of geology, and of comparative anatomy, and of biology. Ought not this to satisfy scientific men? Must we also admit their explanations and inferences? If we admit that the human embryo passes through various phases, must we admit that man was once a fish, then a bird, then a dog, then an ape, and finally what he now is? If we admit the similarity of struc-

Charles Hodge
(Presbyterian Historical Society)

ture in all vertebrates, must we admit the evolution of one from another, and all from a primordial germ? It is to be remembered that the facts are from God, the explanation from men; and the two are often as far apart as Heaven and its antipode. . . .

The third cause of the alienation between religion and science, is the bearing of scientific men towards the men of culture who do not belong to their own class. When we, in such connections, speak of scientific men, we do not mean men of science as such, but those only who avow or manifest their hostility to religion. There is an assumption of superiority, and often a manifestation of contempt. Those who call their logic or their conjectures into question, are stigmatized as narrow-minded, bigots, old women, Bible worshippers, etc.

Professor [Thomas] Huxley's advice to metaphysicians and theologians is, to let science alone. This is his Irenicum. But do he and his associates let metaphysics and religion alone? They tell the metaphysician that his vocation is gone; there is no such thing as mind, and of course no mental laws to be established. Metaphysics are merged into physics. Professor Huxley tells the religious world that there is overwhelming and crushing evidence (scientific evidence, of course) that no event has ever occurred on this earth which was not the effect of natural causes. Hence there have been no miracles, and Christ is not risen. He says that the doctrine that belief in a personal God is necessary to any religion worthy of the name, is a mere matter of opinion. [John] Tyndall, [William] Carpenter, and Henry Thompson, teach that prayer is a superstitious absurdity; Herbert Spencer, whom they call their "great philosopher," *i.e.,* the man who does their thinking, labors to prove that there cannot be a personal God, or human soul or self; that moral laws are mere "generalizations of utility," or, as Carl Vogt says, that self respect, and not the will of God, is the ground and rule of moral obligation. . . .

So much, and it is very little, on the general question of the relation of science to religion. But what is to be thought of the special relation of Mr. Darwin's theory to the truths of natural and revealed religion? We have already seen that Darwinism includes the three elements, evolution, natural selection, and the denial of design in nature. These points, however, cannot now be considered separately.

It is conceded that a man may be an evolutionist and yet not be an atheist and may admit of design in nature. But we cannot see how the theory of evolution can be reconciled with the declarations of the Scriptures. Others may see it, and be able to reconcile their allegiance to science with their allegiance to the Bible. Professor Huxley, as we have seen, pronounces the thing impossible. As all error is antagonistic to truth, if the evolution theory be false, it must be opposed to the truths of religion so far as the two come into contact. Mr. [John] Henslow, indeed, says Science and Religion are not antagonistic because they are in different spheres of thought. This is often said by men who do not admit that there is any thought at all in religion; that it is merely a matter of feeling. The fact, however, is that religion is a system of knowledge, as well as a state of feeling. The truths on which all religion is founded are drawn within the domain of science, the nature of the first cause, its relation to the world, the nature of second causes, the origin of life, anthropology, including the origin, nature, and destiny of man. Religion has to fight for its life against a large class of scientific men. All attempts to prevent her exercising her right to be heard are unreasonable and vain.

It should be premised that this paper was written for the single purpose of answering the question, What is Darwinism? The discussion of the merits of the theory was not within the scope of the writer. What follows, therefore, is to be considered only in the light of a practical conclusion.

1. The first objection to the theory is its *primâ facie* incredibility. That a single plant or animal should be developed from a mere cell, is such a wonder, that nothing but daily observation of the fact could induce any man to believe it. Let any one ask himself, suppose this fact was not thus familiar, what amount of speculation, of arguments from analogies, possibilities, and probabilities, could avail to produce conviction of its truth. But who can believe that all the

plants and animals which have ever existed upon the face of the earth, have been evolved from one such germ? This is Darwin's doctrine. . . .

2. There is no pretense that the theory can be proved. Mr. Darwin does not pretend to prove it. He admits that all the facts in the case can be accounted for on the assumption of divine purpose and control. All that he claims for his theory is that it is possible. His mode of arguing is that if we suppose this and that, then it may have happened thus and so. Amiable and attractive as the man presents himself in his writings, it rouses indignation, in one class at least of his readers, to see him by such a mode of arguing reaching conclusions which are subversive of the fundamental truths of religion. . . .

4. All the evidence we have in favor of the fixedness of species is, of course, evidence not only against Darwinism, but against evolution in all its forms. It would seem idle to discuss the question of the mutability of species, until satisfied what species is. This, unhappily, is a question which it is exceedingly difficult to answer. Not only do the definitions given by scientific men differ almost indefinitely, but there is endless diversity in classification. Think of four hundred and eighty species of humming-birds. Haeckel says that one naturalist makes ten, another forty, another two hundred, and another one, species of a certain fossil; and we have just heard that Agassiz had collected eight hundred species of the same fossil animal. Haeckel also says, that there are not two zoölogists or any two botanists who agree altogether in their classification. . . .

The conclusion of the whole matter is, that the denial of design in nature is virtually the denial of God. Mr. Darwin's theory does deny all design in nature, therefore, his theory is virtually atheistical; his theory, not he himself. He believes in a Creator. But when that Creator, millions on millions of ages ago, did something,—called matter and a living germ into existence,—and then abandoned the universe to itself to be controlled by chance and necessity, without any purpose on his part as to the result, or any intervention or guidance, then He is virtually consigned, so far as we are concerned, to nonexistence. It has already been said that the most extreme of Mr. Darwin's admirers adopt and laud his theory, for the special reason that it banishes God from the world; that it enables them to account for design without referring it to the purpose or agency of God.

Selection 33

# The Compatibility of Evolution with Theology

### *Lyman Abbott (1915)*

I was not long in coming to the conclusion that animal man was developed from a lower order of creation. This was the view of the scientific experts, and on questions on which I have no first-hand knowledge I accept the conclusions of those who have. Such scientific objections as the failure to discover a "missing link" I left the scientists to wrestle with. The objection that evolution could not be reconciled with Genesis gave me no concern, for I had long before decided that the Bible is no authority on scientific questions. To the sneer, "So you think your ancestor was a monkey, do you!" I replied, "I would as soon have a monkey as a mud man for an ancestor." This sentence, first uttered, I believe, in a commencement address before the Northwestern University in Chicago, brought upon me an avalanche of condemnation—but no reply. In truth, no reply was possible. For the question whether God made the animal man by a mechanical process in an hour or by a process of growth continuing through centuries is quite immaterial to one who believes that into man God breathes a divine life. For a considerable time I held that this inbreathing was a new and creative act. Darwin's "The Expression of the Emotions in Man and Animals" did nothing to convince me that spiritual man is a development from unspiritual qualities. [Unitarian theologian James] Drummond's "Ascent of Man," with its emphasis on struggle for others as a factor in spiritual development, a factor of which Darwin took little or no account, led me to see that such a spiritual development is at least quite probable, and, without being dogmatic on that point, I became a radical evolutionist; by which I mean I accepted to the full John Fiske's aphorism: "Evolution is God's way of doing things."

This doctrine of evolution not only tallied with the conclusions I had previously reached respecting the authority of the Bible, but clarified it. If evolution is God's way of doing other things, why not God's way of giving to mankind a revelation of himself and his will? . . .

Source: Lyman Abbott, *Reminiscences* (Boston: Houghton-Mifflin Co., 1915), 458–62, 485–86.

The doctrine that growth, not manufacture, is God's way of doing things changed also my conception of God, of creation, of Jesus Christ, and of the Gospel. The picture of a King on a great white throne, into whose presence I should come by and by when this earthly life is over, disappeared, and in its place came the realization of a Universal Presence, animating all nature as my spirit animates my body, and inspiring all life as a father inspires his children or a teacher his pupils. . . .

Lyman Abbott

As I no longer looked up to an imaginary heaven for an imaginary God, so I no longer looked back to a creation completed in six days or six geological epochs. I saw in creation, as later expressed to me by a friend, "a process, not a product." Every day is a creative day. Every new flower that blooms is a new creation. Nor did I any longer look back over an intervening epoch of eighteen centuries for a revelation of God either in history or in human experience. I saw him in modern as truly as in ancient history, in the life of America as truly as in the life of Israel. I saw him in the "Eternal Goodness" of [John Greenleaf] Whittier as truly as in the One Hundred and Third Psalm; in the mother teaching her child as truly as in Isaiah teaching a nation. And when I was asked what difference I thought there was between inspiration to-day and inspiration in Bible times, I replied that I could not answer. As I neither knew how God spoke to Abraham nor how he spoke to Phillips Brooks, I could not tell wherein was the difference between the two, or whether there was any difference. . . .

I have described this change in my faith at some length because I believe that it is typical of a change which has taken place in the theological beliefs and religious experiences of many thousands during the last half-century.

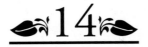

# Liberalism and Christian Orthodoxy

If it is to remain faithful to its original intentions, how much change can a religion allow? That is a question world religions have to face continually. All human institutions, including religions, must strike a balance between liberalism and conservatism. Too much change in essential, core teachings, merely to meet immediate vicissitudes or cultural differences, can alter the religion until it is hardly recognizable. One might say that Buddha would find Buddhism unrecognizable, especially as practiced in China and Japan. Does not all the violence and bitter hatred in Shiite Islam absolutely contravene the Koran? Then again, how many religions have reformations that attempt to bring faith back to the essentials? The Protestant Reformation, that great attempt to restore New Testament Christianity and strip away the excrescences, corruptions and superstitions of the Dark Ages, served exactly such a purpose. These are perennial issues for world religions, and Christians have wrestled with them since the days of the apostles.

Trends toward increasing liberalism, in both Protestantism and Roman Catholicism, have already been noted. This drift was inevitable as America changed dramatically after the Industrial Revolution. No longer was America a generally homogeneous nation. Applied science made possible the astounding expansion of an industrial economy and the rapid growth of cities into great concentrations of humanity and machines. Churches that had enjoyed a secure niche in the more leisurely tempo of rural and small-town America were suddenly and uncomfortably confronted with a new industrial order, including all of its accompanying problems of massive immigration, city slums, unemployment, and shifting populations. Industrialization brought a general fragmentation of life as a multitude of new attractions competed for people's time. If the churches could not develop new techniques for reaching the teeming masses they knew they would soon be anachronisms.

In addition, the old economic and social programs and views met new and unaccustomed challenges, especially after the Civil War. Protestantism still held the loyalty of the middle classes, but it found difficulty in attracting the lower classes. Samuel Gompers of the American Federation of Labor (AFL) said, "My associates have come to look upon the church and the ministry as the apologists and defenders of the wrong committed against the interests of the people."[1] Such comments stung, whether or not they were accurate. In reaction to these and other pressures the churches developed new methods, some of which modified the accepted message of the Christian faith. There is no better example of this than the ministry and teachings of "the father of American religious liberalism," Horace Bushnell (selection 21).

A number of clergymen, disturbed by Bushnell's example and not wanting to compromise essential doctrines, grappled with the problem of modifying and updating the method while preserving intact the orthodox Christian message. This is essentially the oft-recurring *adiaphora* ("things indifferent") argument in Christian thought. By separating essential things from nonessentials Christians might develop more relevant ceremonies, ethics (weighing actions neither expressly commanded nor forbidden), and doctrines (tolerating divergence in teachings that might be biblical but of minor importance). Many leaders have successfully remained orthodox while tailoring their message to new times or cultures.

## A theology of social activism

After the Civil War the important and prestigious pulpits of the nation were frequently occupied by heirs of the *New Theology*, men whose theology tended more or less to liberal views. Washington Gladden (1836–1918) in the First Congregational Church of Columbus (selection 37), Phillips Brooks (1835–1893) at Trinity Episcopal Church in Boston, and Henry Ward Beecher (1813–1887) at Plymouth Congregational Church in Brooklyn were the forerunners of the Social Gospel movement and the twentieth century mood of socially activistic Protestantism generally.

Beecher best exemplifies the characteristics of the new mood and theology. Beecher, the fourth son of Lyman (selections 12 and 25), graduated from Lane Seminary in 1837 and for the next ten years followed the revivalistic tradition of his father in several Indiana churches. The newly formed Plymouth Church in Brooklyn called him in 1847, and by his pulpit oratory he soon attracted a large and wealthy congregation. He was a child of revivalism, and all else was subservient to achieving results. In 1882 he said, "I gradually formed a theology by practice—by trying it on, and the things that really did God's work in the hearts of men I set down as good theology, and the things that did not, whether they were true or not, they were not true to me." This approach led Beecher to the conclusion that sincerity, not doctrine, was the proper test of a person's life. He said, "There is a growing conviction that greatheartedness is more akin to the gospel spirit than dogma or doctrine." His theology was frequently criticized, and Beecher led his church out of the Congregational denomination in 1882, stating that he was a free man with dependence on no one.

Beecher, like a number of others in that day, was persuaded that doctrines divided people; therefore he avoided disputes as much as he could. Because of this he never preached on Jesus' death on the cross. Softening Christology, Beecher made Jesus into a superb example, the king of love, and a wonderful unseen friend, all of which fit well in that sentimental age. The harsh realities of life? Beecher avoided them. How Jesus would save and influence a person was an individual concern, not something that he dealt with in his sermons. It was by personal experience that we can know God and Christ, and each individual must do that personally. Creeds were of little help, as far as he was concerned. He wrote, "The creeds of the future will begin where the old ones ended: upon the nature of man, his condition on earth, his spiritual nature, its range, possibilities, education. . . ."[2]

With such a popularized Christian teaching—a lowest-common-denominator approach—Beecher and others prepared the way for the Social Gospel and for modernism. By eschewing doctrine and minimizing its importance, making only sincerity the test of truth, regarding humans as essentially good and without serious sin or problems, Beecher enervated the gospel and reduced it to a watery concoction of self-help Pelagianism, or as Sydney Ahlstrom writes, "a benign and genteel form of religious humanism."[3] Of liberals such as Beecher, Ahlstrom writes, "Often incredibly naïve in their evaluations of man, society, and the national destiny, they did little to prepare Americans for the brutal assaults of the twentieth century. In this respect they laid the groundwork for tragedy and disillusion."[4] H. Richard Niebuhr's dictum stands: "The renovation of which [liberalism] spoke was not so much the restoration of health to a diseased body as the clearing out of the accumulated rubbish of traditional beliefs or customs. . . . A God without wrath brought men without sin into a kingdom without judgment through the ministrations of a Christ without a cross."[5]

Another of the admired pulpiteers of that day was Theodore Thornton Munger (1830–1910), pastor of the United Congregational Church in New

# The Twentieth Century

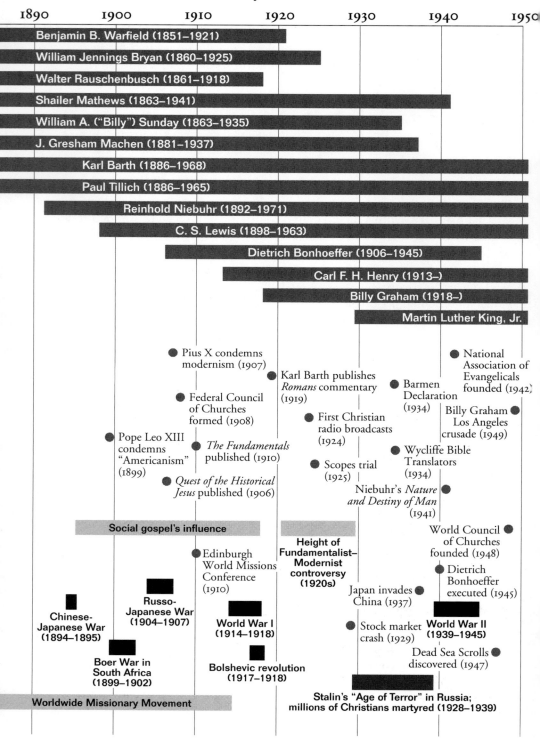

| 1890 | 1900 | 1910 | 1920 | 1930 | 1940 | 1950 |

Benjamin B. Warfield (1851–1921)

William Jennings Bryan (1860–1925)

Walter Rauschenbusch (1861–1918)

Shailer Mathews (1863–1941)

William A. ("Billy") Sunday (1863–1935)

J. Gresham Machen (1881–1937)

Karl Barth (1886–1968)

Paul Tillich (1886–1965)

Reinhold Niebuhr (1892–1971)

C. S. Lewis (1898–1963)

Dietrich Bonhoeffer (1906–1945)

Carl F. H. Henry (1913–)

Billy Graham (1918–)

Martin Luther King, Jr.

Pius X condemns modernism (1907)

Karl Barth publishes *Romans* commentary (1919)

Barmen Declaration (1934)

National Association of Evangelicals founded (1942)

Federal Council of Churches formed (1908)

First Christian radio broadcasts (1924)

Billy Graham Los Angeles crusade (1949)

Pope Leo XIII condemns "Americanism" (1899)

*The Fundamentals* published (1910)

Wycliffe Bible Translators (1934)

Scopes trial (1925)

*Quest of the Historical Jesus* published (1906)

Niebuhr's *Nature and Destiny of Man* (1941)

Social gospel's influence

World Council of Churches founded (1948)

Edinburgh World Missions Conference (1910)

Height of Fundamentalist–Modernist controversy (1920s)

Dietrich Bonhoeffer executed (1945)

Japan invades China (1937)

Chinese-Japanese War (1894–1895)

Russo-Japanese War (1904–1907)

World War I (1914–1918)

Stock market crash (1929)

World War II (1939–1945)

Boer War in South Africa (1899–1902)

Bolshevic revolution (1917–1918)

Dead Sea Scrolls discovered (1947)

Worldwide Missionary Movement

Stalin's "Age of Terror" in Russia; millions of Christians martyred (1928–1939)

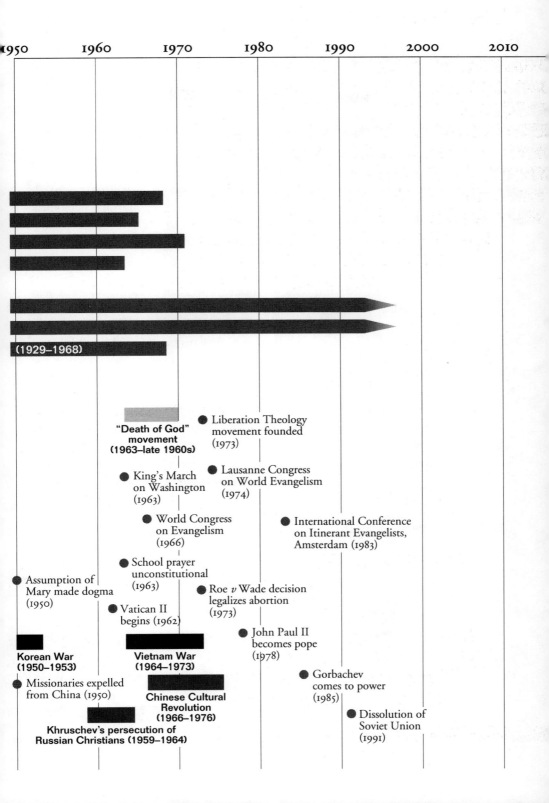

1950    1960    1970    1980    1990    2000    2010

(1929–1968)

**"Death of God" movement (1963–late 1960s)**

● Liberation Theology movement founded (1973)

● King's March on Washington (1963)

● Lausanne Congress on World Evangelism (1974)

● World Congress on Evangelism (1966)

● International Conference on Itinerant Evangelists, Amsterdam (1983)

● School prayer unconstitutional (1963)

● Assumption of Mary made dogma (1950)

● Roe *v* Wade decision legalizes abortion (1973)

● Vatican II begins (1962)

● John Paul II becomes pope (1978)

**Korean War (1950–1953)**

**Vietnam War (1964–1973)**

● Gorbachev comes to power (1985)

● Missionaries expelled from China (1950)

**Chinese Cultural Revolution (1966–1976)**

● Dissolution of Soviet Union (1991)

**Khruschev's persecution of Russian Christians (1959–1964)**

Haven, Connecticut, and chief biographer of Horace Bushnell, Munger's hero. An avowed Darwinian and exponent of progress, Munger was an irenic person. "The New Theology" (selection 34), written in 1883, was well-reasoned and, for many liberals, too moderate in tone and intentions.

## The Warfield response

Some years later, at the height of the popularity of modernism, an outstanding exemplar of Protestant orthodoxy was asked to state his case in a liberal journal, the *Harvard Theological Review*. Benjamin B. Warfield (1851–1921), successor to Charles Hodge in systematic theology at Princeton Theological Seminary, was born in Kentucky and educated at Princeton. He had been a professor at Western Seminary in Pittsburgh from 1879 to 1887. An accomplished linguist of Hebrew, Greek, and modern languages, he was at home in New Testament criticism, theology, and church history. A committed Calvinist with a high regard for the Westminster Confession of Faith, Warfield held to the doctrines of original sin, predestination, and a limited atonement. One of the leading scholars holding to an inerrant Scripture, he held running battles with others who advocated the new higher critical views of the Bible.

When Warfield was asked in 1914 to provide an answer to an article in the *Harvard Theological Review* by Professor Douglas Macintosh of Yale it is possible the editors did not foresee what Warfield would produce (selection 35). While he did deal with Macintosh's "substance of doctrine" and found that he "has naturally no difficulty in moulding Christianity to his own taste," in essence what Macintosh brought forth, Warfield saw, was "indistinguishable from that which is generally professed in the circles of so-called 'Liberal Christianity.'"[5] But then Warfield took this opportunity to define what authentic Christianity was. In doing so he gathered the outstanding scholars of that day— Adolf Harnack, Ernst Troeltsch, Alfred F. Loisy, Eduard von Hartmann, John Caird, William Wrede, Adolf von Dobschütz, and others—quoting them, and producing a long and profound article which not only made the Yale professor look utterly foolish, but shredding liberalism as well. Using scholarship that was not only equal to the general level of the *Review* but superior, Warfield met the liberals on their own ground.

## Select Bibliography

Bowden, Henry W. *Church History in the Age of Science: Historiographical Patterns in the United States.* Chapel Hill: University of North Carolina Press, 1971.

Carter, Paul A. *The Spiritual Crisis of the Golden Age.* DeKalb, Ill.: Northern Illinois University Press, 1971.

Cauthen, Kenneth. *The Impact of American Religious Liberalism,* 2d ed. Lanham, Md.: University Press of America, 1983.

Hutchison, William R., ed. *American Protestant Thought in the Liberal Era.* 1968; repr., Lanham, Md.: University Press of America, 1985.

_____. *The Modernist Impulse in American Protestantism.* New York: Oxford University Press, 1982.

May, Henry F. *Protestant Churches and Industrial America.* New York; Octagon, 1963.

Roth, Robert J. *American Religious Philosophy.* New York: Harcourt, Brace and World, 1967.

# The New Theology

## Theodore T. Munger (1883)

The purpose of this Essay is to state, so far as is now possible, some of the main features of that phase of present thought popularly known as "The New Theology": to indicate the lines on which it is moving, to express something of its spirit, and to give it so much of definite form that it shall no longer suffer from the charge of vagueness. . . .

I pass now to the positive features of the New Theology.

1. It claims for itself a somewhat larger and broader use of the reason than has been accorded to theology.

And by reason we do not mean mere speculation nor a formal logic, but that full exercise of our nature which embraces the intuitions, the conscience, the susceptibilities, and the judgment, *i.e.,* man's whole inner being. Especially it makes much of the intuitions—the universal and spontaneous verdicts of the soul; and in this it deems that it allies itself with the Mind through which the Christian revelation is made.

The fault of the theology now passing is that it insists on a presentation of doctrines in such a way as perpetually to challenge the reason. By a logic of its own—a logic created for its own ends, and not a logic drawn from the depth and breadth of human life—it frets and antagonizes the fundamental action of human nature. If Christianity has any human basis it is its entire reasonableness. It must not only sit easily on the mind, but it must ally itself with it in all its normal action. If it chafes it, if it is a burden, if it antagonizes, it detracts from itself; the human mind cannot be detracted from. Man is a knower; the reason never ceases to be less than itself without losing all right to use itself as reason. Consequently a full adjustment between reason and Christianity is steadily to be sought. If there is conflict, uneasiness, burdensomeness, the cause is to be looked for in interpretation rather than in the human reason. For, in the last analysis, revelation—so far as its acceptance is concerned—rests on reason, and not reason on revelation. The logical order is, first reason, and then revelation—the eye before sight. It is just here that a narrow and formal theol-

Source: Theodore T. Munger, "The New Theology," in *The Freedom of Faith* (Boston: Houghton, Mifflin, 1883), 3, 11–25, passim.

ogy inserts its hurtful fallacy; it says, Use your reason for ascertaining that a revelation is probable, and has been made, after which the only office of the mind is to accept the contents of the revelation without question, *i.e.*, without other use of the reason than some small office of collating texts and drawing inferences. But this is formal and arbitrary. The mind accepts revelation because it accepts the *substance* of revelation. It does not stand outside upon some structure of logical inference that a revelation has been made, and therefore is to be accepted, but instead it enters into the material of the revelation, and plants its feet there. The reason believes the revelation because *in itself* it is reasonable. Human nature—so far as it acts by itself—accepts Christianity because it establishes a thorough *consensus* with human nature; it is agreeable in its nature to human nature in its normal action. It wins its way on the manward side by winning the assent of the whole reasonable nature of man. The largest play must be allowed to this principle. . . .

2. The New Theology seeks to interpret the Scriptures in what may be called a more natural way, and in opposition to a hard, formal, unsympathetic, and unimaginative way.

Its strongest denial and its widest divergence from the Old Theology lie here. It holds profoundly to inspiration, but it also holds that the Scriptures were written by living men, whose life entered into their writings; it finds the color and temper of the writer's mind in his work; it finds also the temper and habit of the age; it penetrates the forms of Oriental speech; it seeks to read out of the mind and conception and custom of the writer instead of reading present conceptions into his words. In brief, it reads the Scriptures as literature, yet with no derogation from their inspiration. It refuses to regard the writers as automatic organs of the Spirit,—"moved," indeed, but not carried outside of themselves nor separated from their own ways and conceptions. It is thus that it regards the Bible as a *living* book; it is warm and vital with the life of a divine humanity, and thus it speaks to humanity. But as it was written by men in other ages and of other habits of speech, it needs to be interpreted; it is necessary to get back into the mind of the writer in order to get at the inspiration of his utterance; for before there is an inspired writing there is an inspired man, through whom only its meaning can be reached. This is a very different process from picking out texts here and there, and putting them together to form a doctrine; yet it is by such a process that systems of theology have been formed, and cast on society for acceptance. The New Theology does not proceed in such a way. The Old Theology reads the Scriptures with a lexicon, and weighs words as men weigh iron; it sees no medium between the form of words and their first or preconceived meaning. It looks into the Bible as one looks through space, beyond the atmosphere, upon the sun,—seeing one point of glowing light, but darkness on every side; one text of burning sense, but no atmosphere of context, or age, or custom, or temper of mind, or end in view. The New Theology does not tolerate the inconsistency of the Old, as it slowly gives up the theory of verbal inspiration, but retains views based on verbal inspiration. It will not remove foundations and prop up the superstructure with assertions.

Again, it does not regard the Bible as a magical book; it is not a diviner's rod; it is not a charmed thing of intrinsic power, representing a far-off God. The New Theology remembers that the mass, the confessional, the priestly office, the intercession of saints, were the product of a theology that held to a mechanical, outside God, and that these superstitions sprang from the demand of the human heart for a God near at hand. It remembers that when these superstitions were cast off and the theology retained the Bible was put in their place, and with something of the same superstitious regard. Hence, it was not read naturally and in a free, off-hand way, as it was inspired and written, but in hard and artificial ways, and was used much as men use charms. The New Theology does not reduce to something less the inspiration of the Bible, nor does it yield to any theology in its sense of its supreme value in the redemption of the world; but it holds it as purely instrumental, and not as magical in its power or method. It is a history of the highest form in which God is manifesting himself in the world, but it is not the manifestation itself; it is not a revelation, but is a history of a revelation; it is a chosen and indispensable means of the redemption of the world, but it is not the absolute means,—that is in the Spirit. It is necessary to make this distinction in order to read it, otherwise it cannot be interpreted; it lies outside the sphere of our rational nature,—a charmed mystery, before which we may sit in awe, but not a voice speaking to our thinking minds. . . .

3. The New Theology seeks to replace an excessive individuality by a truer view of the solidarity of the race.

It does not deny a real individuality, it does not predicate an absolute solidarity, but simply removes the emphasis from one to the other. It holds that every man must live a life of his own, build himself up into a full personality, and give an account of himself to God: but it also recognizes the blurred truth that man's life lies in its relations; that it is a derived and shared life; that it is carried on and perfected under laws of heredity and of the family and the nation; that while he is "himself alone" he is also a son, a parent, a citizen, and an inseparable part of the human race; that in origin and character and destiny he cannot be regarded as standing in a sharp and utter individuality. It differs from the Old Theology in a more thorough and consistent application of this distinction. That holds to an absolute solidarity in evil, relieved by a doctrine of election of individuals; this holds to a solidarity running throughout the whole life of humanity in the world,—not an absolute solidarity, but one modified by human freedom. It is not disposed wholly to part company with the Old in respect to the "fall in Adam" (when the Scriptures, on this point, are properly interpreted), and hereditary evil, and the like; it sees in these conceptions substantial truths, when freed from their excessiveness and their formal and categorical shapes, but it carries this solidarity into the whole life of man. If it is a fallen world, it is also a redeemed world; if it is a lost world, it is a saved world; the Christ is no less to it than Adam; the divine humanity is no smaller than the Adamic humanity; the Spirit is as powerful and as universal as sin; the links that bind the race to evil are correlated by links equally strong binding it to righteousness. It goes, in a certain manner, with the Old Theology in its views of common evil, but it diverges from it in its conceptions of the redemptive and delivering forces by ascribing to them corresponding sweep. To repeat: it does not admit that Christ is less to the race than Adam, that the Gospel is smaller than evil; it does not consign mankind as a mass to a pit of common depravity, and leave it to emerge as individuals under some notion of election, or by solitary choice, each one escaping as he can and according to his "chance," but the greater part not escaping at all. . . .

---

## Selection 35

---

# The Essence of Christianity

### *Benjamin B. Warfield (1914)*

In order to reach the truth we need only take one step more and frankly recognize that these declarations are central to Jesus' conception of His mission. And this step we must take not less on account of the declarations themselves (Jesus says expressly that He "came" for the distinct purpose of "giving His life as a ransom for many" and with great explicitness declares the sacrificial character of His death) than on account of numerous other less direct but no less real references to the significance of His mission as redemptive, and in order that the whole subsequent historical development may not be rendered unintelligible (the very disposition of the matter of the Gospels is determined by

Source: In the *Harvard Theological Review*, 7.4 (October 1914): 586–94, passim.

this presupposition, and the whole preaching of the disciples turns on it as its hinge). No doubt Jesus is thus implicated in the presentation of Christianity as specifically a redemptive religion; "an appearance is created," to use Paul Wernle's phrase in an analogous connection, "that Jesus Himself is responsible for the momentous dogmatic development, and encumbered the simple, eternal will of God with a minimum of dogma and ecclesiasticism"; an appearance, we may add, which is not deceptive, as Wernle would have us believe, and with an amount of "dogma" which cannot justly be called a "minimum." This is, however, only to permit Jesus to come to His rights in the matter of His teaching; and to allow Him to found the religion which He tells us He came to found, and not to insist on thrusting an essentially different one upon Him because we happen ourselves to like it better. These declarations of Jesus as to the redemptive significance of His death cannot be denied to Him; their meaning cannot be eviscerated by studiously minimizing expositions, and they cannot be deprived of their cardinal position in the religion which He founded. In point of fact, Jesus announced His mission as not to the righteous but sinners; and what He offered to sinners was not mere exemption—or if even that word retains too much reminiscence of a price paid, say immunity—but specifically redemption.

In the mind of Jesus as truly as in the minds of His followers, the religion which He founded was by way of eminence the religion of redemption. Perhaps we could have no better evidence of this than the tenacity with which those who would fain retain the name of Christianity while yet repudiating its specific character, cling to the term "redemptive" also as descriptive of the nature of their new Christianity, identified by them with the religion of Jesus. Professor Macintosh, for example, wishes still to describe his new religion as "the religion of moral redemption"; though he discriminates the notion which the term connotes with him as its broad sense, as over against "the narrow sense" which it bears in its customary application to Christianity. By "redemption" he means, however, merely "reformation"; and these are not only the narrow and the broad of it; they are specifically different conceptions, and the employment of the two terms as synonyms cannot fail to mislead. . . .

. . . Professor Macintosh tells us, to be sure, that if this is Christianity, "he would have to confess not only that he is not a Christian, but that he does not see how he ever could be a Christian." It is a sad confession, but by no means an unexampled one. Every Inquiry Room supplies its contingent of like instances, and Christianity had not grown very old before it discovered that the preaching of Christ crucified was unto the Jews a stumbling-block and unto the Greeks foolishness. The only novel feature in the present situation lies in the proposal that if one cannot or will not accept the Christianity of the crucified Son of God, we shall just call what he can or will accept "Christianity" and let it go at that. This may seem an easy adjustment; but it is attended with the inconvenience of transferring our interest from things to mere names. The thing which has hitherto been known as Christianity appears to remain the same, however we deal with the name by which it has hitherto been known. And that thing enshrines the Cross in its heart. Paul Feine does not in the least exaggerate when, in the opening words of the section in his *Theology of the New Testament* which speaks of Jesus' own teaching as to His death, he writes:—

> It has been the belief and the teaching of the Christian Church of all ages and of all Confessions, that Jesus, the Son of God, in His sacrificial death on the cross wrought the reconciliation of men with God, and by His resurrection begot anew those who believe in Him unto a living hope of eternal life. This belief forms the content of the hymns and prayers of Christian devotion through all the centuries. It filled with new life the dying civilization of Greece and Rome and conquered to Christianity the youthful forces of the Germanic stock. In the proclamation of Jesus the Divine Saviour who died for us on the Cross, still lies even today the secret of the successes of Christian missions among the heathen. The symbol of this belief greets us in the form of the Cross from the tower of every church, from every Christian grave-stone and in the thousands of forms in which the Cross finds employment in daily life; this belief meets us in the gospel of the great Christian festivals and in the two sacraments of the church. . . .

Enough; there can be no doubt what Christianity has been up to today; and there can be no doubt that what it is now proposed to transfer the name to is an essentially different religion. Have we not had it for a generation past dinned into our ears that it is an essentially different religion? that precisely what Paul did, when he substituted "the religion about Jesus," that is, the religion of the Cross, for "the religion of Jesus," that is, the "Liberal" reconstruction of what Jesus Himself taught, was to introduce a new religion, a religion, to recall Wrede's characterization, more unlike the religion of Jesus than the religion of Jesus was unlike Judaism?

It seems merely frivolous to declare in one and the same breath that Paul introduced an essentially new religion when he supplanted "the simple gospel of Jesus" with the religion of the Cross, and that this new religion of the Cross is not essentially deserted when a return is made from it to "the simple religion of Jesus." The two religions are, in point of fact, essentially different, and no attempt to confuse them under a common designation can permanently conceal this fact. He who looks to be perfected through his own assumption of what he calls a Christlike attitude towards what he calls a Christlike super-human reality—though he considers that the term "Christlike" may without fatal loss be a merely conventional designation—is of a totally different religion from him who feels himself a sinner redeemed by the blood of a divine Saviour dying for him on the Cross. It may be, as Troeltsch seems to suggest, that "Liberal Christianity" lacks the power to originate a church and can live only as a kind of parasitical growth upon some sturdier stock. It may be that it is not driven by internal necessity to separate itself off from other faiths, on which it rather depends for support. It is otherwise with those who share the great experience of reconciliation with God in the blood of His dear Son. They know themselves to be instinct with a life peculiar to themselves and cannot help forming a community, distinguished from all others by this common great experience. We have quoted the opening words of Feine's remarks on Jesus' teaching as to His sacrificial death. The closing words are worth pondering also. They run:

> Let it be said in closing that in the two declarations of the ransom-price and the cup of the Lord's Supper there lies church-building power. Jesus did not organize His community; He founded no church in His earthly labors. But the Christian Church is an inevitable product of the declaration of the expiatory effect of His death for many. For those who have experienced redemption and reconciliation through the death of Jesus must by virtue of this gift of grace draw together and distinguish themselves over against other communities.

There is indeed no alternative. The redeemed in the blood of Christ, after all said, are a people apart. Call them "Christians," or call them what you please, they are of a specifically different religion from those who know no such experience. It may be within the rights of those who feel no need of such a redemption and have never experienced its transforming power to contend that their religion is a better religion than the Christianity of the Cross. It is distinctly not within their rights to maintain that it is the same religion as the Christianity of the Cross. On their own showing it is not that.

# 15

## Concerns for the Poor and Downtrodden

The feverish years after the Civil War saw a breathtaking expansion of American ingenuity, industry, and wealth. The railroads provide only one example of many. At the conclusion of the war in 1865 there were about 35,000 miles of railways in the United States, mostly east of the Mississippi. But by 1900, in only thirty-five years, the mileage was 192,556, or more than that for all Europe combined. American ingenuity was coming to its zenith. Mass-production techniques, pioneered by Eli Whitney, were being perfected and utilized by the captains of industry. Between 1860 and 1900 more than 440,000 patents were issued. Expanding markets and daring leadership stimulated industrialization. The rapid growth of population provided millions of eager consumers for the new products, and entrepreneurs equally eager for wealth stepped forward to exploit them.

In 1866 Horatio Alger, a former clergyman, gave up his pulpit and began to write his well-known "rags-to-riches" books intended to inspire youth. Eventually he turned out more than a hundred volumes of juvenile fiction that sold over 20 million copies, each employing the formula that honesty, virtue and hard work are rewarded with wealth, success, and honor. Some did not leave the ministry to preach wealth; Russell H. Conwell (1843–1925), founder of Temple University, began his ministry at Grace Baptist Church in Philadelphia in 1879. Within a few years he began to give his address, "Acres of Diamonds," across the nation, eventually delivering it more than 5000 times:

Now then, I say again that the opportunity to get rich, to attain unto great wealth, is here in Philadelphia now, within the reach of every man and woman who hears me speak tonight, and I mean just what I say. I have not come to this platform even under these circumstances to recite something to you. I have come to tell you what in God's sight I believe to be the truth, and if the years of life have been of any value to me in the attainment of common sense, I know that I'm right; that the men and women sitting here, who found it difficult perhaps to buy a ticket to this lecture or gathering tonight, have within their reach "acres of diamonds," opportunities to get largely wealthy. There never was a place on earth more adapted than the city of Philadelphia today, and never in the history of the world did a poor man without capital have such an opportunity to get rich quickly and honestly as he has now in our city.[1]

Conwell and Alger could back up their thesis by pointing to the multitude of entrepreneurs who had indeed found acres of diamonds through ingenuity and hard work, men like Andrew Carnegie, the personification of the age of steel. Brought penniless from Scotland as a lad by his parents, he was a superb organizer, entering the burgeoning steel industry just as the new Bessemer process was coming in. By 1900 Carnegie was producing one-fourth of America's steel and making $25 million a year. Those were the pre-income tax days, when governmental bureaucracy was small, and millionaires were truly rich, each dollar having fifteen to twenty times the buying power it has today.

Despite Conwell's and Alger's boundless optimism, not all—indeed few—could get rich. Once the companies were founded, there were only so many that one industry could need. Ruthlessness in industry was too often the rule, as amply demonstrated by John D. Rockefeller's policy of rule or ruin in the oil business. His Standard Oil Company was undoubtedly heartless, but its rivals were no less so in that age of dog-eat-dog competition. A kind of social-economic Darwinism prevailed in the jungle world of business, where only the fittest survived. By 1877 Rockefeller controlled 95 percent of all the oil refineries in the nation, and could raise or lower prices at will. His profits were enormous. So-called piratical practices were employed by "corsairs of finance," and business ethics were depressingly low in the last three decades of the nineteenth century.

### Immigrants, women, and blacks

The economic transformation of America enormously increased the nation's wealth. Standards of living rose sharply, and the American worker enjoyed more physical comforts than similar workers in other nations, but his surroundings were often still bleak, his pay merely adequate, his workday ten and twelve hours long, and his labor backbreaking. The cities mushroomed as the insatiable factories demanded more and more labor, and the new immigrants poured into the vacuum created by new jobs.

Probably no single group was more profoundly affected by the new Industrial Age than women. Millions of young women entered the job market, working over machines in factories, as stenographers and secretaries in offices, achieving a new economic and social independence and, with their careers, usually deferring marriage. In factories with twelve-hour working days the labor of children as young as ten or eleven years old was one of the cruelest aspects of that age. Frightful abuses were reported constantly, and few laws protected the brutalized youth. On the backs of poor people vast industrial empires were built, and huge fortunes accumulated. The existence of an oligarchy of money was amply demonstrated by the fact that by 1900 about one-tenth of Americans owned and controlled nine-tenths of the nation's wealth.

One group particularly lagged far behind the rest of the nation—the blacks. Until World War I approximately 90 percent of the nation's blacks lived in the South, and two-thirds of them were rural. And many of these found their meaning to life in their Christian faith. While the many issues affecting the black church are complex,[2] the church certainly was by far the most important black institution after the family unit. It provided much more than spiritual care; the church gave a sense of racial unity, provided a much-needed sanctuary in a hostile world, helped poor members to cooperate economically, and assisted black education as actively as any other institution. After 1877, as political suppression, Jim Crow laws, and white antagonism constantly grew, the church took on ever greater significance for Afro-Americans.

As might be imagined, black leaders from 1870 to the Second World War varied in their approaches to the advancement of their people. Some, including Henry Turner, Jabez P. Campbell, and W. E. B. DuBois, were extremely distressed at the slow progress and the white oppression of blacks. But they were opposed by the accommodationist views of Booker T. Washington (1856–1915), whose position was attacked as "Uncle Tomism" by many who feared that their race was being condemned to perpetual manual labor.

Washington was the son of a slave mother and a white father, and had slept under a board sidewalk in order to save money for his education at Hampton Institute. Called in 1881 to organize a new black normal and industrial school in Alabama named Tuskegee Institute, he began with forty students in a tumble-down shanty. In time Washington became convinced that vocational training, unlike classical education, would prevent blacks from learning egalitarian ideas and provide them with jobs. At the Atlanta Exposition of 1895 he further pleased whites by declaring that blacks were interested in hard work, not social advancement. Washington hoped that dedication and sobriety would bring about white recognition of human equality. Between 1890 and 1915, the years of his greatest influence, he had a firm hold on the black clergy's loyalty. Although he was raised a Baptist and was very knowledgeable of the Bible and Christian faith, Washington was privately disdainful of many of the black clergy in the South, as selection 36 indicates.

## A gospel of confidence and hope

While the *Social Gospel* nurtured an interest in these "huddled masses yearning to breathe free," there was little new in Christian social concern. Jesus commanded his followers to offer self-sacrificing, loving concern for the poor and downtrodden (for example, Luke 6:27–36), and the early church carried out measures to alleviate their distress (see, for example, Acts 2:45–46; 6:1; Gal. 2:10; James 1:27). The Second Great Awakening and the work of the evangelical united front expressed intense social concern, especially in the reform movements mounted by Lyman Beecher, Charles G. Finney, and the Tappan brothers. A multitude of truly compassionate leaders ministered to a hundred human needs and ills from 1810 to the Civil War. Antislavery, with its slogans, hymns, and crusading zeal was a decisive prelude to the Social Gospel. An unbroken line of commitment to the poor and oppressed stretched from Beecher, Finney, Theodore Dwight Weld and Elijah Lovejoy to Washington Gladden, Walter Rauschenbusch and the dozens of other Social Gospel leaders.

Sydney E. Ahlstrom has defined the spirit and background of the Social Gospel: "It reflected and depended upon the singular spirit of confidence and hope that prevailed for only a few decades before the Great War and the Great Depression shattered the mood. . . . Similarly, a single set of social problems stirred its passions: the urban dislocations occasioned by America's unregulated industrial expansion. The Gilded Age was a prerequisite."[3]

In the annals of the Social Gospel, Gladden (1836–1918) was among the first to enunciate the specific intentions of the movement (selection 37). A graduate of Williams College, he never attended seminary and was pastor of churches in Massachusetts before going to the First Congregational Church of Columbus, Ohio, where he preached from 1882 until his death in 1918. He is probably best remembered for his widely-used hymn, "O Master, Let Me Walk with Thee." From early days he was a pronounced liberal in theology and became a great admirer of Horace Bushnell (selection 21). In time he became a leader in two closely related liberal movements: the new theology (selection 34), and the Social Gospel. He wrote over thirty books, mostly tracts for the times, among them *Applied Christianity* (1886), *Who Wrote the Bible?* (1891), *Social Facts and Forces* (1897), *How Much Is Left of the Old Doctrines?* (1899), *Christianity and Socialism* (1905), and *Present Day Theology* (1913).

Rauschenbusch (1861–1918) is noted as the foremost theological interpreter of the Social Gospel. A Baptist minister and graduate of Rochester Seminary, he applied for foreign missionary service but was rejected because of his reputed liberal view of the Old Testament. Eventually he accepted a call at an annual salary of only $900 to serve a small immigrant German Baptist Church on the edge of New York City's notorious "Hell's Kitchen" district. Among the squalid tenements "an endless procession of men 'out of work, out of clothes, out of shoes, and out of hope' wore down the threshold and wore away the heart of the sensitive young pastor and his wife."[4] For eleven years he labored there, trying to help these people, and he became convinced that the wretched social problems of the great cities of America demanded a rethinking of the gospel as he had known it. In 1897 he joined the faculty of Rochester Seminary, becoming professor of church history in 1902.

Rauschenbusch was a leader in the Social Gospel movement before the turn of the century, but in 1907 he achieved national prominence when he wrote *Christianity and the Social Crisis* (selection 38). Paramount among his ideas was the Kingdom of God, which is a completely instrumental interpretation of the church, plus his insistence that ethics and religion are inseparable: "The Kingdom of God is not confined within the limits of the Church and its activities. It embraces the whole of human life. It is the Christian transfiguration of the social order. The Church is one social institution alongside of the family, the industrial organization of society, and the State. The Kingdom of God is in all these, and realizes itself through them all."[5]

## Select Bibliography

Cross, Robert D. *The Church and the City, 1865–1910.* Indianapolis: Bobbs-Merrill, 1967.

Handy, Robert T. *The Social Gospel in America, 1870–1920.* New York: Oxford University Press, 1966.

Hopkins, Charles H. *The Rise of the Social Gospel in American Protestantism, 1865–1915.* 1940; repr., New York: AMS, 1982.

May, Henry F. *Protestant Churches and Industrial America*, rev. ed. New York: Harper, 1967.

Sharpe, Dores R. *Walter Rauschenbusch.* New York: Macmillan, 1942.

Weisenburger, Francis P. *Ordeal of Faith: The Crisis of Church-going America, 1865–1900.* New York: Philosophical Library, 1959.

White, Ronald C., Jr., and C. Howard Hopkins. *The Social Gospel: Religion and Reform in Changing America.* Philadelphia: Temple University Press, 1976.

# The Colored Ministry: Its Defects and Needs

## Booker T. Washington (1890)

Tuskegee, Ala. [Aug. 14, 1890]

What is the actual condition of the colored ministry in the South, is a question that should interest every one. As a part answer to this question I give the following extracts taken from the leading editorial of the Alabama "Baptist Leader," the organ of the colored Baptists of Alabama, edited by the Rev. A. N. McEwen, of Montgomery, a well-informed and reliable minister: "The greatest object of over two-thirds of the Baptist ministers of Alabama is to collect their salaries. They care no more for the moral and intellectual training of the people than they care for the snap of their finger. They care no more for schools, for public enterprises, than if there were no such things. . . . In some parts of the country where our missionaries travel, they find preachers who do not take a paper of any sort, nor read the Bible; in fact, they cannot read, and yet they are attempting to lead the people." So far as it goes, the foregoing extract tells the truth; but in order to grasp the situation it is well to bear in mind that there are in the fifteen Southern States, including the District of Columbia, at least 7,000,000 colored people to be reached with the Gospel. In their religious opinion these people are almost equally divided between the Baptist and Methodist denominations. This is about the numerical force: Colored Baptists, 1,120,000 church members, 10,000 churches, and 7,000 ordained ministers; Methodists (divided into the African, Zion, Wesleyan, Northern, and Colored Methodist branches), with about the same numerical strength as the Baptists, making a total of 2,240,000 church members in these two denominations. . . .

With few exceptions, the preaching of the colored ministry is emotional in the highest degree, and the minister considers himself successful in proportion as he is able to set the people in all parts of the congregation to groaning, uttering wild screams, and jumping, finally going into a trance. One of

Source: *The Christian Union*, 42 (August 14, 1890): 199–200. Reprinted in *The Booker T. Washington Papers*, edited by Louis R. Harlan (Chicago: University of Illinois Press, 1974), vol. 3 (1889–1895), 71–75.

the principal ends sought by most of these ministers is their salary, and to this everything else is made subservient. Most of the church service seems to resolve itself into an effort to get money. Not one in twenty has the business standing in the communities where they reside, and those who know them best mistrust them most in matters of finance and general morality.

With such spiritual leaders, the mere fact that so large a proportion of the seven million colored people in the South are church members is misleading, and is no evidence that a large proportion of these church members are not just as ignorant of true Christianity, as taught by Christ, as any people in Africa or Japan, and just as much in need of missionary efforts as those in foreign lands. . . .

It should be borne in mind that the masses of the colored people, and those most in need of help, live in the country, and that at least four-fifths of the educated colored ministers go into the cities and towns. In fact, during my eight years' residence and traveling in the country districts, I have not come into contact with a single educated minister preaching in the country, and I repeat, for emphasis, that, outside of the Baptist and Methodist denominations, the educated ministers do

Booker T. Washington (Billy Graham Center Museum, Wheaton, Ill.)

not reach in their own congregations an average of over fifty persons, though they do do much general work for the uplifting of the people, and give them examples of what a church should be. I have no unfriendly word for the theological work now being done, nor should I ask that the standard of scholarship be lowered, for we need broad and deep theologians; but it is painfully evident that something needs to be done to give the masses trained and helpful ministers—to supplement the present ministerial training. I am thoroughly convinced that if a school, to be known as a Bible Seminary or Bible Training School, were established at some central point in the South, on a thoroughly Christian but *strictly* undenominational basis, with a one or two years' course covering such branches as would fit a student to get a comprehensive idea of the Bible, to teach him how to prepare a sermon, how to read a hymn, how to study, and, most important, how to reach and help the people outside of the pulpit in an unselfish Christian way, it would be a great power for good. To begin with, one teacher could do the work that I have suggested for forty or fifty students, and I am sure that such a seminary would be crowded with students from the beginning. When the school grew to the point where two or three teachers were demanded (and it would be well to have, as early as possible, the leading denominations represented in the force of teachers) $1,500 or $2,500 would supply the teaching force, and at the same time thirty or forty men could be sent out each year with a training that would enable them to go into the country and elsewhere among the masses of the people and help them in a most effectual way. As such a seminary would be nonsectarian, all denominations would enter it, and it would send forth every year a stream of young men who would fill Baptist and all other pulpits. In other words, they would reach the masses. In the present seminaries the tuition alone of ten or a dozen sometimes costs $3,000 or $4,000. With the proposed Bible seminary this sum could be made to educate many times this number.

---

## Selection 37

# The Social Gospel

## *Washington Gladden (1902)*

Any treatment of social questions which failed to bring the responsibility for right social actions home to individuals would, indeed, be defective treatment; on the other hand, any discussion of the problems of the individual life which did not keep the social environment steadily in view would be utterly inadequate.

I am therefore unable to understand how Christianity, whether as a law or as a gospel, can be intelligently or adequately preached or lived in these days without a constant reference to social questions. No individual is soundly converted until he comprehends his social relations and strives to fulfill them; and the work of growth and sanctification largely consists in a clearer apprehension of these relations and a more earnest effort to fill them with the life of the divine Spirit. The kingdom of heaven is *within* us and *among* us; the preposition, in Christ's saying, seems to have the double meaning. It cannot

Source: Washington Gladden, *Social Salvation* (Boston: Houghton, Mifflin, 1902), 14–15, 25–28, 206–8, 226.

be among us unless it is within us, and it cannot be within us without being among us.

It would seem, therefore, that the minister's work, in these days, must lie, very largely, along the lines of social amelioration. He is bound to understand the laws of social structure. It is just as needful that he should understand the constitution of human society as that he should understand the constitution of the human soul; the one comes under his purview no less directly than the other. He does not know definitely what sin is, unless he understands the nature of the social bond; he does not surely know what salvation means until he has comprehended the reciprocal action of society upon the individual and of the individual upon society. The men who are working out their own salvation are doing it largely through the establishment of right relations between themselves and their neighbors, and he cannot help them in this unless he has some clear idea of what these right relations are.

The truth which Mr. Brierley emphasizes in the passage which I last read is the truth which we must never forget. The church, he says, will have these social subjects "continually within its scope, but ever to bring them under its own light, to view them *sub specie æternitatis.*" Yea, verily. We have absolutely no business whatever with any of these things except as they are vitally and inseparably related to that kingdom of heaven for whose coming we pray, whose presence we ought to be quick to discern, and whose spread it is our first business to seek. "When the minister has become merely political," says Mr. Brierley, "it is because he has lost grip of religion." That proposition ought to require no argument. The minister who has become merely or mainly political, or sociological, or economical, or scientific, has abandoned his vocation. The minister to whom religion is not the central and culminating power in all his teaching has no right in any Christian pulpit. It is *the religion* of politics, of economics, of sociology that we are to teach,—nothing else. We are to bring the truths and the powers of the spiritual world, the eternal world, to bear upon all these themes. This is what we have to do with these social questions, and we have nothing else to do with them.

The first thing for us to understand is that God is in his world, and that we are workers together with him. In all this industrial struggle he is present in every part of it, working according to the counsel of his perfect will. In the gleams of light which sometimes break forth from the darkness of the conflict we discern his inspiration; in the stirrings of goodwill which temper the wasting strife we behold the evidence of his presence; in the sufferings and losses and degradations which wait upon every violation of his law of love we witness the retributions with which that law goes armed. In the weltering masses of poverty; in the giddy throngs that tread the paths of vice; in the multitudes distressed and scattered as sheep having no shepherd; in the brutalized ranks marching in lock-step through the prison yard; in the groups of politicians scheming for place and plunder,—in all the most forlorn and untoward and degrading human associations, the One who is never absent is that divine Spirit which brooded over the chaos at the beginning, nursing it to life and beauty, and which is

> "nearer to every creature he hath made,
> Than anything unto itself can be."

Nay, there is not one of these hapless, sinning multitudes in whose spirit he is not present to will and to work according to his good pleasure; never overpowering the will, but gently pressing in, by every avenue open to him, his gifts of love and truth. As he has for every man's life a plan, so has he for the common life a perfect social order into which he seeks to lead his children, that he may give them plenty and blessedness and abundance of peace as long as the moon endureth. Surely he has a way for men to live in society; he has a way of organizing industry; he has a way of life for the family, and for the school, and for the shop, and for the city, and for the state; he has a way for preventing poverty, and a way for helping and saving the poor and the sick and the sinful; and it is his way that we are to seek and point out and follow. We cannot know it perfectly, but if we are humble and faithful and obedient, we shall come to understand it better and better as the years go by. The one thing for us to be sure of is that God has a way for human beings to live and work together, just as truly as he has a way for the stars over our heads and the crystals under our feet; and that it is man's chief end to find this way and follow it.

No one who has lived and labored for many years in ill-governed cities, in the interests of virtue, can fail to be aware of the evil influence which bad government exerts upon the characters of those who live under it. The tone of public morality is affected; the convictions of the youth are blurred; the standards of honor and fidelity are lowered. That which in the family and in the Sunday-school and in the day-school and in the pulpit we are teaching our children to regard as sacred, the bad city government, by the whole tenor of its administration, openly despises; the things which we tell them are detestable and infamous, the bad city government, by its open connivance or inaction, proclaims to be honorable. The whole weight of the moral influence of a municipal government like that which has existed until recently in New York, like that which exists to-day in Philadelphia, and in many other cities, is hostile to honesty, honor, purity, and decency. The preacher of righteousness finds, therefore, in bad municipal government, one of the deadliest of the evil forces with which he is called to contend. The problem of the city is a problem in which he has a vital interest, a question on which he has an undoubted right to speak.

The American city of the nineteenth century has been notable for two things, the rapidity of its growth and the corruptness of its civic administration. The population of the whole land has been growing apace, but the cities have grown at the expense of the rural districts.

Let us not underrate our problem. These people of the cities—many of them ignorant, depraved, superstitious, unsocial in their tempers and habits; many of them ignorant of the language in which our laws are written, and unable freely to communicate with those who wish to influence them for good; having no conception of government but that of an enemy to be eluded or an unkind providence from which dole may be extorted; and no idea of a vote higher than that of a commodity which can be sold for money—these are the "powers that be" who must give us good government in our cities, if we are ever to get it.

---

## Selection 38

# The Social Gospel

### *Walter Rauschenbusch (1907)*

The gospel, to have full power over an age, must be the highest expression of the moral and religious truths held by that age. If it lags behind and deals in outgrown conceptions of life and duty, it will lose power over the ablest minds and the young men first, and gradually over all. In our thought to-day the social problems irresistibly take the lead. If the Church has no live and bold thought on this dominant question of modern life, its teaching authority on all other questions will dwindle and be despised. It cannot afford to have young men sniff the air as in a stuffy room when they enter the sphere of religious thought. When the world is in travail with a higher ideal of justice, the Church dare not ignore it if it would retain its moral leadership. On the other hand, if the Church

Source: Walter Rauschenbusch, *Christianity and the Social Crisis* (New York: Macmillan, 1907), 339–42, 419–22.

does incorporate the new social terms in its synthesis of truth, they are certain to throw new light on all the older elements of its teaching. The conception of race sin and race salvation become comprehensible once more to those who have made the idea of social solidarity in good and evil a part of their thought. The law of sacrifice loses its arbitrary and mechanical aspect when we understand the vital union of all humanity. Individualistic Christianity has almost lost sight of the great idea of the kingdom of God, which was the inspiration and centre of the thought of Jesus. Social Christianity would once more enable us to understand the purpose and thought of Jesus and take the veil from our eyes when we read the synoptic gospels. . . .

As we have seen, the industrial and commercial life to-day is dominated by principles antagonistic to the fundamental principles of Christianity, and it is so difficult to live a Christian life in the midst of it that few men even try. If production could be organized on a basis of coöperative fraternity; if distribution could at least approximately be determined by justice; if all men could be conscious that their labor contributed to the welfare of all and that their personal well-being was dependent on the prosperity of the Commonwealth; if predatory business and parasitic wealth ceased and all men lived only by their labor; if the luxury of unearned wealth no longer made us all feverish with covetousness and a simpler life became the fashion; if our time and strength were not used up either in getting a bare living or in amassing unusable wealth and we had more leisure for the higher pursuits of the mind and the soul—then there might be a chance to live such a life of gentleness and brotherly kindness and tranquillity of heart as

Walter Rauschenbusch (Billy Graham Center Museum, Wheaton, Ill.)

Jesus desired for men. It may be that the coöperative Commonwealth would give us the first chance in history to live a really Christian life without retiring from the world, and would make the Sermon on the Mount a philosophy of life feasible for all who care to try.

This is the stake of the Church in the social crisis. If society continues to disintegrate and decay, the Church will be carried down with it. If the Church can rally such moral forces that injustice will be overcome and fresh red blood will course in a sounder social organism, it will itself rise to higher liberty and life. Doing the will of God it will have new visions of God. With a new message will come a new authority. If the salt lose its saltness, it will be trodden under foot. If the Church fulfils its prophetic functions, it may bear the prophet's reproach for a time, but it will have the prophet's vindication thereafter.

The conviction has always been embedded in the heart of the Church that "the world"—society as it is—is evil and some time is to make way for a true human society in which the spirit of Jesus Christ shall rule. For fifteen hundred years those who desired to live a truly Christian life withdrew from the evil world to live a life apart. But the principle of such an ascetic departure from the world is dead in modern life. There are only two other possibilities. The Church must either condemn the world and seek to change it, or tolerate the world and conform to it. In the latter case it surrenders its holiness and its mission. The other possibility has never yet been tried with full faith on a large scale. All the leadings of God in contemporary history and all the promptings of Christ's spirit in our hearts urge us to make the trial. On this choice is staked the future of the Church. . . .

In asking for faith in the possibility of a new social order, we ask for no Utopian delusion. We know well that there is no perfection for man in this life: there is only growth toward perfection. In personal religion we look with seasoned suspicion at any one who claims to be holy and perfect, yet we always tell men to become holy and to seek perfection. We make it a duty to seek what is unattainable. We have the same paradox in the perfectibility of society. We shall never have a perfect social life, yet we must seek it with faith. We shall never abolish suffering. There will always be death and the empty chair and heart. There will always be the agony of love unreturned. Women will long for children and never press baby lips to their breast. Men will long for fame and miss it. Imperfect moral insight will work hurt in the best conceivable social order. The strong will always have the impulse to exert their strength, and no system can be devised which can keep them from crowding and jostling the weaker. Increased social refinement will bring increased sensitiveness to pain. An American may suffer as much distress through a social slight as a Russian peasant under the knout [flogging whip]. At best there is always but an approximation to a perfect social order. The kingdom of God is always but coming.

But every approximation to it is worth while. Every step toward personal purity and peace, though it only makes the consciousness of imperfection more poignant, carries its own exceeding great reward, and everlasting pilgrimage toward the kingdom of God is better than contented stability in the tents of wickedness.

And sometimes the hot hope surges up that perhaps the long and slow climb may be ending. In the past the steps of our race toward progress have been short and feeble, and succeeded by long intervals of sloth and apathy. But is that necessarily to remain the rate of advance? In the intellectual life there has been an unprecedented leap forward during the last hundred years. Individually we are not more gifted than our grandfathers, but collectively we have wrought out more epoch-making discoveries and inventions in one century than the whole race in the untold centuries that have gone before. If the twentieth century could do for us in the control of social forces what the nineteenth did for us in the control of natural forces, our grandchildren would live in a society that would be justified in regarding our present social life as semi-barbarous. Since the Reformation began to free the mind and to direct the force of religion toward morality, there has been a perceptible increase of speed. Humanity is gaining in elasticity and capacity for change, and every gain in general intelligence, in organizing capacity, in physical and moral soundness, and especially in responsiveness to ideal motives, again increases the ability to advance without disastrous reactions. The swiftness of evolution in our own country proves the immense latent perfectibility in human nature.

Last May a miracle happened. At the beginning of the week the fruit trees bore brown and greenish buds. At the end of the week they were robed in bridal garments of blossom. But for weeks and months the sap had been rising and distending the cells and maturing the tissues which were half ready in the fall before. The swift unfolding was the culmination of a long process. Perhaps these nineteen centuries of Christian influence have been a long preliminary stage of growth, and now the flower and fruit are almost here. If at this juncture we can rally sufficient religious faith and moral strength to snap the bonds of evil and turn the present unparalleled economic and intellectual resources of humanity to the harmonious development of a true social life, the generations yet unborn will mark this as that great day of the Lord for which the ages waited, and count us blessed for sharing in the apostolate that proclaimed it.

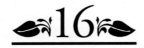

# Pluralism and the American Catholics

Before 1800 the citizens of America could be divided generally into two groups: Protestants, and those outside the Protestant pale, whether they be secularists, agnostics, or atheists. Other groups were minuscule.

As to Jews in America, estimates must suffice, but they suggest there were 1500 Jews in 1776, 6000 by 1800, 15,000 by 1825, 50,000 by 1848, 150,000 by 1860, and 250,000 by 1875, when the vast immigration of Jews began.

There were perhaps 25,000 Roman Catholics in America by 1776, 70,000 by 1800, 318,000 by 1830, 563,000 by 1840, 3 million by 1865 (9.65 percent of the total population), 6 million by 1880, 12 million by 1900 (15.78 percent of the whole), 23 million by 1930 (18.76 percent of the whole), and almost 36 million by 1958 (21 percent of the whole).

Prior to 1850, only two languages had been spoken by the vast majority of those coming to the United States: English and German; the first had prevailed, and the second was phased out as the younger generations rapidly learned and spoke English. But after the Civil War, entirely new languages—Russian, Italian, Greek, Yiddish, Swedish, and dozens of others—were brought by those "huddled masses yearning to breathe free." Americans were confused and apprehensive. Some of the newcomers were of the Eastern Orthodox faith and others were Jewish, but the majority were Roman Catholics. And so, the faith to which the majority belonged naturally received the greatest concern.

As early as 1829 a reporter of the *Home Missionary* magazine warned that the Jesuits were making "rapid strides" in Missouri, and this and similar reports alarmed many readers. In 1834 the inventor of the telegraph, Samuel F. B. Morse, published a book entitled *Foreign Conspiracy Against the Liberties of the United States.* He charged that the Roman Catholic Church was a political organization whose aim was to subvert any nation that opposed it, and that it was unalterably opposed to democratic principles. He further charged that Europe's Roman Catholic despots were so angered over the spread of democratic ideas that they plotted to check them by altering the character of America through unlimited immigration, and that they were already beginning to send the most ignorant, degenerate, and lazy of their peoples to her shores.

Much was happening during the 1830s as Americans contemplated increased Roman Catholic presence. In 1834 a mob burned down the Ursuline convent in Charlestown, Massachusetts, after stories were spread (later proven totally false) of dissolute life in the convent. In 1836 the *Awful Disclosures* of Maria Monk were published, in which she claimed she had been forced to be a priest's mistress in Montreal, and after this a great number of similarly lurid and concocted tales came off the presses. The nation was divided over the issue. Some feared the worst of papal power and wanted to limit Catholic immigration, while others were willing to try the experiment.

The issue would not die, and became a national one. The *Native American Party* sprang up in 1837, demanding that immigration be limited and that all aliens be required to live in America for twenty-one years before they were eligible for citizenship. The *Order of United Americans*, organized in the late 1840s, sought to limit all offices and honors to "native-born Protestant citizens." From this group emerged the "Know-Nothing" party which backed Millard Fillmore for the presidency in 1856. These were the years during which the potato famine struck Ireland and overwhelming numbers of Irish Catholics came to America. Protestants were not alone in resisting the tides of Irish. Native-born Roman Catholics often reviled the new Irish, disgusted with their frequent brawls, uncleanness, and crude ways. There was particular hatred between Irish and the German Catholics who had immigrated earlier. This dislike reached even into the American Roman Catholic hierarchy.

### Fitting into Protestant America

By 1855 dioceses had been formed in most American cities of any size, and the Catholic church flourished in some areas, while struggling in others. In 1852 the first plenary council met in Baltimore, and of the thirty-two bishops attending, only nine had been born in the United States. But each time that supposedly encouraging signs appeared of the willingness of Roman Catholics and their church to fit well into the American scene, opposing signs also appeared. We have noted that Pius IX, in his *Syllabus of Errors* (selection 28) promulgated in 1864, condemned religious liberty; the suggestion that Protestantism was acceptable to God; cooperation with Bible societies; separation of

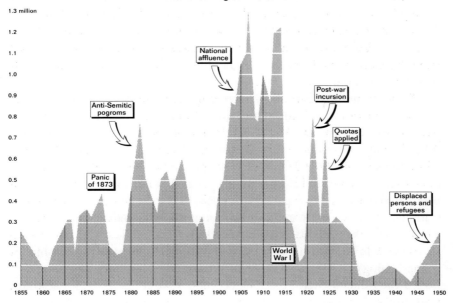

church and state; state control over public education, and other practices at the heart of modern democratic society.

Then the Vatican Council of 1870 disturbed many Catholics, both in Europe and in the United States. The principal matter before the bishops was *papal infallibility*, and many of them believed it the wrong time to approve such a dogma. The members of the American hierarchy were especially reluctant, knowing that if the dogma were made official it would likely stir up more prejudice against Roman Catholics.

Intemperate statements and anti-Protestantism in some Catholic leaders also contributed to the antagonism felt by many Americans. The *American Catholic Quarterly Review* in 1877 stated that the Declaration of Independence was little more than a cluster of vague clichés, and in 1882 a pastoral letter from bishops of the province of Cincinnati declared that the concept of citizens governing themselves was a perverse and questionable notion.[1] Archbishop John Hughes of New York said that any Catholic clergyman who befriended Protestants was a "Protestant priest."[2] German Catholics were most vocal in condemning everything American; a priest in Cincinnati, Anton Walburg, said in 1889 that culture in the United States was a "hotbed of fanaticism, intolerance, and radical ultra views on matters of politics and religion." Walburg pointed to Germany as a fine example of what a Catholic nation should be.[3] Perhaps the most bitter attacks were those directed against the public school system. Bishop Bernard McQuaid declared that the public schools were "a huge conspiracy against religion, individual liberty, and enterprise." Redemptorist Father Michael Muller called the public schools "hotbeds of immorality" where "courtesans have disguised themselves as school-girls in order the more surely to ply their foul vocation."[4]

Of the numerous Catholic leaders during the nineteenth century who attacked American institutions and incited more dislike against Rome, few were more incendiary than Archbishop John Hughes (1797–1864) of New York. A headstrong and stubborn man, he convened a series of debates with Protestant leaders in which he denounced religious and civil liberty, the separation of church and state, and similar topics. Hughes is remembered most for his part in the controversy over parochial schools. In 1840 he demanded that Roman Catholics in New York City be given a proportionate share of tax money for education for the parochial schools. He attacked the public school system constantly as a Protestant organization, and ironically he was responsible for strengthening that system. Weary of his attacks, the New York legislature reaffirmed the principle that no public tax money would be given for sectarian education and created a city board of education to oversee the public schools. But the demands for public money continued. In 1876 Bishop John B. Purcell of Cincinnati insisted that Roman Catholics be tax exempt so far as taxes for the maintenance of public schools were concerned. Other demands and plans kept the controversy boiling for a century.

Such men in the hierarchy as Hughes, McQuaid, and Purcell, plus the mounting tides of immigration, made Anglo-Saxon Protestants ever more fearful. The reasons for the concerns were complex. One was a dread that some day Protestants might be a minority in a nation they had founded and set upon a steady course. Protestants also grew increasingly alarmed at the influx because it threatened a number of folk moralities that had been widely observed throughout the nation, such as temperance and the observance of Sunday. They had long been taught the dangers of alcohol (selection 25), and they noted that the immigrants brought with them much alcoholism and the "Continental Sunday" on which church attendance was minor and the day given over to anything. In addition, they feared that the great national imperative—world evangelization—would be imperiled if the country's morals were watered down.

These concerns were nowhere better enunciated than by Josiah Strong (1847–1916) in his book *Our Country,* which stunned the nation in 1885 by its penetrating analysis of its problems (selection 39). Strong was no benighted reactionary bumpkin but a farsighted and broadminded leader. Early on he realized the damage being caused by urban slums and crowding, rampant greed, and industrialization. A Congregational pastor, he was one of the first to be disturbed by the poverty of the immigrants and their exploitation by the capitalist factory owners. He felt this oppression was corrupting the entire nation. An early exponent of the Social Gospel, Strong became the secretary of the Evangelical Alliance, and in 1908 he was at the forefront in the formation of the Federal Council of Churches.

Strong carried forward, fifty years later, the vision of Lyman Beecher that the American people had become the emissaries of two brilliant hopes for all humankind—"Civil liberty" and "spiritual Christianity." The first hope, he said, was completely dependent upon the preservation of the second. Strong declared the Anglo-Saxons to be a race of "unequalled energy, with all the majesty of numbers and wealth behind it—the representative, let us hope, of the largest liberty, the purest Christianity, the highest civilization." He expressed his prediction and hope that the aggressive spirit behind liberty and Christianity "will spread itself over the earth."[5]

While this would be sneered at as racist by many today, Strong did not mean to dismiss other races as inferior. He held that all immigrants, by the chemistry of the "melting pot," became Anglo-Saxons when they accepted the ideals of the nation. He wrote that Anglo-Saxon superiority "is due in large measure to its highly mixed origin," since it is "almost universally admitted by ethnologists that the mixed races of mankind are superior to the pure ones."[6] Strong took this as a challenge to Christians not to demean other peoples, but to spread the gospel quickly and elevate the entire world to the high standards of life that America had been privileged to enjoy. Strong's writings, and the influence of others of like mind, inspired more than 2000 students to offer themselves for missionary service by 1887. In the following year the *Student Volunteer Movement* was formed to further the effort, having as its motto: "The evangelization of the world in this generation."

## Americanizing the church

In 1891 Pope Leo XIII issued his encyclical *Rerum Novarum* (selection 40). While the background for this document is complex and has been much debated, basically it addressed the economic predicament of immigrants and the Roman Church's opposition to secret societies, to which many Catholics belonged. The Knights of Labor, the nation's first large labor union, had been founded in 1869, and had more than half a million members by 1886, mostly unskilled laborers and Catholics. In 1884 the Vatican had condemned the

Knights as a secret society in Quebec Province, Canada, but the great majority of the American hierarchy opposed a similar condemnation in the United States, as they feared it would alienate labor from the church. In 1887 James Gibbons (1834–1921), cardinal archbishop of Baltimore, personally prevailed upon the pope not to condemn the Knights in the U.S.A. When the encyclical appeared in 1891, it took a surprisingly liberal stance, espousing the workingman's cause but condemning socialism and the Marxian dialectic of inevitable class war. The role of the church was stressed, as directing Christian charity and giving spiritual motivation and social control. It recognized the right of labor to form associations for their betterment. Many were shocked at the advanced stand Leo XIII had taken.

Against the anti-Protestantism of Hughes, McQuaid, and others, some Catholic leaders tried to quell passions on both sides, understanding well that reciprocal hatred and bigotry achieved nothing. Three who tried to bring about the Americanization of the church were John Ireland (1838–1918), archbishop of St. Paul; Bishop John J. Keane (1839–1918), and especially Gibbons, who was the most distinguished member of the American hierarchy in the half century after the Civil War.

After his ordination in 1861, Gibbons rose quickly in the ranks of the Catholic church, becoming vicar-apostolic of North Carolina at age 34. In 1876 he wrote *The Faith of Our Fathers,* an effective argument for his plan to have the church recognize the benefits of America. The next year he became archbishop of Baltimore, and in 1886 he was elevated to cardinal, the second American to be so honored. After having wide influence for some years, the liberal triumvirate of Gibbons, Ireland, and Keane was finally chastened by Pope Leo XIII in 1899. Suddenly what these three had tried to do for years—fostering understanding and healing, liberalizing theology, and stimulating wider fraternization with non-Catholics—was stopped.[7]

In 1916 Cardinal Gibbons wrote *A Retrospect of Fifty Years,* looking back on his career and all that had happened (selection 41). Despite the rebuke from Leo XIII, Gibbons once again attempted to answer the sentiments held by Josiah Strong and millions of others.

## Select Bibliography

Abell, Aaron I. *American Catholicism and Social Action: A Search for Social Justice, 1865–1950.* Garden City, N.Y.: Hanover House, 1960.

Cross, Robert D. *The Emergence of Liberal Catholicism in America.* Chicago: Quadrangle, 1968.

Ellis, John T. *American Catholicism*, 2d ed. Chicago: University of Chicago Press, 1969.

Hennesey, James J. *American Catholics: A History of the Roman Catholic Community in the United States.* New York: Oxford University Press, 1981.

Maynard, Theodore. *The Catholic Church and the American Idea.* New York: Appleton-Century-Crofts, 1953.

Shields, Currin V. *Democracy and Catholicism in America.* New York: McGraw-Hill, 1958.

# Our Country:
## Its Possible Future and Its Present Crisis

### Josiah Strong (1891)

### Perils—Romanism

There are many who are disposed to attribute any fear of Roman Catholicism in the United States to bigotry or childishness. Such see nothing in the character and attitude of Romanism that is hostile to our free institutions, or find nothing portentous in its growth. Let us, then, first, compare some of the fundamental principles of our free institutions with those of the Roman Catholic church.

I. *The Declaration of Independence teaches Popular Sovereignty. It says that "governments derive their just powers from the consent of the governed."* Roman Catholic doctrine invests the Pope with supreme sovereignty. In "Essays on Religion and Literature," edited by Archbishop [Henry] Manning, 1867, we read, p. 416; "Moreover, the right of deposing kings is inherent in the supreme sovereignty which the Popes, as vicegerents of Christ, exercise over all Christian nations."

In Art. VI., Sec. 2 of the Constitution we find: *"This Constitution and the laws of the United States which shall be made in pursuance thereof. . . . shall be the supreme law of the land."* The Canon Law of the Church of Rome is essentially the constitution of that church, binding upon Roman Catholics everywhere. The bull, *"Pastoralis Regiminis,"* published by Benedict XIV., is a part of the Canon Law and decrees that those who refuse to obey *any* "commands of the Court of Rome, if they be ecclesiastics, are *ipso facto* suspended from their orders and offices; and, if they be laymen, are smitten with excommunication." . . .

Here is a distinct issue touching the highest allegiance of the Roman Catholic citizens of the United States, whether it is due to the Pope or to the constitution and the laws of the land. In his Syllabus of Errors, Proposition 42, issued

Source: Josiah Strong, *Our Country: Its Possible Future and Its Present Crisis* (New York: Baker and Taylor, 1891), 62–64, 70–73, 76–77, 81–82, 84–85.

December 8, 1864, Pius IX. said: "It is an error to hold that, In the case of conflicting laws between the two powers, the civil law ought to prevail." The reigning pontiff, in an encyclical issued January 10, 1890, says: "It is wrong to break the law of Jesus Christ in order to obey the magistrate, or under pretence of civil rights to transgress the laws of the church." Again Leo XIII. says: "But if the laws of the state are openly at variance with the law of God—if they inflict injury upon the church. . . . or set at naught the authority of Jesus Christ which is vested in the Supreme Pontiff, then indeed it becomes a duty to resist them, a sin to render obedience." . . .

The two greatest living statesmen, [England prime minister William] Gladstone and [German chancellor Otto von] Bismarck, hold that the allegiance demanded by the Pope is inconsistent with good citizenship. Says the former: "—the Pope demands for himself the right to determine the province of his own rights, and has so defined it in formal documents as to warrant any and every invasion of the civil sphere; and that this new version of the principles of the Papal church inexorably binds its members to the admission of these exorbitant claims, without any refuge or reservation on behalf of their duty to the Crown." He also says: "That Rome requires a convert who now joins her to forfeit his moral and mental freedom, and to place his loyalty and civil duty at the mercy of another."

The Constitution of the United States guarantees *Liberty of Conscience*. Nothing is dearer or more fundamental. The first amendment to the Constitution says: *"Congress shall make no law respecting an establishment of religion or prohibiting the free exercise thereof."* Pius IX. declared it to be an error that, "Every man is free to embrace and profess the religion he shall believe true, guided by the light of reason." And from this dictum no good Roman Catholic can differ. The same Pope in his encyclical of December 8, 1864, said: "Contrary to the teaching of the Holy Scriptures, of the Church, and of the Holy Fathers, these persons do not hesitate to assert that 'the best condition of human society is that wherein no duty is recognized by the government *of correcting by enacted penalties the violators of the Catholic Religion,* except when the maintenance of the public peace requires it.' From this totally false notion of social government, they fear not to uphold that erroneous opinion most pernicious to the Catholic Church, and to the salvation of souls, which was called by our predecessor, Gregory XVI., the insanity (deliramentum), namely, that 'liberty of conscience and of worship is the right of every man; and that this right ought, in every well-governed state, to be proclaimed and asserted by the law.'" Much more to the same effect might be quoted from Pius IX. and Leo XIII. . . .

In the *Pontificale Romanum* is the bishop's oath, in which occur these words: "Heretics, schismatics and rebels against our said Lord or his successors I will to my utmost persecute (persequar) and oppose." What if Methodist and Episcopal bishops took an oath to *persecute* Roman Catholics and all others who refuse to accept the standards of their respective churches! If Romanists were persecuted in Protestant countries, would they not demand the religious liberty for themselves which they refuse to others? Their policy is very frankly stated by M. Louis Venillot, a distinguished French Roman Catholic writer, highly esteemed at Rome, who says: "When there is a Protestant majority we claim religious liberty because such is their principle; but when we are in majority we refuse it because that is ours." . . .

We have made a brief comparison of some of the fundamental principles of Romanism with those of the Republic. And,

1. We have seen the supreme sovereignty of the Pope opposed to the sovereignty of the people.

2. We have seen that the commands of the Pope, instead of the constitution and laws of the land, demand the highest allegiance of Roman Catholics in the United States.

3. We have seen that the alien Romanist who seeks citizenship swears true obedience to the Pope instead of "renouncing forever all allegiance to any foreign prince, potentate, state or sovereignty," as required by our laws.

4. We have seen that Romanism teaches religious intolerance instead of religious liberty.

5. We have seen that Rome demands the censorship of ideas and of the press, instead of the freedom of the press and of speech.

6. We have seen that she approves the union of church and state instead of their entire separation.

7. We have seen that she is opposed to our public school system.

Manifestly there is an irreconcilable difference between papal principles and the fundamental principles of our free institutions. Popular government is self-government. A nation is capable of self-government only so far as the individuals who compose it are capable of self-government. To place one's conscience, therefore, in the keeping of another, and to disavow all personal responsibility in obeying the dictation of another, is as far as possible from *self*-government, and, therefore, wholly inconsistent with republican institutions, and, if sufficiently common, dangerous to their stability. It is the theory of absolutism in the state, that man exists for the state. It is the theory of absolutism in the church that man exists for the church. But in republican and Protestant America it is believed that church and state exist for the people and are to be administered by them. Our fundamental ideas of society, therefore, are as radically opposed to Vaticanism as to imperialism, and it is as inconsistent with our liberties for Americans to yield allegiance to the Pope as to the Czar. It is true the Third Plenary Council in Baltimore denied that there is any antagonism between the laws, institutions and spirit of the Roman church and those of our country, and in so doing illustrated the French proverb that "To deny is to confess." No Protestant church makes any such denials. . . .

It is undoubtedly safe to say that there is not a member of the hierarchy in America, who does not accept the infallibility of the Pope and who has not sworn to obey him. Now this dogma of papal infallibility as defined by the Vatican Council and interpreted by Pius IX. and Leo XIII. carries with it logically all of the fundamental principles of Romanism which have been discussed. Infallibility is necessarily intolerant. It can no more compromise with a conflicting opinion than could a mathematical demonstration. Truth cannot make concessions to error. Infallibility represents absolute truth. It is as absolute as God himself, and can no more enter into compromise than God can compromise with sin. And if infallibility is as intolerant as the truth, it is also as authoritative. Truth may be rejected, but even on the scaffold it is king, and has the right and always must have the right to rule absolutely, to control utterly every reasoning being. If I believed the Pope to be the infallible vicar of Christ, I would surrender myself to him as unreservedly as to God himself. How can a true Roman Catholic do otherwise? A man may have breathed the air of the nineteenth century and of free America enough to be out of sympathy with the absolutism and intolerance of Romanism, but if he accepts the Pope's right to dictate his beliefs and acts, of what avail are his liberal sympathies? He is simply the instrument of the absolute and intolerant papal will. His sympathies can assert themselves and control his life only as he breaks with the Pope, that is, ceases to be a Roman Catholic. I fear we have little ground to expect that many would thus break with the Pope, were a distinct issue raised. Everyone born a Roman Catholic is suckled on authority. His training affects every fiber of his mental constitution. He has been taught that he must not judge for himself, nor trust to his own convictions. If he finds his sympathies, his judgment and convictions in conflict with a papal decree, it is the perfectly natural result of his training for him to distrust himself. His will, accustomed all his life to yield to authority without question, is not equal to the conflict that would follow disobedience. . . .

We have seen the fundamental principles of our free institutions laid side by side with some of those of Romanism, expressed in the words of the highest possible authorities in the Roman Catholic Church; and thus presented they have declared for themselves the inherent contradiction which exists between them.

It has been shown that it is the avowed purpose of Romanists to "make America Catholic."

It has been shown that this could not be done without bringing into active conflict the diametrically opposed principles of Romanism and of the Republic, thus forcing all Romanists in the United States to choose between the two masters, both of whom they now profess to serve.

It has been shown that Roman Catholic training, from childhood up, is calculated to disqualify the mind for independent action, and renders it highly improbable that any considerable number of even moderate and liberal Romanists would, in the supposed event, forsake their allegiance to the Pope.

---

## Selection 40

# *Rerum Novarum*

### *Pope Leo XIII (1891)*

That the spirit of revolutionary change, which has long been disturbing the nations of the world, should have passed beyond the sphere of politics and made its influence felt in the cognate sphere of practical economics is not surprising. The elements of the conflict now raging are unmistakable: in the vast expansion of industrial pursuits and the marvellous discoveries of science; in the changed relations between masters and workmen; in the enormous fortunes of some few individuals, and the utter poverty of the masses; in the increased self-reliance and closer mutual combination of the working classes; as also, finally, in the prevailing moral degeneracy. The momentous gravity of the state of things now obtaining fills every mind with painful apprehension; wise men are discussing it; practical men are proposing schemes; popular meetings, legislatures, and rulers of nations are all busied with it—and actually there is no question which has taken a deeper hold on the public mind. . . .

Source: John A. Ryan and Joseph Husslein, eds., *The Church and Labor* (New York, 1920), 57–94, *passim*.

## Socialists and Private Property

To remedy these wrongs the Socialists, working on the poor man's envy of the rich, are striving to do away with private property, and contend that individual possessions should become the common property of all, to be administered by the State or by municipal bodies. They hold that by thus transferring property from private individuals to the community, the present mischievous state of things will be set to rights, inasmuch as each citizen will then get his fair share of whatever there is to enjoy. But their contentions are so clearly powerless to end the controversy that were they carried into effect the workingman himself would be among the first to suffer. They are, moreover, emphatically unjust, because they would rob the lawful possessor, bring State action into a sphere not within its competence, and create utter confusion in the community.

It is surely undeniable that, when a man engages in remunerative labor, the impelling reason and motive of his work is to obtain property, and thereafter to hold it as his very own. If one man hires out to another his strength or skill, he does so for the purpose of receiving in return what is necessary for sustenance and education; he therefore expressly intends to acquire a right full and real, not only to the remuneration, but also to the disposal of such remuneration, just as he pleases. Thus, if he lives sparingly, saves money, and, for greater security, invests his savings in land, the land, in such case, is only his wages under another form; and, consequently, a workingman's little estate thus purchased should be as completely at his full disposal as are the wages he receives for his labor. But it is precisely in such power of disposal that ownership consists, whether the property consist of land or chattels. Socialists, therefore, by endeavoring to transfer the possessions of individuals to the community, strike at the interests of every wage earner, for they deprive him of the liberty of disposing of his wages, and thus of all hope and possibility of increasing his stock and of bettering his condition in life. . . .

## Man's Natural Right and His Social and Domestic Duties

The rights here spoken of, belonging to each individual man, are seen in a much stronger light if they are considered in relation to man's social and domestic obligations. . . .

That right of property, therefore, which has been proved to belong naturally to individual persons, must also belong to a man in his capacity of head of a family; nay, such a person must possess this right so much the more clearly in proportion as his position multiplies his duties. For it is a most sacred law of nature that a father must provide food and all necessaries for those whom he has begotten; and, similarly, nature dictates that a man's children, who carry on, as it were, and continue his own personality, should be provided by him with all that is needful to enable them honorably to keep themselves from want and misery in the uncertainties of this mortal life. Now, in no other way can a father effect this except by the ownership of profitable property, which he can transmit to his children by inheritance. . . .

## The Church Alone Can Solve the Social Problem

We approach the subject with confidence, and in the exercise of the rights which belong to Us. For no practical solution of this question will ever be found without the assistance of Religion and of the Church. It is We who are the chief guardian of Religion, and the chief dispenser of what belongs to the Church, and we must not by silence neglect the duty which lies upon Us. Doubtless this most serious question demands the attention and the efforts of others besides Ourselves—of the rulers of States, of employers of labor, of the wealthy, and of the working population themselves for whom We plead. But We affirm without hesitation that all the striving of men will be vain if they leave out the Church. . . .

## The Christian Interdependence of Capital and Labor

The great mistake that is made in the matter now under consideration, is to possess oneself of the idea that class is naturally hostile to class; that rich and poor are intended by nature to live at war with one another. So irrational and so false is this view, that the exact contrary is the truth. Just as the symmetry of the human body is the result of the disposition of the members of the body, so in a State it is ordained by nature that these two classes should exist in harmony and agreement, and should, as it were, fit into one another, so as to maintain the equilibrium of the body politic. Each requires the other; capital cannot do without labor, nor labor without capital. Mutual agreement results in pleasantness and good order; perpetual conflict necessarily produces confusion and outrage. Now, in preventing such strife as this, and in making it impossible, the efficacy of Christianity is marvelous and manifold. First of all, there is nothing more powerful than Religion (of which the Church is the interpreter and guardian) in drawing rich and poor together, by reminding each class of its duties to the other, and especially of the duties of justice. Thus Religion teaches the laboring man and the workman to carry out honestly and well all equitable agreements freely made, never to injure capital, nor to outrage the person of an employer; never to employ violence in representing his own cause, nor to engage in riot and disorder; and to have nothing to do with men of evil principles, who work upon the people with artful promises, and raise foolish hopes which usually end in disaster and in repentance when too late. Religion teaches the rich man and the employer that their work-people are not their slaves; that they must respect in every man his dignity as a man and as a Christian; that labor is nothing to be ashamed of, if we listen to right reason and to Christian philosophy, but is an honorable employment, enabling a man to sustain his life in an upright and creditable way; and that it is shameful and inhuman to treat men like chattels to make money by, or to look upon them merely as so much muscle or physical power. . . .

## Save the Laborers from the Cruelty of Speculators in Labor

If we turn now to things exterior and corporeal, the first concern of all is to save the poor workers from the cruelty of grasping speculators, who use human beings as mere instruments for making money. It is neither justice nor humanity so to grind men down with excessive labor as to stupefy their minds and wear out their bodies. Man's powers like his general nature, are limited, and beyond these limits he cannot go. His strength is devoted and increased by use and exercise, but only on condition of due intermission and proper rest. Daily labor, therefore, must be so regulated that it may not be protracted during longer hours than strength admits. How many and how long the intervals of rest should be, will depend upon the nature of the work, on circumstances of time and place, and on the health and strength of the workman. Those who labor in mines and quarries, and in work within the bowels of the earth, should have shorter hours in proportion, as their labor is more severe and more trying to health. . . .

## Multiply Workingmen's Associations

In the last place—employers and workmen may themselves effect much in the matter of which We treat, by means of those institutions and organizations which afford opportune assistance to those in need, and which draw the two orders more closely together. Among these may be enumerated: Societies for mutual help; various foundations established by private persons for providing for the workman, and for his widow or his orphans, in sudden calamity, in sickness, and in the event of death; and what are called "patronages," or institutions for the care of boys and girls, for young people, and also for those of more mature age.

The most important of all are Workmen's Associations; for these virtually include all the rest. History attests what excellent results were effected by the Artificers' Guilds of a former day. They were the means not only of many advantages to the workmen, but in no small degree of the advancement of art, as numerous monuments remain to prove. . . .

As far as regards the Church, its assistance will never be wanting, be the time or the occasion what it may; and it will intervene with greater effect in proportion as its liberty of action is the more unfettered; let this be carefully noted by those whose office it is to provide for the public welfare. Every minister of holy Religion must throw into the conflict all the energy of his mind, and all the strength of his endurance; with your authority, Venerable Brethren, and by your example, they must never cease to urge upon all men of every class, upon the high as well as the lowly, the Gospel doctrines of Christian life; by every means in their power they must strive for the good of the people; and above all they must earnestly cherish in themselves, and try to arouse in others, Charity, the mistress and queen of virtues. For the happy results we all long for must be chiefly brought about by the plenteous outpouring of Charity; of that true Christian Charity which is the fulfilling of the whole Gospel law, which is always ready to sacrifice itself for others' sake, and which is man's surest antidote against worldly pride and immoderate love of self; that Charity whose office is described and whose God-like features are drawn by the Apostle St. Paul in these words: *Charity is patient, is kind, . . . seeketh not her own, . . . suffereth all things, . . . endureth all things.*

On each of you, Venerable Brethren, and on your Clergy and people, as an earnest of God's mercy and a mark of our affection, We lovingly in the Lord bestow the Apostolic Benediction.

Given at St. Peter's in Rome, the fifteenth day of May, 1891, the fourteenth year of our Pontificate.

Leo XIII., Pope.

# On the Separation of Church and State

## *James Cardinal Gibbons (1916)*

The political authority exercised by the mediæval Popes, then presupposed a united Christendom, and was part of the universally recognized international law. Yet, legitimate and beneficial as it was, it was seized upon by the Reformers as one of their chief arguments against the Papacy, and became one of their pretexts for repudiating Rome's spiritual authority. Ever since, the same weapon has been persistently and effectually employed by Protestant writers and divines against the Catholic religion. In consequence there are many persons today who, while they are profoundly impressed and attracted by the beauty, the discipline, the deep spiritual influence, and efficient moral force of the Catholic Church, yet hesitate to enter, simply because of their views regarding the political power claimed by the Pope in the Middle Ages. The power was lost when the unity of Christendom on the rise of the modern States ceased to be a fundamental principle of the law of nations; and when Germany, France, Russia, England and America shall be welded into a world-wide Christian confederation on the plan of the Holy Roman Empire, then, and not before, need statesmen discuss the possibility of a revival of the mediæval Papacy.

Catholics, then, may subscribe to the fundamental article of English Protestantism. "The Pope of Rome hath no jurisdiction in this Realm," if it be understood of the realm of purely temporal affairs; and while we insist that he has the right to the free exercise of his spiritual authority over Catholics, we believe that in civil matters which do not contravene the moral law, we Catholics owe a full and unreserved allegiance to the civil authorities. The same Divine Voice, as I have often preached in the discharge of my pastoral office, which gives us the command to render unto God the things of God, gives us the other command, of equally binding force, to render unto Cæsar the things of Cæsar.

But an objection is repeatedly cast up to Catholics which, repugnant though it is to my inmost feelings of loyalty and reverence towards the Holy Father, I must take into consideration; for utterly impracticable and absurd as it is in our eyes, it seems to haunt the minds of many outside the Church. Suppose,

Source: James Cardinal Gibbons, *A Retrospect of Fifty Years*, 2 vols. (Baltimore: John Murphy, 1916), 1:227–33, *passim*.

it is said, the Pope were to issue commands in purely civil matters, should not Catholics be bound to yield him obedience? The Pope will take no such act, we know, even though it is a part of Catholic Faith that he is infallible in the exercise of his authority; but were he to do so he would stand self-condemned, a transgressor of the law he himself promulgates. He would be offending not only against civil society, but against God, and violating an authority as truly from God as His own. Any Catholic who clearly recognized this, would not be bound to obey the Pope; or rather his conscience would bind him absolutely to disobey, because with Catholics conscience is the supreme law which under no circumstances can we ever lawfully disobey. . . .

The Jesuit Cardinal [Robert] Bellarmine says: "In order to resist and defend oneself, no authority is required. . . . Therefore, as it is lawful to resist the Pope if he assaulted a man's person, so it is lawful to resist him if he assaulted souls or troubled the State, and much more if he strove to destroy the Church. It is lawful, I say, to resist him by not doing what he commands and hindering the execution of his will." My venerable and learned predecessor in the See of Baltimore, Archbishop [Francis] Kenrick, speaks in a similar strain; the Pope's "power was given for edification, not for destruction; if he used it for love of domination (quod absit) scarcely will he meet with obedient populations."

We may put aside, then, as an absurdity the injurious supposition that the Pope would ever interfere in purely civil affairs. But is there not a twilight zone over which both Church and State put forth claims? True; and I grant that here a collision of authorities comes more within the horizon of possibility. . . .

The admission, however, of the merely theoretical possibility of such a collision keeps alive the apprehension of timid Protestants, and is sufficient to determine some of them to deprive Catholics forever of the honor of the Presidency. But if no man were to be considered eligible for the Presidency unless we were certain that under no conceivable circumstances would his conscience come into conflict with any possible legislation, then the first consideration to qualify a man as candidate for the office would be that he should have no conscience at all. . . .

The Catholic Church states in form of doctrine what all history shows to be inevitable—that where the Church and State are practically two names for the nation, viewed as a body of worshippers and as a political entity, it is impossible to prevent an intimate union. If my Protestant friends will show me a free nation that really believes in one religion and has no union of religion with the State, I will believe the Catholic doctrine unwarranted.

But while the union is ideally best, history assuredly does not prove that it is always practically best. There is a union that is inimical to the interests of religion, and consequently to the State; and there is a separation that is inimical to the interests of religion, and consequently to the State; and there is a separation that is for the best interests of both. In our country separation is a necessity; and it is a separation that works best for the interests of religion, as Mr. [William Howard] Taft recently stated, as well as for the good of the State. I fully agree with him, and I can understand, too, and sympathize with the great Catholic leader of France, the Count [Adrien Albert Marie] de Mun, who recently exclaimed: "In America separation means the reign of liberty; in France the reign of impiety."

American Catholics rejoice in our separation of Church and State; and I can conceive no combination of circumstances likely to arise which should make a union desirable either to Church or State. We know the blessings of our present arrangement; it gives us liberty and binds together priests and people in a union better than that of Church and State. Other countries, other manners; we do not believe our system adapted to all conditions; we leave it to Church and State in other lands to solve their problems for their own best interests. For ourselves, we thank God we live in America, "in this happy country of ours," to quote Mr. [Theodore] Roosevelt, where "religion and liberty are natural allies."

# 17

# The Fundamentalist-Modernist Controversy

While divisions between Protestants who were conservative in their theology and those who were liberal had been going on since before 1800, the matter came to a head in the last decades of the nineteenth century and the first decades of the twentieth. We have seen that early indications of a difference in viewpoint toward theological matters are detectable in the writings of Charles Chauncy, pastor of Boston's First Church, who attacked Jonathan Edwards in his 1743 work, *Seasonable Thoughts on the State of Religion in New-England,* and later espoused universalism. But the things which impelled Chauncy to dissent were as nothing compared with the towering controversies engendered by such nineteenth-century issues as the advent of the evolutionary theory, higher criticism, and the new theology. Among other tendencies which increasingly manifested themselves in liberal theologies during the nineteenth century were: convictions that humans are basically good, that evil and sin are "growing pains" that humanity is gradually overcoming, that sincerity is the test for truth, that doctrines are relatively unimportant, that doctrines previously considered essential could be abandoned, and that the church must be socially involved.

## Liberalism and the Roman Church

Protestants were not alone in these struggles. While the perimeters were somewhat different, the Roman Catholic Church world wide was dealing with similar bifurcations. The great difference between the outcome of the two major bodies' struggles was that the Roman Church was better able to define, through the pope and Vatican councils, the allowable boundaries of discursive thinking. The Scriptures had been the absolute standards among Protestants, but when higher criticism attacked the Bible's authority, a relativism set in among those willing to accept the conclusions of the critics. As we have seen (pp. 186–87), Pope Pius IX determined to oppose the rise of democratic liberalism that was sweeping across Europe around 1850, and defend Catholic cultural and political ideals. Growing more stringent with each year, the pope in 1864 issued the *Syllabus of Errors* (selection 28) which condemned not only such expected issues as atheism, pantheism, and infidelity, but also state-run education, religious liberty, democracy, civil marriage, and a host of other progressive ideas. While liberal Catholics in Europe and America tried to restrict the condemnations to the European political scene, that was not easy to do, and those who continued to violate the dictates of the church risked excommunication.

## The Presbyterian heresy trials

In America some fragmented Protestant denominations sought to enforce orthodoxy against the newer ideas through ecclesiastical machinery, particularly through examining the views of ordinands and trying ordained ministers in church courts for teaching heretical beliefs. The best example of this was probably the heresy trials of the Presbyterian Church in the U.S.A. Heresy trials in that denomination were not new. Lyman Beecher was brought before the Presbytery of Cincinnati in 1835 for denying original sin, imputed guilt, and humanity's inability to save itself, and he was acquitted. After the Civil War such proceedings became more common. In 1874 Professor Francis L. Patton (1843–1932) of McCormick Theological Seminary prosecuted David Swing (1830–1894), pastor of Chicago's Fourth Presbyterian Church, before Chicago Presbytery on charges that some elements in his preaching were not in accord with the Confession of Faith. A gifted speaker, Swing won acquittal, although the experience moved him to leave the Presbyterian ministry.

Much more notoriety was attached to the case of Charles A. Briggs (1841–1913), a professor of biblical theology at Union Theological Seminary, New York. Briggs had been veering from the traditional view of biblical inspiration since 1870 and was an exponent of higher criticism and a follower of German theology. In the era of good feelings after the Old School–New School Presbyterian reunion of 1869, Princeton Theological Seminary had cooperated with Union Seminary in publishing the *Presbyterian Review*. In a series of articles on biblical higher criticism, Archibald A. Hodge (1823–1886), the son of Charles Hodge, and Benjamin B. Warfield (selection 35) of Princeton made the case for the Mosaic authorship of the Pentateuch and for verbal inspiration of the Scriptures, stressing that the Bible was without error in its original autographs, which of course, are no longer extant. Briggs opposed these positions and accused his colleagues of an "orthodoxism." In 1891 when Briggs sharply criticized these views in his own inaugural address at Union, he was prosecuted for heresy before the Presbytery of New York. When that tribunal acquitted him the case was appealed to the General Assemblies of 1892 and 1893. He was suspended from the ministry, and he decided to enter the Episcopal Church, receiving priest's orders. The General Assembly, meeting in Portland, then adopted the Princeton position of Biblical inerrancy as the official stance of the denomination.

The Presbyterians were not done with controversy. About the same time as the trial of Briggs, Professor Henry Preserved Smith (1847–1927) of Lane Theological Seminary in Cincinnati was charged with heresy and found guilty in 1892 by his presbytery. A few years later Arthur Cushman McGiffert (1861–1933), a professor at Union Seminary, was criticized by the General Assembly for making written statements at variance with the Westminster Confession and asked to recant or withdraw from the Presbyterian ministry. He became a Congregationalist in 1899. One man who was especially outspoken in defending his liberalism was the well-known writer, poet, and theologian Henry Van Dyke (1852–1933), whose Christmas story, "The Other Wise Man," was a favorite around the world. Van Dyke was critical of many doctrines, so he probably would have been tried for heresy had he not become a professor of English at Princeton University in 1899, thus escaping further scrutiny.

Across the Presbyterian Church, as in many other denominations, battles were being fought over doctrines. In 1910 the General Assembly, in a determined attempt to safeguard the denomination's orthodoxy, ruled that the following articles of faith were necessary for ordination: the inerrancy of the Scriptures, the virgin birth of Jesus, the miracles of Jesus, his substitutionary atonement, and his resurrection. By this point the term *modernism* was frequently used to describe the system of thought liberals had developed. The term referred to a reinterpretation of traditional Christian beliefs to make them compatible with current thinking and intelligible in the light of modern historical and scientific knowledge. Modernists saw only two options for the church: (1) The church must either accept a modern revision of the faith, even if it meant jettisoning most historic beliefs, or (2) it must give up the faith altogether. Positively, liberals and modernists held at the core of their theology the fatherhood of God and the brotherhood of all humans. Because Jesus had a unique insight into the Father, he is for humans the older brother, the example to follow, the epitome of all that humans can become through spiritual development. Since all people are God's children, they are all brothers and sisters and must show love and compassion toward one another. By thus injecting into the mainstreams of culture the moral righteousness that issues from this love, humans are preparing for a developing future time of peace and enlightenment. Such a liberal interpretation of Christianity was taught in most older seminaries and many influential pulpits of America before the First World War.

## The fundamentalist response

Not all church people had accepted this, however. Determined attempts to fight modernism were mounted in a number of denominations. One of the best known was when two wealthy brothers in Los Angeles, Milton and Lyman Stewart, in 1910 financed the free distribution of 3 million copies of a series of twelve booklets collectively entitled *The Fundamentals*. The editors brought together the best in conservative scholarship, including Princeton's Warfield, and defined the gospel in terms that would satisfy all evangelicals. So as to address the issues of the day in the most pronounced manner, the booklets highlighted six basic doctrines as the essential Christian beliefs, much as the Presbyterian General Assembly had done in 1910. The name *fundamentalist* originally referred to one who was concerned with the defense of these six essentials, although the term has taken on other meanings over the years.

World War I interrupted the debates over doctrine within Protestantism, but after the war *fundamentalism* took up the defense of the faith again and passed into the organizational phase of its history. During the 1920s and 1930s, great struggles were waged over control of denominational seminaries and colleges, and a number of new institutions were founded to replace those considered too liberal. Another major development within the evangelical wing was the adoption of *dispensationalism*, a system of biblical interpretation brought to America from England by the Plymouth Brethren leader John Nelson Darby (1800–1882). Protestant thought had stressed the sovereignty of God and the unity of a divine covenant of grace that stretched through all history. Dispensationalism organized God's dealings with humankind under several distinct historical periods or dispensations of testing. One dispensation operated under the Mosaic law, the current dispensation under God's grace. Making decisive distinctions among Jews, gentiles, and the Church, dispensationalism was promoted by C. I. Scofield (1843–1921) and his greatly influential Scofield Reference Bible (1909) and by the Bible Institute movement.

Two of the following readings are from the 1920s when the contest between modernism and fundamentalism was at its height, and the third is from a later period, reflecting on the conflict. Shailer Mathews (1863–1941, selection 42) was professor of historical theology and dean of the Divinity School of the

University of Chicago. Believing that higher critical study had shown the Bible to be quite different from what had previously been thought, Mathews wrote, "As a result of historical critical study the Bible had already lost its authority as an infallible revelation to be used as a theological oracle, but now the basis of religious loyalty itself was subject to examination. If one accepted evangelical orthodoxy it could only be because of the authority of a group or a literature rather than because of any demonstration of its truth."[1]

William Jennings Bryan (1860–1925) was the Joshua of fundamentalism. Reared in a pious home, educated in a denominational college, and guided throughout his life by the traditions and practices of evangelicalism, Bryan was a sincere and well-meaning man who should not have allowed himself, at the end of his life, to become entangled in the Tennessee trial of John Scopes, a young teacher under indictment for teaching evolution contrary to laws of the state. Defending Scopes was a team of nationally known lawyers including the famous Clarence Darrow, and the trial became not only a national joke but a confrontation between Darrow and Bryan. Over several very hot days in July 1925 the two battled over the Genesis record (selection 43), and after the trial the exhausted Bryan died within five days of apoplexy, doubtless brought on by the heat and strain.

Looking back on the embittered period, Carl F. H. Henry (1912– ) reflects in selection 44 on the lessons to be learned by evangelicals. A distinguished theologian, Henry graduated from Wheaton College and received his Ph.D. from Boston University. He taught at Northern Baptist Seminary, Fuller Theological Seminary, and other schools, and was the first editor of the influential evangelical journal, *Christianity Today*. This selection, part of a series in that journal, stresses the demands upon those who claim to support "Biblical supernaturalism."

## Select Bibliography

Furniss, Norman F. *The Fundamentalist Controversy, 1918–1931.* New Haven: Yale University Press, 1954.

Gasper, Louis. *The Fundamentalist Movement.* The Hague: Mouton, 1963.

Horton, Michael Scott. *Made in America: The Shaping of Modern American Evangelicalism.* Grand Rapids: Baker, 1991.

Hutchison, William R. *The Modernist Impulse in American Protestantism.* Cambridge, Mass.: Harvard University Press, 1976.

Loetscher, Lefferts A. *The Broadening Church: A Study of Theological Issues in the Presbyterian Church Since 1869.* Philadelphia: University of Pennsylvania Press, 1954.

Longfield, Bradley J. *The Presbyterian Controversy: Fundamentalists, Modernists, and Moderates.* New York: Oxford University Press, 1991.

McLoughlin, William G., ed. *The American Evangelicals, 1800–1900: An Anthology.* New York: Harper and Row, 1968.

Machen, J. Gresham. *Christianity and Liberalism.* 1923; repr., Grand Rapids: Eerdmans, n.d.

Marsden, George M. *Fundamentalism and American Culture: The Shaping of Twentieth-Century Evangelicalism: 1870–1925.* New York: Oxford University Press, 1980.

Rouse, Ruth, and Stephen C. Neill, eds. *A History of the Ecumenical Movement, 1517–1948*, 2d ed. Philadelphia: Westminster, 1967.

Sandeen, Ernest R. *The Roots of Fundamentalism: British and American Millenarianism 1800–1930.* Chicago: University of Chicago Press, 1970.

# The Faith of Modernism

## Shailer Mathews (1924)

It is poor psychology to deny that convictions underlie attitudes. Sooner or later the human heart requires the support of reason. It demands an answer to the insistent questions, What and why do I believe? Can Modernism organize any positive answers to such questions?

Not in the manner of the dogmatic mind. The Modernist movement does not seek to organize a system of theology or to draw up a confession. Modernists do not constitute a new denomination. Yet just as chemists without appeal to any authority recognize a body of facts and hypotheses which are held by those who use proper methods of chemical research, so the Modernists, because of unity of point of view and method, may be said to have reached unformulated but none the less common beliefs. Whoever attempts to epitomize this concurrence of faith will of course be giving only his own impression as to what seems to be common property of these having the same point of view and the same method of study. Such an impression, however, can be gained by a study of the literature scattered throughout all communions and countries. . . .

The religious affirmations of the Modernist are not identical with any theology. They represent an attitude rather than doctrine, they involve creative living under the inspiration of Christian connections rather than a new orthodoxy. The Modernist undertakes to project, not simply to defend permanent Christian faith. He knows that if it faces its real tasks the church cannot simply re-affirm the past. He sees something more imperative than theological regularity in the expansion of Christianity until it touches all human interest. Yet he would be consistent. If Christians find their impulses and loyalties inspired by a literal acceptance of the inherited doctrinal patterns, he would welcome their coöperation in the Christian service. It would be inconsistent for him to demand that others should accept his theology as a new orthodoxy. He must do unto others as he would have them do to him; namely, recognize the fundamental unity constituted by membership in the Christian group and devotion to the driving and reproductive convictions centering about Christ

Source: Shailer Mathews, *The Faith of Modernism* (New York: Macmillan, 1924), 169–82, passim.

which it embodies. Let men use and permit others to use such doctrinal patterns as will make these convictions and loyalties effective in human affairs. . . .

In developing an intellectual apparatus for justifying the Christian life, we shall not feel the need of stressing certain doctrinal patterns which expressed the Christian convictions and attitudes of men in different circumstances and controlled by different social practices. We shall shape new patterns whenever they are needed, from life itself. But we shall not forget they are patterns.

The Modernist will cherish faith in Jesus Christ as the revealer of the saving God, but until he is convinced of the historicity of the infancy sections of Matthew and Luke, and holds different conceptions of generation from those given at present by biology, he will not base that faith upon the virgin birth as the one and only means by which God can enter into human experience.

The Modernist will not insist upon miracles, but he believes that God is active and mysteriously present in the ordered course of nature and social evolution.

Because the Modernist thinks of God as immanent within His world, he counts upon divine help in every struggle for larger freedom and justice. The death of Christ, therefore gets far richer significance for him as a revelation of such participation than is possible from analogies drawn from the sacrifices of the ancient world, the practices of feudal lords, the punishments of an absolute monarch and the demands of a severe creditor.

Because he thus sees the character of Jesus in God, and therefore believes in the possibilities of a life like that of Jesus, the Modernist will practice good will himself and urge it as the only safe and promising motive for social, economic and national life. And he will never doubt that God's good will shall some day reign on earth.

While he believes in the inevitableness of suffering from any violation of the will of God the Modernist cannot think of a literal hell with fire and burning. The ravages of disease are more terrible analogies.

Because he believes in the mystery as well as the reality of the present continued life of Christ, the Modernist will not stake this faith upon untested traditions, but will ground it on literary criticism, history and his own experience, and will therefore hope for a similar advance through death.

In fact, Modernists will very likely have no common theology whatever. They have the same attitudes and convictions as those of the historical Christian community, but they will not codify them in words of authority. They will get uniformity of point of view and expression through a common method of thought. With limitations they may prefer to use the same terms, but they are concerned primarily with Christian attitudes and convictions rather than with doctrinal patterns. They do not believe that it is possible for any body of men to express authoritatively what a group believes, so long as there is a minority of one who differs. The community of interest, the solidarity of undertaking which the Modernist knows the Christian religion involves, he will increasingly find in the activities of the Christian group to which he belongs. In this choice he will feel with certainty that he is reproducing the spirit of him who taught that his friends were those who kept his commandment to love and forgive.

---

## Selection 43

---

# The Scopes Trial

### *William Jennings Bryan and Clarence Darrow (1925)*

CLARENCE DARROW, early in the trial: There is not a single line of any constitution that can withstand bigotry and ignorance when it seeks to destroy the rights of the individual; and bigotry and ignorance are ever active. Here we find today as brazen and as bold an attempt to destroy learning as was ever made in the Middle Ages, and the only difference is we have not provided that they shall be burned at the stake. But there is time for that, your Honor. We have to approach these things gradually.

Now let us see what we claim with reference to this law. If this proceeding, both in form and substance, can prevail in this court, then, your Honor, any law, no matter how foolish, wicked, ambiguous, or ancient, can come back to Tennessee. All the guarantees go for nothing. All of the past has gone to waste, been forgotten, if this can succeed.

I am going to begin with some of the simpler reasons why it is absolutely absurd to think that this statute, indictment, or any part of the proceedings in this case are legal; and I think the sooner we get rid of it in Tennessee the better for the people of Tennessee, and the better for the pursuit of knowledge in the world; so let me begin at the beginning.

The first point we made in this suit is that it is unconstitutional on account of divergence and the difference between the statute and the caption and because it contains more than one subject.

Source: Leslie Allen, ed., *Bryan and Darrow at Dayton* (New York: A. Lee, 1925), 16–19, 64–66, passim.

Every Constitution with which I am familiar has substantially this same proposition, that the caption and the law must correspond.

Lots of things are put through the Legislature in the night time. Everybody does not read all of the statutes, even members of the Legislature—I have been a member of the Legislature myself, and I know how it is. They may vote for them without reading them, but the substance of the act is put in the caption, so it may be seen and read, and nothing may be in the act that is not contained in the caption. There is not any question about it, and only one subject shall be legislated on at once. Of course, the caption may be broader than the act. They may make a caption and the act may fall far short of it, but the substance of the act must be in the caption, and there can be no variance.

Now let us see what they have done. There is not much dispute about the English language, I take it. Here is the caption:

Public Act, Chapter 37, 1925, an act prohibiting the teaching of the evolution theory in all the universities, normals, and all the public schools of Tennessee which are supported in whole or in part by the public school funds of the State, and to prescribe penalties for the violation thereof.

Now what is it—an act to prohibit the teaching of the evolution theory in Tennessee? Is this the act? Is this statue to prevent the teaching of the evolution theory?

William Jennings Bryan (Billy Graham Center Museum, Wheaton, Ill.)

There is not a word said in the statute about evolution. There is not a word said in the statute about preventing the teaching of the theory of evolution—not a word.

This caption says what follows is an act forbidding the teaching of evolution, and the Catholic could have gone home without any thought that his faith was about to be attacked. The Protestant could have gone home without any thought that his religion could be attacked. The intelligent, scholarly Christians, who by the millions in the United States find no inconsistency between evolution and religion, could have gone home without any fear that a narrow, ignorant, bigoted shrew of religion could have destroyed their religious freedom and their right to think and act and speak; and the nation and the State could have laid down peacefully to sleep that night without the slightest fear that religious hatred and bigotry were to be turned loose in a great State.

Any question about that? Anything in this caption whatever about religion, or anything about measuring science and knowledge and learning by the Book of Genesis, written when everybody thought the world was flat? Nothing.

They went to bed in peace, probably, and they woke up to find this, which has not the slightest reference to it; which does not refer to evolution in any way; which is, as claimed, a religious statute.

That is what they found and here is what it is:

"Be it enacted by the General Assembly of the State of Tennessee, that it shall be unlawful for any teacher in any of the universities, normals, and all other public schools in the State, which are supported in whole or in part by the public school funds of the state, to teach"—what, teach evolution? Oh, no.—"To teach the theory that denies the story of the divine creation of man as taught in the Bible, and to teach instead that man has descended from a lower order of animals."

That is what was foisted on the people of this State, under a caption which never meant it, and could give no hint of it; that it should be a crime in the State of Tennessee to teach any theory,—not evolution, but any theory of the origin of man, except that contained in the divine account as recorded in the Bible.

But the State of Tennessee, under an honest and fair interpretation of the Constitution, has no more right to teach the Bible as the Divine Book than that the Koran is one, or the Book of Mormon, or the Book of Confucius, or the Buddha, or the Essays of Emerson, or any one of the 10,000 books to which human souls have gone for consolation and aid in their troubles.

WILLIAM JENNINGS BRYAN: Our position is that the statute is sufficient. The statute defines exactly what the people of Tennessee decided and intended and did declare unlawful, and it needs no interpretation.

The caption speaks of the evolutionary theory, and the statute specifically states that teachers are forbidden to teach in the schools supported by taxation in this State any theory of creation of man that denies the Divine record of man's creation as found in the Bible, and that there might be no difference of opinion—there might be no ambiguity—that there might be no such confusion of thought as our learned friends attempt to inject into it. The Legislature was careful to define what is meant by the first of the statute.

It says 'to teach that man is a descendant of any lower form of life.' If that had not been there, if the first sentence had been the only sentence in the statute, then these gentlemen might come and ask to define what that meant or to explain whether the thing that was taught was contrary to the language of the statute in the first sentence. But the second sentence removes all doubt, as has been stated by my colleague.

The second sentence points out specifically what is meant, and that is the teaching that man is the descendant of any lower form of life; and if the defendant taught that, as we have proved by the textbook that he used and as we have proved by the students that went to hear him, if he taught that man is a descendant of any lower form of life, he violated the statute, and more than that, we have his own confession that he knew he was violating the statute.

After summarizing the evidence, MR. BRYAN continued:

We do not need any expert to tell us what the law means. An expert cannot be permitted to come in here and try to defeat the enforcement of a law by testifying that it isn't a bad law, and it isn't—I mean a bad doctrine—no matter how these people phrase that doctrine, no matter how they eulogize it. This is not the place to try to prove that the law ought never to have been passed. The place to prove that was at the Legislature.

If these people were so anxious to keep the State of Tennessee from disgracing itself, if they were so afraid that by this action taken by the Legislature, the State would put itself before the people of the nation as ignorant people and bigoted people—if they had half the affection for Tennessee that you would think they had as they come here to testify—they would have come at a time when their testimony would have been valuable, and not at this time to ask you to refuse to enforce a law because they did not think the law ought to have been passed.

And if the people of Tennessee were to go into a state, into New York, the one from which this impulse comes to resist this law, or go into any state . . . and try to convince the people that a law they had passed ought not to be enforced (just because the people who went there didn't think it ought to have been passed), don't you think it would be resented as an impertinence? . . .

The people of this State passed this law. The people of this State knew what they were doing when they passed the law, and they knew the dangers of the doctrine that they did not want it taught to their children. And, my friends, it isn't proper to bring experts in here to try to defeat the purpose of the people of this State by trying to show that this thing that they denounce and outlaw is a beautiful thing that everybody ought to believe in. . . .

These people want to come here with experts to make your Honor believe that the law should never have been passed, and because in their opinion it ought not to have been passed, it ought not to be enforced. It isn't a place for expert testimony. We have sufficient proof in the book. Doesn't the book state the very thing that is objected to and outlawed in this State? Who has a copy of that book?

JUDGE RAULSTON: Do you mean the Bible?

MR. BRYAN: No, sir, the biology.

A VOICE: Here it is, Hunter's Biology.

MR. BRYAN: No, not the Bible. You see, in this State they cannot teach the Bible. They can only teach things that declare it to be a lie, according to the learned counsel. These people in the State, Christian people, have tied their hands by their Constitution. They say we all believe in the Bible, for it is the overwhelming belief in the State, but we will not teach that Bible, which we believe—even to our children, through teachers that we pay with our money.

No, no, it isn't the teaching of the Bible, and we are not asking it.

The question is, Can a minority in this State come in and compel a teacher to teach that the Bible is not true and make the parents of these children pay the expenses of the teacher to tell their children what these people believe is false and dangerous?

Has it come to a time when the minority can take charge of a state like Tennessee and compel the majority to pay their teachers while they take religion out of the heart of the children of the parents who pay the teachers?

[The defendant John Scopes was found guilty by the jury and fined $100, but later the Tennessee Supreme Court overturned the conviction on a technicality.]

# Dare We Renew the Controversy?
## *The Evangelical Responsibility*

### Carl F. H. Henry (1957)

A higher spirit to quicken and to fulfill the theological fortunes of this century will require more than the displacement of modernism, more than the revision of neo-orthodoxy, more than the revival of fundamentalism. Recovery of apostolic perspective and dedication of the evangelical movement to biblical realities are foundational to this hope.

## Exalt Biblical Theology

Evangelical theology has nothing to fear, and much to gain, from aligning itself earnestly with the current plea for a return to biblical theology. To measure this moving front of creative theology sympathetically, to understand its concern and courage and to name its weaknesses without depreciating its strength will best preserve relevant theological interaction with the contemporary debate.

The evangelical movement must make its very own the passionate concern for the reality of special divine revelation, for a theology of the Word of God, for attentive hearing of the witness of the Bible, for a return to biblical theology.

## Positive Preaching

Rededication to positive and triumphant preaching is the evangelical pulpit's great need. The note of Christ's lordship over this dark century, of the victory of Christianity, has been obscured. If it be evangelical, preaching must enforce the living communication of the changeless realities of divine redemption. The minister whose pulpit does not become the life-giving center of his community fails in his major mission. Perspective on Christianity's current gains and final triumph will avoid a myopic and melancholy discipleship. The Christian pulpit must present the invisible and exalted Head of the body of Christ; linked to him this earthly colony of heaven moves to inevitable vindi-

Source: Carl F. H. Henry, "Dare We Renew the Controversy? The Evangelical Responsibility" in *Christianity Today*, 1 (July 22, 1957): 23–26, 38.

cation and glory. The perplexing problems of our perverse social orders find their hopeful solution only in this regenerative union. Out of its spiritual power must spring the incentives to creative cultural contributions.

## Social Concern

We need a new concern for the individual in the entirety of his Christian experience. He is a member of all life's communities, of faith, of the family, of labor, of the state, of culture. Christianity is by no means the social gospel of

Carl F. H. Henry (Billy Graham Center Museum, Wheaton, Ill.)

modernism, but is nonetheless vibrant with social implications as a religion of redemptive transformation. To express and continue the vitality of the gospel message, marriage and the home, labor and economics, politics and the state, culture and the arts, in fact, every sphere of life, must evidence the lordship of Christ.

Obviously, the social application of Christian theology is no easy task. For one thing, fundamentalism fails to elaborate principles and programs of Christian social action because it fails to recognize the relevance of the gospel to the sociocultural sphere. Modernism defines Christian social imperatives in secular terms and uses the Church to reorganize unregenerate humanity. Its social sensitivity gave modernism no license to neglect the imperative of personal regeneration. Evangelistic and missionary priorities, on the other hand, gave fundamentalism no license to conceal the imperative of Christian social ethics. Despite the perils, no evasion of responsibility for meaningfully relating the gospel to the pressing problems of modern life is tolerable. . . .

## Sound Doctrine and New Life

Evangelical insistence that the unity of the body of Christ requires a basic doctrinal agreement and a regenerate membership is sound. The ecumenical temperament encourages the breakdown of denominational barriers at too great a price whenever it minimizes doctrinal positions. Interdenominationalism in our century has sprung from a peculiar assortment of motives. Fundamentalists stimulated denominational desertion through discontent with theologically inclusive programs ventured by liberal leadership in the established denominations. Such was not in actuality an antithesis to denominationalism, since denominational tenets were not called into question. Indeed, most evangelicals prefer to support New Testament programs within their own denominational lines, allowing interdenominational cooperation to spring from multidenominational dedication to common evangelical priorities. The compromise of priorities in denominational circles, however, led to interdenominationalism at the expense of denominationalism and quickened the sense of an extradenominational unity based on common doctrine and faith.

The liberal interdenominational urge had a different motivation, namely, a virtual depreciation of denominationalism as unworthy sectarianism insofar as any fixed creedal positions are affirmed. This exaltation of the experiential unity of the Church through the disparagement of doctrinal soundness is the great peril of ecumenical ecclesiology today. Its constant danger is the elevation of the concern for unity above the concern for truth.

## Precision in Beliefs

Evangelical emphasis on an indispensable doctrinal basis for Church unity needs, however, to be defined with greater precision. Such concern accounts for evangelical uneasiness over the creedal vagrancy of the World Council of Churches whose nebulous emphasis is only on "Jesus Christ as Lord and Savior." Since the evangelical movement includes churches that are both creedal and noncreedal in heritage, a specific creedal unity has not been elaborated, although common theological tenets are listed. This evangelical listing of a doctrinal minimum raises difficulties for creedal churches, inasmuch as they consider no article of faith dispensable. To Reformed churchmen, evangelical formulas often appear open to objectionable development. They prefer a strict creedal fellowship, a restriction that excludes progress toward the unity of diverse evangelical elements. The evangelical failure to fully elaborate essential doctrines has resulted in fragmentation by granting priority to secondary emphases (in such matters as eschatology). Evangelical Christianity has been slow to establish study conferences in biblical doctrine, to encourage mutual growth and understanding. Ironically, study sessions on theological issues are now often associated with movements whose doctrinal depth and concern are widely questioned. The significance of Christian doctrine, its dispensability or indispensability, its definition as witness or revelation, the elements identified respectively as core and periphery—these are issues on which evangelical Christianity must be vocal.

## Fellowship of Disciples

Evangelical Christianity too frequently limits the term "evangelical" to those identified with a limited number of movements. This needlessly stresses a sense of Christian minority and discourages cooperation and communication with unenlisted evangelicals. But the tension of American church history in this turbulent century cannot be automatically superimposed upon all world evangelical communities. Ecumenical leadership in the Federal Council of Churches and its successor, the National Council of Churches, failed to reflect the viewpoint of that considerable genuinely evangelical segment of its constituency. In the World Council of Churches, leaders on the Continent also have often found themselves theologically far to the right of American spokesmen, and have found American evangelicals in the World Council disappointingly unvocal. Long before the establishment of organizations like the World Evangelical Fellowship, many European churches have approached the World Council in quest of an enlarging evangelical fellowship. Evangelical world alternatives to inclusive movements arose after most large historic denominations were already enlisted in the World Council. Does evangelical loyalty within these committed denominations necessarily depend upon public repudiation of the World Council, and upon entrance instead into minority movements quite withdrawn from the stream of influential theological discussion? Even the National Association of Evangelicals in the United States must accept the absence of Southern Baptists and Missouri Lutherans, whose antipathy for theological inclusivism keeps these denominations also outside the National Council. The question that obviously remains, of course, is whether an evangelical who prefers identification with the broader movements can justify his participation, if he knows his own spiritual heritage, except in the capacity of a New Testament witness? Must not a silent evangelical in this climate always ask himself whether the silence which once perhaps was golden, now, through a dulling of love for truth and neighbor, has become as sounding brass or tinkling cymbal[?] Indeed, must not the evangelical always and everywhere address this question to himself in whatever association he is placed?

Lack of evangelical communication across the lines of inclusive and exclusive movements is not wholly due to the exclusivists. Ecumenical enthusiasts have encouraged neither fellowship nor conversation with exclusivist evangelicals. This coldness contributed needlessly to the fundamentalist suspicion of all outside their own constituency, and did little to mitigate the incivility that some fundamentalists reserved for such individuals. The unity of the believing Church requires communication between evangelicals on a basis of mutual tolerance and respect.

## Concern for Unity

Unfortunately for the evangelical cause, the concern for the unity of the Church is now largely associated in the public mind with the inclusive vision. The failure of evangelicals to hear what the Spirit says in the New Testament to the churches has created the void now being filled by inclusivist conceptions of unity. The evangelical church needs with new earnestness to seek unity in its fragmenting environment, needs to reflect to the disunited world and to the disunited nations the sacred unity of the body of Christ.

Although evangelicals have criticized the broad basis of ecumenical merger and unity, they have achieved in their own ranks few mergers on the theological-spiritual level. Without conceding that denominationalism is evil or that health increases in proportion to the reduction of denominations, may there not be evidence that evangelical Christianity is overdenominationalized? If doctrinal agreement enhances the deepest unity of believers, may we not expect progress in the elimination of unnecessary divisions by emphasizing the spiritual unity of the Church? Evangelical Christianity, if it takes seriously its own emphasis on the unity of the body, must show visible gains in demonstrating unity in church life.

Contemporary Christianity would gain if the discussion of ecclesiastical tolerance were set in a New Testament context. The scriptural respect for individual liberty in matters of religious belief must not obscure definite requirements for identification with the body of Christian believers. The New Testament upholds specific doctrinal affirmations as indispensable to genuine Christian confession. In this biblical setting, divisiveness is depicted primarily as a theological question, not (as is usually the case today) as a matter of ecclesiastical attitude and relationship. The modernist tendency to link Christian love, tolerance and liberty with theological inclusivism is therefore discredited. Modernist pleas for religious tolerance and the caustic indictments of fundamentalist bigotry often were basically a strategic device for evading the question of doctrinal fidelity. This flaunting of tolerance, however, was discredited when inclusivist leaders suppressed or excluded evangelicals not sympathetic to the inclusive policy. The "tolerance plea" swiftly dismissed as divisive what was not clearly so in fact. Divisiveness meant disapproval of the inclusive policy, tolerance meant approval. But the New Testament does not support the view that devotion to Christian liberty and progress and to the peace and unity of Christ's Church is measured by the devaluation of doctrine in deference to an inclusive fellowship. From the biblical point of view, doctrinal belief is a Christian imperative, not a matter of indifference.

The fact must not be ignored, however, that different evangelical conceptions of the visible Church are prevalent. Although historically the Christian churches have all insisted upon a minimal theological assent for admission to membership, Reformed churches share Calvin's view that even in the Church wheat and tares—professing and believing Christians—will dwell together until their final separation in the judgment. Baptist churches have traditionally placed greater emphasis on a regenerate membership and on a pure church. Even the disciplinary procedure of the more broadly conceived Reformed churches, however, considers church members flouting or indifferent to creedal standards as guilty as grave sin. Christian churches in the past stressed both a minimal requirement for membership and a maximal indulgence for avoidance of discipline or exclusion. But modernist leaders asserted the inevitability of doctrinal change. Heresy trials became an oddity in contemporary church history, not because of an absence of heresy, but because of the lack of zeal to prosecute heretics.

We dare not own any other authority over life and deed but the living God. We dare not own any other God than the righteous and merciful God revealed in Jesus Christ. We dare not own another Christ but Jesus of Nazareth, the Word become flesh who now by the Spirit is the exalted head of the body of believers. We dare not own any other Spirit than the Spirit who has breathed out Scripture through chosen men, that doubt may vanish about what God is saying to the Church and to the world. We dare not own any other Scripture than this Book. Let other men proclaim another god, another Christ, another spirit, another book or word—that is their privilege and their peril. But if once again the spiritual life of our world is to rise above the rubble of paganism into which it is now decaying, it will be only through the dynamic of revelation, regeneration, and redemption, through the sacred message which once brought hope. We have a task to do, a task of apostolic awesomeness; let us rise to the doing. The hour for rescue is distressingly late.

# Challenges of the New Millennium

It is almost impossible to cover all the changes, shifts, and developments that have occurred within American religion in the late twentieth century. Since World War II they have included "the death of God," "the great moral revolution," "the new morality," "the age of Aquarius," radicalism in every area, *Roe v. Wade* and abortion on demand, liberation theology, the "peace-of-mind" cultists, "feminism," the political rise of the "Christian right," the "Moral Majority," the decline of mainstream Protestant denominations and the growth of conservative churches, "the knowledge explosion," TV's "wasteland" and the "dumbing down" of America, enormous greed and self-centeredness of the 1980s, odious scandals involving venal television "evangelists," the AIDS epidemic . . .

These only sample the developments that made an impact on religion and changed its outward forms. Fundamental shifts in American religious and moral values in the 1960s accompanied President John F. Kennedy's New Frontier and President Lyndon B. Johnson's Great Society. Old foundations of national self-confidence, moral traditionalism, patriotic idealism, and even historic Judaeo-Christian theism, were awash in skepticism and the tides of change. Presuppositions that had been bedrock for thousands of years were suddenly open to doubt. Conservatives in religion held to the old convictions as best they could, but changes in attitude and declining zeal were apparent in this arena as well.

## End of an era?

Sydney Ahlstrom wrote that the period of the 1960s through the 1980s ended "a distinct quadricentennium—a unified four-hundred-year period—

287

in the Anglo-American experience. . . . Histories of the rise of organized Puritanism begin their accounts with the decisive first decade in the reign of Queen Elizabeth I; and the terms 'post-Puritan' and 'post-Protestant' are first popularly applied to America in the 1960s."[1] Without question there have been radical turns in religion and morals, stimulated by U.S. Supreme Court decisions that dealt decisively with long-established Protestant practices in the schools and nation. It is easy to make simplistic judgments about these matters; some have even spoken of the late 1900s as "post-Christian." But simplistic answers will not do; religion and public morals are multi-faceted and multi-layered matters, yielding to no easy analyses. As when Samuel Clemens, better known by his pseudonym "Mark Twain,"was surprised to find his own obituary appearing in a newspaper, grand epitaphs of the late twentieth century as *post-Christian* have seemed "highly exaggerated" amid concurrent signs of renewed vitality.

All sides hurled demands at the Christian church. In contrast, such previous times as the nineteenth century, were golden ages in that religious issues were far simpler and competition for the hearts of people far less intense. The late 1900s definitely was no golden age for the U.S. church. Secular humanism, materialism, and cultic teachings confronted the Christian standard. Troubling problems included increasing secularization that blurred the boundary separating Christian from worldly standards, government intrusion into the churches, and sanctity of human life issues (especially the rights of the unborn). Christians also had to frame a response to issues raised by feminism, homosexuality, and the influences of the arts and the entertainment industry, especially on youth.

Perhaps discouraging things were happening, but U.S. Christians could also identify evidence of the Holy Spirit's work elsewhere in the world. A number of countries in the former Soviet bloc opened to the gospel as never before. Missionaries, print ministries, and Christian radio reached unprecedented numbers of people there. In Latin America evangelical Christianity grew at a phenomenal rate. African Christianity continued to advance. World evangelism remained a top priority, with opportunities opening on every hand.

Thus, the Christian had reason for a conviction that events were not moving on the horizontal plane alone. There is a vertical, usually unseen, dimension. An excellent modern example of the unseen and unknown work of God was in China. When the Christian church was forced underground by the Communist takeover in 1949 and missionaries had to leave the country, restrictions on Chinese Christians were severe. All through the 1950s, 1960s, and 1970s no word was heard from behind the "Bamboo Curtain," and the church of China was feared to have expired, its people martyred. But the reopening of China to Western visitors in 1977 showed large gains in the church, despite all the repression. The church has adapted to new cultures and trends for two thousand years, and there is no reason why it should not continue to show similar ability to adapt and grow in the future.

## Evangelization, organization, and politicization

In America, enormous diversity was apparent everywhere among its people. Religion takes a variety of forms. The Christian faith itself displays great variety. Generalizations are difficult to make, and summary statements must be offered with caution. But many expectantly looked for another American awakening. If communist governments could collapse almost overnight, with the U.S. Central Intelligence Agency having little suspicion of it in advance, what other momentous events might come at the hand of a sovereign Lord.

Three selections have been chosen to illustrate some trends of this complex time. The first is by Billy Graham (1918– ), who spoke to more people face to face—100 million—than any other individual in history, and who has been seen and heard by countless millions more on television and radio. Graham has written a number of books; 15.5 million copies of which have been distributed in 38 languages around the world. From 1955 opinion surveys by the George Gallup organization listed Graham on the "Ten Most Admired Men in the World" at least thirty-five times, more than any other individual.

Graham's career as an evangelist came to national attention in late September 1949 when he conducted three weeks of meetings in Los Angeles. A huge tent holding 6000 was erected on a downtown lot, and the meetings began well, with good crowds. When the meetings were due to close, Southern California's best-known radio personality, Stuart Hamblen, announced over his radio show that he had been attending the meetings and "Tonight at the end of Billy's invitation, I'm going to hit the sawdust trail." The conversion of two other well-known figures gave Graham massive media attention, and the meetings were extended. The aging William Randolph Hearst sent a two-word telegram to the editors of all Hearst papers: "Puff Graham," and the thirty-one-year-old evangelist was catapulted to international notice.

Graham again came to world attention in 1954 with his Greater London Crusade. At the beginning opposition from the British media was vicious. Even before Graham arrived in Britain the papers were printing wild, fictitious stories about him. After several weeks, the meetings were going well. Harringay Arena, a 12,000-seat sports complex, was filled for as many as two or three services each evening for six nights a week. The press, still attempting to relate

Graham to "hysterical snake-handling fanatics," were baffled by the dignity and genuineness of the meetings and became increasingly aware that they had made fools of themselves. The tone of their reporting began to change, and opposition melted. For twelve weeks Graham filled Harringay, and on the last evening 120,000 overflowed Wembley Stadium to see the archbishop of Canterbury standing at the American evangelist's side as Graham gave the invitation. Altogether nearly 2 million heard him preach, and 40,000 commitments to Christ were recorded.

These breakthroughs made Graham increasingly welcome around the world. He conducted almost 400 major crusades, reaching every continent. One of the most spectacular in numbers was in Seoul, Korea in 1973, where 300,000 gathered for the first service. In 1974 Graham called together 4000 Christian leaders from 150 nations to the Lausanne Congress on World Evangelism. He then began a world ministry on an unprecedented scale. Twenty years after the first London crusade, the Lausanne Congress showed Graham to be a world Christian statesman, welcomed by national leaders everywhere. Of his numerous books, a section from *Approaching Hoofbeats,* written in 1983, is given (selection 45), since it can represent as well the increasing interest in published books on eschatology in the last quarter of the century.

In selection 46 Les Parrott, III, assistant professor of clinical psychology at Seattle Pacific University, and Robin D. Perrin, assistant professor of sociology at Seattle Pacific, examine the phenomena of megachurches with huge Sunday attendances, the decline of the old-line Protestant denominations, and the vitality of a number of fellowships which promised to develop into new denominations should their exponential growth continue. An outstanding example, Calvary Chapel, began in 1965 and by the early 1990s had grown to 350 Calvary Chapel groups, in every state and around the globe. Taking an entirely different approach to worship and aimed directly at well-off, laid-back, bored "baby-boomers," contemporary marketing strategies characterized this movement. But what are the problems of such megachurches? With their charismatic leaders aging, Parrot and Perrin asked, would these anti-institutional, back-to-the-Bible fellowships eventually institutionalize as they became ever larger? Would that quench their fervor? If not, how would they avoid it? And would they be able to replace their current leaders with equally visionary younger leaders when that time came?

In selection 47 Augustus Cerillo, Jr., professor of history at California State University, Long Beach, and Murray W. Dempster, professor of social ethics at Southern California College in Costa Mesa, present a wide-ranging treatment of the "new religious right" and its astonishing political growth during the 1970s and 1980s. This survey touches on a number of important issues connected with the political awareness of millions of American Protestants.

## Select Bibliography

Ball, William Bentley, ed. In *Search of a National Morality: A Manifesto for Evangelicals and Catholics*. Grand Rapids, Baker, 1992.

Belli, Humberto, and Ronald Nash. *Beyond Liberation Theology*. Grand Rapids: Baker, 1992.

Chichester, David. *Patterns of Power: Religion and Politics in American Culture*. Englewood Cliffs, N.J.: Prentice Hall, 1988.

Diuk, Nadia, and Adrian Karatnycky. *New Nations Rising: The Fall of the Soviets and the Challenge of Independence*. New York: Wiley and Sons, 1993.

Ellul, Jacques. *The Presence of the Kingdom*, exp. ed. Colorado Springs: Helmers and Howard, 1989.

_____. *The Technological Society*. New York: Random House, 1967.

Kantzer, Kenneth S., and Carl F. H. Henry. *Evangelical Affirmations*. Grand Rapids: Zondervan, 1989.

Marty, Martin E. *Religion and Republic: The American Circumstance*. Boston: Beacon, 1989.

Nash, Ronald. *Freedom, Justice, and the State*. Lanham, Md.: University Press of America. 1980.

Perkins, John M. *Let Justice Roll Down*. Ventura, Calif.: Regal, 1976.

Wald, Kenneth D. *Religion and Politics in the United States*. New York: St. Martin's, 1987.

# Approaching Hoofbeats

### *Billy Graham (1983)*

There is definitely a "mystery of iniquity" attached to the four horses in chapter 6 of Revelation. We may not fully understand everything that will happen when they come upon the earth. But Revelation does not end with chapter 6! For John points us in chapter 19 to another horse and rider—One who rides to bring the kingdom of God in all its fullness to earth. Like the first horse in chapter 6, this horse is white. But there the resemblance ends, for the rider of this horse is Jesus Christ Himself, coming in glory and power to the earth.

Let us see what the aged apostle is trying to tell us in the account of the rider on the white horse in Revelation 19. Chapters 7 to 18 deal with that catastrophic saga of history, perhaps just ahead, about which Jesus insisted we are to make no mistake, when "there will be great distress, unequaled from the beginning of the world until now—and never to be equaled again. If those days had not been cut short, no one would survive, but for the sake of the elect those days will be shortened" (Matthew 24:21, 22). It will be a time of nuclear conflagrations, biological holocausts and chemical apocalypses rolling over the earth, bringing man to the edge of the precipice. History will "bottom out" in the battle of Armageddon. We already see its shadow creeping over the earth.

Will man exterminate himself? He *almost* will, as Jesus stated. But just before man does so, Christ will come back! The demonized leaders "of the whole world" will have mobilized both as antagonists and protagonists of that coming world anti-God system—probably headed by the Antichrist. They'll be "gathered," we're told, "together to the place that in Hebrew is called Armageddon" (Revelation 16:16).

Franklin D. Roosevelt spoke of "the war to end all wars," and now Ellen Goodman, the columnist, speaks of a possible ominous war ahead, "to end all life." *It won't happen.* God has other plans for the human race! Life is not going to be brought to a catastrophic end. God's intervention will see to that.

Everywhere I go, people ask, "Are you an optimist or a pessimist?" My reply is that I'm an unswerving optimist. In the words of Robert Browning, "The

Source: Billy Graham, *Approaching Hoofbeats: The Four Horsemen of the Apocalypse* (Waco, Tex.: Word, 1983), 221–25.

best is yet to be." I believe that, too, and in the final pages of this book I want to explain why.

It is estimated that forty wars are going on somewhere in the world at any given time. Any one of them could be the beginning of "the beginning of the end!"

So we have to ask: Can paradise be restored? Is there light at the end of the tunnel? As the late Sir Winston Churchill asked a young American clergyman thirty years ago, "Young man, can you give me any hope?"

## Back to the Bible

For the answer to Churchill's question, I take you into the future by going back to the Bible.

In Revelation 19:10–13 the ancient apostle writes, "'The testimony of Jesus is the spirit of prophecy.' I saw heaven standing open and there before me was a white horse, whose rider is called Faithful and True. With justice he judges and makes war. His eyes are like blazing fire, and on his

Billy Graham
(Billy Graham Evangelistic Association)

head are many crowns. He has a name written on him that no one but he himself knows. He is dressed in a robe dipped in blood, and his name is the Word of God."

So the four horses of the Apocalypse of Revelation 6 have gone on before. Other judgments have fallen. Now God is about to make His final move. The identity of the rider on the white horse in Revelation 19 is the Lord Jesus Christ, Israel's Messiah, head of the church, the King of Kings and Lord of Lords. The white horse of deception in Revelation 6 darkens into a dirty gray in comparison to the impeccable, immaculate white horse here in Revelation 19. Whereas the red horse in Revelation 6 inflicts war to kill and defoliate, this white horse, with the mounted "King of Kings" draped in a robe dipped in blood, declares war on the killers—to establish His kingdom of salvation and peace. Whereas the black horse of Revelation 6 carries famine and disease, the white horse of Revelation 19 brings healing and the Bread of life. And whereas the pale horse of Revelation 6 brings death and hell, the white horse of chapter 19 brings life and heaven to all who place their faith in Him.

When will the Man on the white horse, as outlined in Revelation 19, appear? The clear teaching of the Word of God is that He will come when man has sunk to his lowest and most perilous point in all history—the time when the four horses of the Apocalypse, with their mounted riders, have run their course and pushed man to the very edge of the precipice. There is an eerie feeling throughout society today that concurs with the late Dr. Albert Schweitzer, who lamented, "Man has lost the capacity to foresee and to forestall. He will end by destroying the earth." Left to himself, that is precisely what man would do. Barbra Streisand put her finger on the problem; she is reported in *Esquire* as having said, "I do believe the world is coming to an end. I just feel that science, technology and the mind have surpassed the soul—the heart. There is no balance in terms of feeling and love for fellowman."

Who is better qualified to make a statement on this theme than the dean of behaviorists, Harvard's B. F. Skinner? At 78, Skinner shocked the American Psychological Convention (1982) by asking in understandable anger and anguish, "Why are we not acting to save the world? Is there to be much more history at all?" Asked afterward, "Has the observer of social conditioning lost his optimism?" his reply was, "I have. . . . When I wrote *Beyond Freedom and Dignity,* I was optimistic about the future. A decade ago there was hope, but today the world is fatally ill. . . . It is a very depressing way to end one's life. . . . The argument that we have always solved our problems in the past and shall, therefore, solve this one is like reassuring a dying man by pointing out that he has always recovered from his illness" *(Philadelphia Inquirer,* 25 September 1982).

## Of War and Peace

In his article on "Psychology and Armageddon" in *Psychology Today* (May 1982) Harvard Professor of Psychiatry Dr. Robert Coles describes a prevailing feeling worldwide that mankind is heading for its final Armageddon. The gamble that man will have taken will be the worst in all history. The Antichrist or system will be a monstrous impostor, the incarnation of iniquity. And all people the world over will think and say, "We've been had!" As I wrote earlier in this book, there is coming a time in the future—whether near or far I do not know (since Jesus warned us not to speculate on dates), when a counterfeit world system or ruler will establish a false utopia for an extremely short time. The economic and political problems of the world will seem to be solved. But after a brief rule the whole thing will come apart. During this demonic reign tensions will mount, and once again the world will begin to explode with a ferocity involving conflict on an unparalleled scale. Even the grip of the world leaders will be unable to prevent it. This massive upheaval will be the world's last war—the battle of Armageddon.

According to secular and scientific writers, there is an inevitability to man's date with Armageddon. "Everybody who's anybody believes that global war is imminent," reckons Phil Surguy of *Today*.

## Arming for Armageddon

If I were not a believer in Christ, I might at this point in history succumb to total pessimism. On 10 August 1982 Ellen Goodman wrote in her column that with "Armageddon perhaps around the corner, what are intelligent people to do? Wrap ourselves in mourning sheets and wait for the end?" Are we to stare up at that intimidating nuclear sword of Damocles that "has hung over us like some apocalypse without the promise of redemption?"

Emphatically not! Jesus urged that when universal holocaust begins "to take place, stand up and lift up your heads, because your redemption is drawing near" (Luke 21:28). Rather than pulling mourning sheets around us, we are to look for redemption in Christ. We are also to work as if these events are far in the future. Jesus promised a blessing on those who would be found working when their Lord returns.

I will not here deal with the who, what, why, how or when of Armageddon. But I know from a vast number of scriptures that Armageddon will be interrupted by the return of Jesus Christ on the white horse leading the armies of heaven, as clearly prophesied in many Bible passages. In no place is it more definitively or dramatically described than in Revelation 19. When John foresaw "heaven standing open and there before me was a white horse, whose rider is called Faithful and True," he went on to describe the rider as "the Word of God" followed by the armies of heaven "riding on white horses and dressed in fine linen, white and clean." Turning his focus back on the coming Messiah, John saw that "out of his mouth comes a sharp sword with which to strike down the nations. 'He will rule them with an iron scepter'" (Revelation 19:11–15). And in case anyone gets confused as to His identity or authority, John makes it unmistakably plain, "On his robe and on his thigh he has this name written: KING OF KINGS AND LORD OF LORDS" (Revelation 19:16).

# The New Denominations

## *Les Parrott III and Robin Perrin (1991)*

No one who looks seriously at the Protestant scene in America can ignore the dynamics of the last 30 years.

Before the sixties there was little reason to question the vitality of American religion. From the beginning, most of this country's denominations have grown faster than the population. Moreover, the years between 1950 and 1964 saw a church-membership surge that verged on "religious revival," giving the lie to the secular prophets who believed that Christianity would "wither in the bright sun of modern culture."

However, in the midsixties, an unexpected and massive change began. Many of this country's culture-affirming "mainline" denominations began to experience membership *declines* for the first time. The declines were sudden, dramatic, and persistent. Between 1965 and 1985, for example, the Presbyterian Church declined 24 percent, the Episcopal Church (U.S.A.) declined 20 percent, the United Methodist Church declined 16 percent, and the Disciples of Christ declined 42 percent.

Meanwhile, conservative churches and religious movements grew. Between 1965 and 1985, the Assemblies of God more than tripled, the Church of God (Cleveland, Tenn.) increased nearly two-and-a-half times, Mormons and Jehovah's Witnesses more than doubled, and the Seventh-day Adventists grew by almost 80 percent. Conservative denominations closer to the mainstream also grew, generally at a slower rate: the Church of the Nazarene grew by 50 percent and the Southern Baptist Convention, America's largest Protestant denomination, grew by 34 percent.

However, to focus on established denominations may be to miss key evidence of religious vitality. The spiritual thrust of experience-centered, Bible-toting believers has generated a spate of new sects and independent churches. Many of these new churches sprouted from the Jesus movements of the seventies. These "Jesus Freak" groups, as they were known among themselves, attempted to substitute a variety of religious experiences for the heightened psychic awareness sought earlier through psychedelic drugs. While the seventies

Source: "The New Denominations," *Christianity Today* (March 11, 1991): 29–33.

spelled the end of the counterculture, many of the new evangelical and charismatic movements that had their beginnings in the Jesus movement continued to grow through the eighties. Some of these groups are today's "megachurches."

Church-growth scholars, parish pastors, and enlightened lay leaders are wondering why these movements have grown. And some futurists are eagerly asking if they will be the denominations of the next century. . . .

One of the strongest movements began amid the bean fields of Santa Ana, California. In 1965, Chuck Smith, a pastor with 17 years of ministry in Foursquare Gospel churches, took over a fundamentalist church whose membership had dwindled to 25. "One year later we had 100, two years later we had 200 . . . today we have over 10,000 tithing families in three Sunday services and meetings every night of the week," says Smith. . . .

Today Calvary Chapel includes a 21-acre campus with a religious bookstore, a Christian school with 1,500 pupils, a fellowship hall, and multiple, hopelessly overcrowded, parking lots.

Beyond the borders of this booming church is a "fellowship" of over 350 other Calvary Chapels. Smith says affiliate churches are in every state and "around the globe"—in Australia, Mexico, Hong Kong, Africa, and even the People's Republic of China where it has delivered 1 million Chinese Bibles to the underground house churches. . . .

In 1973, the seeds of another movement were planted in the fertile soil of religious openness in Southern California. This church began as a Bible-study group led by Kenn Gullikson, a well-known "Jesus movement" pastor. This study group in the San Fernando Valley took root, grew steadily, and became the original Vineyard Christian Fellowship. . . .

The second phase of Vineyard development began with a group of members from a Friends church led by an ex-music arranger for the Righteous Brothers, John Wimber. These people, "in openness to the Holy Spirit," reported a trickle of miraculous healings that eventually became a flood. . . .

In 1983, Wimber's congregation moved to its current Anaheim location, where it has grown to over 5,000 members. One visit to the nondescript warehouse-style church causes outsiders to ask what is so special. The answer: John Wimber's leadership. Under his lofty vision and aggressive plan to grow 10,000 new Vineyards, the movement is experiencing the expansion pains of an incipient denomination. Approximately 500 men have been ordained. There are more than 300 churches in the U.S. and Canada. . . .

Another movement that shows signs of becoming a denomination is Larry Lea's Church on the Rock, begun in a Dallas suburb in 1980 with 13 members. A decade later, the church's membership is 8,000. And there now are at least

70 other affiliated churches across the United States under the umbrella association known as Church on the Rock North America (CRNA). The ministry averages about six new churches a year, and it has plans to establish congregations in other countries. . . .

Where do the members of these "new denominations" come from? Given the growth of conservative churches and the decline of liberal denominations, the natural assumption is that evangelical churches have grown at the expense of the mainline. One might also assume that evangelical churches do better at attracting converts. . . .

Why would a good Presbyterian baby boomer attend a Vineyard Fellowship or a Calvary Chapel? What makes these movements so attractive?

One of the most significant explanations comes from Dean Kelley, a Methodist minister, in his book *Why the Conservative Churches Are Growing*. Kelley explains the growth of evangelical churches by blaming the mainline churches for not being more "serious." He argues that conservative movements are growing because they make serious demands on their members. This attracts people who want explanations to life's "ultimate questions"—explanations that are validated by commitment.

In comparison, Kelley argues, many mainline churches are theologically unsure of themselves. They are seemingly unconcerned with members' moral conduct, generally do not proselytize, expect little commitment from their members, and do not encourage emotional expression. As a result, they are less effective in providing "ultimate answers."

Another explanation for the growth of these movements is found in the work of sociologist H. Richard Niebuhr. He made a distinction between "church" and "sect" to explain the development of the various Protestant denominations in this country. Niebuhr argued that every movement is in the middle of a secularization process. As this process takes place, there are always a few members who feel the movement has drifted from the ideal. These idealists eventually break off from the parent church in an attempt to recreate the original vision. In this "charismatic" stage of the "sect" there is typically a high level of commitment, more involvement of lay members, reliance on spiritual gifts, complete reliance on God and a desire to spread the Good News, a spirit of regeneration, exclusiveness of beliefs and actions, reliance on charismatic leadership, and conservative interpretation of religious doctrine.

As a new movement grows and prospers, it will eventually be transformed and "secularized." There will be greater reliance on tradition and on the church as an institution. The charismatic founder will pass on and, with him, the spirit of regeneration—upon which the movement was founded. Structure will replace spontaneity. This transformation will produce a new category of disgruntled visionaries who will once again start the process.

Institutional secularization, according to sociologists Rodney Stark and William Simms Bainbridge (authors of *The Future of Religion)*, "has never been the end of a [religious movement], but merely a shift in fortunes among [denominations] as faiths that have become too worldly are supplanted by more vigorous and less worldly [denominations]."

Examined in his light, the "new denominations" can be seen as a natural and inevitable outgrowth of the more secularized mainline denominations. The new denominations—like wildflowers in a formal garden—are somewhat antagonistic to the established denominations.

This vibrant and exciting alternative to "the way things have always been" is attractive to Christians who have become disillusioned with the "churchiness" of the established denominations. At Calvary Chapel, one former Catholic says, "Religion before this was cold and sterile. Now [church] is alive and I go . . . because I want to, not because I have to."

More specific explanations that account for the new denominations are difficult because of the variety among these congregations. Although they are different from one another, one significant growth factor is their marketing strategy. Planned or unplanned, each of these church groups have developed an appeal to a specific segment of the public. The Vineyard and Calvary Chapel, for example, are well known for the "culture current" style—casual dress, laid-back attitude, new or revised forms of worship, and contemporary music. This style is especially targeted toward the baby-boom generation. The membership of these movements reflects the current attitudes of our culture. The mean age of the respondents from Perrin's study, for example, is 36. This is 10 to 15 years younger than the membership of most other denominations.

Leadership is another recognized explanation for the growth of these movements. Sectarian movements are, by definition, highly dependent on a charismatic leader. The extraordinary talents and vision of these men can explain, in part, why these movements are growing. Whatever their specific talents and characteristics, these men have drawn followers to their new denominations in dramatic numbers.

As these movements enter the next century, one challenge is inevitable. It will come when they are faced with the prospect of replacing their founders. Like all first-generation movements highly dependent on a charismatic leader, the new denominations are in a precarious position. On the one hand, their followers have been drawn by the anti-institutional, back-to-the-Bible fervor of their charismatic founders. On the other hand, the absence of institutionalization and structure leaves them with little to hold these movements together when the charismatic founders are gone.

Charismatic leadership is often more brilliant than stable. According to renowned German sociologist Max Weber, the individualistic nature of charismatic authority must be regulated if a community is to develop permanence. The need for stability leads to the modulation or, as Weber put it, the "routinization" of charisma.

If these infant denominations are to live beyond their founders, they will have to tend toward the object of their original rebellion, the institutionalized church. These movements abhor this idea. Each group shuns the thought of being denominational, choosing, instead, to portray themselves as loosely organized groups with more emphasis on fellowship than structure.

"Denominations create hierarchies and power games," explains Chuck Smith, now 63, "and as long as I am around we will remain an informal fellowship." The Church on the Rock enjoys "the benefits of a denomination without the hassles," say its leaders. The Vineyard strives for "only implicit and minimal structure," says Gullikson, and the "entanglements of a denomination would only trip us up."

The catch is that the empowering effects found in organizational structures—essential to the future success of any organism—are also likely to bring a decline in the emotional and spiritual fervor that is currently fueling these movements. The longer they burn, the smaller their flame.

---

## Selection 47

---

# Salt and Light

### *Augustus Cerillo, Jr., and Murray Dempster (1989)*

The year 1976 proved to be a significant one as the nation celebrated the two-hundredth anniversary of its birth. "The bicentennial observance," as Richard Pierard noted, "gave the nation an opportunity to relax and to recover from the twin traumas of Watergate and Vietnam." Focusing on what was good about America, the year-long patriotic celebration restored some measure of cohesion among the American people.

Source: Augustus Cerillo, Jr., and Murray W. Dempster, *Salt and Light: Evangelical Political Thought in Modern America* (Grand Rapids: Baker, 1989), 107–12.

The year was also designated by *Newsweek* as "the year of the evangelicals." The bicentennial year ushered in an era of "born-again" politics that spanned from the beginning of Jimmy Carter's presidency in 1976 to the end of Ronald Reagan's administration in 1988. Democratic presidential candidate Jimmy Carter, in the election of 1976, unashamedly identified himself as a "born-again" Christian, and made the political significance of his evangelical faith a recurrent theme of his campaign. Carter's Republican opponent, President Gerald R. Ford, also claimed a "born-again" experience. Such "born-again" rhetoric sent the nation's secular establishment, especially the media elites, scurrying to decipher the language and thought forms of an evangelical sub-culture that most had assumed was a relic of the nation's religious past.

What can we learn about evangelical political involvement from the bicentennial election? First, "born-again" politics did not occur in a historical vacuum. Both Ford and Carter rode the crest of the evangelical political resurgence that began after World War II even as they contributed to accelerating its impact on American public life. Second, the election revealed that political partisanship and ideology took priority over religious loyalty in evangelical voting psychology. Although Carter's Southern Baptist style of religious piety clearly was closer to the religious identity of evangelicals than was Ford's high church tradition, evangelical voters, according to the best estimates, preferred Ford over Carter 60 to 40 percent. Third, evangelical voters for the first time in modern presidential politics received the media-imposed consecration as a special interest group to be watched in the future. Ironically, at the very time evangelicals were gaining national recognition, in reality, they were in political and theological disarray.

During the years Carter occupied the White House, evangelical political conservatives, liberals, and radicals continued to divide over social and political issues such as women's rights, the moral legitimacy of nuclear weapons, the achievement of social, economic, and racial justice through government programs, the politics of abortion, and the civil rights of homosexuals. Attempts to resolve these differences through working out the sociopolitical implications of commonly held theological convictions only seemed to deepen the disarray by playing into another set of evangelical battles over biblical inerrancy, the practical implementation of the kingdom of God, and the political nature and moral mission of the church. Differences over these and other issues, the inability to forge a comprehensive evangelical political philosophy, and a widening and bitter rift between black and white evangelicals caused the collapse of Evangelicals for Social Action (ESA) as a cohesive integrative structure to coordinate social action across the entire evangelical political spectrum. After 1976 the ESA, reconstituted as a membership organization with a national coordinating office and regional affiliations, increasingly pursued a more radical agenda.

This organizational and philosophical shift in ESA was accompanied by a proliferation of concrete experiments in evangelical social action ministries. John Perkins' Voice of Calvary stimulated black community development through economic cooperatives while the radical Sojourners' house-church combined simple living in the slums of Washington, D.C., with legal advocacy for the capital's urban poor. Radicals also organized Liberty to the Captives to fight torture and oppression and Dunamis to enlist a community of "pastor-prophets" to provide both prayerful support and a prophetic word to governmental leaders.

Long-standing World Vision International supplemented its traditional social welfare ministry with programs of indigenous economic development and was joined by several newly created evangelical organizations to relieve world hunger. A significant number of evangelicals participated in Bread for the World, an ecumenical Christian citizens' movement seeking to influence U.S. government policies that directly affect the poor. The Association for Public Justice, another Christian citizens' organization, was formed to integrate practical social action and public policy analysis with a comprehensive, biblically based political philosophy. Evolving directly out of ESA, the Evangelical Women's Caucus championed the feminist cause for equal rights for women in church and society. Convicted Watergate felon Charles Colson's Prison Fellowship sought to evangelize prison inmates and worked for penal reform.

Such worthy social action projects rallied support from a variety of politically active evangelicals. But the very growth of these practical ministries further fragmented the evangelical political witness around special interest groups and prevented a renewed effort at political coalition making.

Evangelical political conservatives, liberals, and radicals, as most of the American public, were caught off guard during the late 1970s and early 1980s by the sudden public emergence and apparent political clout of the ultraconservative fundamentalist new right. Fundamentalists shared with other evangelicals a common doctrinal orthodoxy, but since the mid-1940s had remained militantly separatistic in their ecclesiastical development and in their relationship to modern culture. Comprised largely of independent Baptist and Presbyterian congregations, these fundamentalists stressed personal evangelism, Bible study, and withdrawal from political and cultural involvement. Nevertheless, during the conservative 1950s, some politicized fundamentalist leaders—Carl

McIntire, Billy James Hargis, Stuart McBirnie, and others—articulated a theologically based attack on liberalism, communism, and Roman Catholicism. These "radical right" crusaders originally appealed to a large number of politically conservative evangelicals, but by the mid-1960s were already in decline.

The links between the fundamentalist new right of the 1970s and 1980s and the old religious right of the 1950s and 1960s are unclear. While the fundamentalist new right did share with the old radical right a religious and social history of cultural marginalization, a common constituency, and a good deal of political rhetoric and ideology, the two movements probably were not part of a continuous social process. The fundamentalist new right can best be viewed as a distinctive response to the social and political upheaval of the late 1960s and early 1970s.

Fundamentalists and their politically conservative evangelical allies responded to the forces of secularization sweeping the country during this period by formulating a conservative social agenda and by organizing a counterattack. They promoted American patriotism, the traditional family, prayer, and Bible reading in the public schools, capital punishment, and Israel's right to exist. They attacked the 1973 *Roe v. Wade* Supreme Court decision that legalized abortion, the feminist push for the Equal Rights Amendment, the public emergence of the gay rights movement, the pornography explosion, and the use of quotas to achieve racial justice. Fundamentalist leaders viewed this agenda as the only way to stop what they perceived as the new anti-Christian religion of "secular humanism" in American public life. More so than their politically active brothers and sisters from the evangelical tradition, these politicized fundamentalists also participated directly in the electoral process. Through effective use of television and grass roots recruitment they mobilized millions of ordinary churchgoers behind their favorite candidates and issues. Recipients of massive secular media exposure, they forged alliances with other Christian, religious, and secular groups in support of conservative political causes.

The three most significant fundamentalist new right political organizations were created in 1979. Superchurch Baptist pastor and television preacher Jerry Falwell, at the urging of Richard Viguerie, Paul Weyrich, and other secular new right activists seeking to broaden the conservative movement in America, organized the Moral Majority to mobilize fundamentalists and evangelicals behind conservative issues and political candidates. Moral Majority was joined by Robert Grant's California-based Christian Voice, which gained notoriety by evaluating candidates according to a "biblical scoreboard," and Ed McAteer's Religious Roundtable, which sponsored workshops to teach pastors how to politicize their congregations. These three political action groups, along with influential television ministries led by Pat Robertson, James Robison, Charles Stanley, and other morally conservative Jewish, Catholic, and Mormon organizations comprised what was called the new religious right, a loosely knit political coalition with a formidable grass roots base.

The power of this new religious right became evident in the election of 1980. Dissatisfied with Democratic President Jimmy Carter's foreign and domestic policies and feeling betrayed by the president's lack of enthusiasm for the conservative social agenda, the new religious right, together with its secular allies, rallied behind the presidential candidacy of Ronald Reagan, former movie actor and California Republican governor. Much to the chagrin of evangelical political radicals, liberals, and some conservatives, the new religious right was able to co-opt the long-standing evangelical political resurgence on behalf of its conservative social and political crusade by monopolizing the secular mass media's coverage of evangelical political involvement. Through its mass-mailing techniques, biblical scorecards, television programs, and grass roots politicking, the new religious right effectively shaped the public mind to equate their positions on political and social issues with the evangelical Christian view. Moreover, in contrast to the radical, liberal, and conservative voices of the evangelical political renaissance, the fundamentalist-led new religious right brought its message and organizing expertise down to the level of the pew in countless fundamentalist, evangelical, pentecostal, and other theologically conservative churches.

Although political analysts have downplayed the importance of the new religious right's contribution to Reagan's victory in 1980, the new religious right believed its organization of the evangelical and conservative religious vote for the president had been decisive in his election. Their postelection euphoria about morally reconstructing the Republic, however, in time gave way to a more sober and realistic recognition that their agenda would take longer to achieve than four years of Reagan rule. Undaunted by the president's inability or unwillingness to make the new religious right's agenda his top priority during his first term, fundamentalist new right leaders continued to build their organizational network, champion conservative causes, and educate their grass roots followers. Buttressed by the newly created American Coalition for Traditional Values under Tim La Haye's leadership, which conducted voter registration drives in local churches, and by Assemblies of God television evangelist Jimmy Swaggart's continuous, hard-hitting attacks against secular humanism, the new religious right mounted an all-out campaign on behalf of President Reagan's re-election bid in 1984. The president's landslide victory over Walter Mondale was hailed by the new religious right as a God-given opportunity to perpetuate the Reagan conservative counterrevolution and to reestablish Judeo-Christian moral values as the foundation of American national life.

Ronald Reagan's conservative philosophy meshed well with the fundamentalist new right's theological and political convictions. Firmly convinced that godly founding fathers had built America's institutions and culture upon biblical values, and that over the past several decades ungodly humanists had steered the nation away from its scriptural foundations, fundamentalist new rightists tended to see themselves as soldiers of the Lord girding up for a last great battle to save American Christian civilization. Combining their interpretation of America's Christian history with their conviction that the Bible contained a divine blueprint of political, economic, and social principles, fundamentalist leaders called on the general public to repent, experience a spiritual awakening, and establish biblical righteousness in the land.

Convinced that the Scriptures supported an individualistic view of society, fundamentalist new right leaders unreservedly advocated a free enterprise economy unhampered by federal bureaucratic regulations. To the delight of the Reagan administration, they also advocated the elimination of most welfare programs, believing that an expanding private economy created sufficient job opportunities for those willing to work. Again in step with the administration in Washington, fundamentalist new rightists viewed a militarily superior United States as the last and best hope for the defeat of communist aggression, the survival of Israel, and the triumph of democracy and capitalism in the world.

# Endnotes

## Introduction

1. Alexis de Tocqueville, *Democracy in America*, trans. H. Reeve (London: Oxford University Press, 1946), 232–37, passim.

2. Ibid., 238.

3. Ibid., 376.

## Chapter One *Hopes for the New World*

1. Jonathan Edwards, *Some Thoughts Concerning the Present Revival of Religion in New-England* (Boston: T. Green, 1742), 96.

2. William Bradford, *Of Plimoth Plantation* (Boston: Wright and Potter), 110.

3. Ibid, 94–95.

## Chapter Two *Problems within American Puritanism*

1. The basic work on New England Covenant theory is Perry Miller, *The New England Mind, The Seventeenth Century* (1939; repr., Cambridge, Mass.: Harvard University Press, 1985), 365–491. See also Edmund S. Morgan, *Visible Saints: The History of a Puritan Idea* (Ithaca, N.Y.: Cornell University Press, 1965).

2. Miller, *New England Mind*, 375, 377.

3. Quoted in Norman Pettit, *The Heart Prepared* (New Haven, Conn.: Yale University Press, 1966), 134.

4. Thomas Hooker, *A Survey of the Summe of Church Discipline* (London: J. Bellamy, 1648), 1:36.

5. Ibid., 1:46.

6. The Seekers was a small quietistic sect that developed in the Netherlands shortly after 1600. Within about fifty years the group was absorbed by the Quakers.

7. H. Shelton Smith, Robert T. Handy, and Lefferts A. Loetscher, *American Christianity: An Historical Interpretation with Representative Documents*, 2 vols. (New York: Scribner's, 1960), 1:114

8. Perry Miller, ed., *The American Puritans: Their Prose and Poetry* (Garden City, N.Y.: Doubleday, 1956), 59.

## Chapter Three *The Great Awakening*

1. Solomon Stoddard, *The Defects of Preachers Reproved in a Sermon Preached at Northampton, May 19, 1723* (New London, Conn.: T. Green, 1724), 13–14.

2. Jonathan Edwards, *The Complete Works of Jonathan Edwards*, 7 vols.: vol. 4, *The Great Awakening: A Faithful Narrative*, edited by C. C. Goen (New Haven, Conn.: Yale University Press, 1972), 146, 158.

3. This biographical information is part of an introduction to Theodore J. Frelinghuysen, *Sermons*, translated by W. Demarest (New York: Tappan and Dennet, 1856), 7.

4. George Whitefield, *Journals* (Edinburgh: Banner of Truth, 1960), 342–43.

5. Boston *News-Letter,* 23 September 1740.

6. Edwin S. Gaustad, *The Great Awakening in New England* (New York: Harper, 1957), 43.

7. Leonard J. Trinterud, *The Forming of an American Tradition* (Philadelphia: Westminster, 1949), 89.

8. From a letter written by Whitefield to introduce Tennent to Governor Jonathan Belcher, Nov. 9, 1740. In George Whitefield, *Works of the Rev. George Whitefield,* 2 vols. (London, 1771–1772), 1:221.

9. Thomas Prince, *The Christian History,* 2 (26 Nov. 1744), 391.

10. For a discussion of *The Distinguishing Marks* see Edwards, *Great Awakening,* 52–65.

## Chapter Five *Revolution and the New Nation*

1. Perry Miller, "The Great Awakening from 1740 to 1750," *Encounter* (March 1956), 5.

2. Winthrop S. Hudson, *Religion in America: An Historical Account of the Development of American Religious Life* (New York: Scribner's, 1981), 76.

3. Thomas A. Bailey,eant: A History of the RRepublic (Boston: Heath, 1961) 74.

4. Conrad Cherry, *God's New Israel: Religious Interpretations of American Destiny* (Englewood Cliffs, N.J.: Prentice-Hall, 1971), 61.

5. Quoted in Leonard J. Trinterud, *The Forming of an American Tradition* (Philadelphia: Westminster, 1949), 250.

6. Edmund S. Morgan, *The Gentle Puritan: A Life of Ezra Stiles, 1727–1795* (New Haven, Conn.: Yale University Press, 1962), 454–55.

## Chapter Six *Threats to Christian Orthodoxy*

1. Jonathan Edwards, *History of the Works of Redemption,* in *The Works of President Edwards,* 4 vols. (Worcester, Mass.: S. Austin, 1847), 1:467.

2. Thomas Jefferson, *Notes on the State of Virginia* (Philadelphia: Jameson, 1788), 31.

3. Ethan Allen, *Reason the Only Oracle of Man, or a Compendious System of Natural Religion* (Bennington, Vt.: Haswell and Russell, 1784), preface.

4. Timothy Dwight, *Travels; in New-England and New-York,* 4 vols. (New Haven, Conn.: S. Converse, 1821–22), 2:388.

5. G. Adolf Koch, *Religion of the American Enlightenment* (New York: Crowell, 1968), 31. This volume was first published in 1933 as *Republican Religion.*

6. Allen, *Reason,* preface.

7. Ibid., 196.

8. Ibid., 352, 418.

9. Ibid., 352.

10. Richard J. Purcell, *Connecticut in Transition: 1775–1818,* rev. ed. (Middletown, Conn.: Wesleyan University Press, 1963), 12.

11. Elihu Palmer, *Principles of Nature; or, a Development of the Moral Causes of Happiness and Misery among the Human Species,* 2d ed. (New York: J. Crookes, 1806), 25.

12. Ibid., 23.

13. Purcell, *Connecticut,* 16.

14. Ashbel Green, *A Sermon Delivered . . . on the 19th of February, 1795* (Philadelphia: Sharpe, 1795), 19.

15. Conrad Wright, *The Beginnings of Unitarianism in America* (Boston: Beacon, 1955), 243.

16. Ibid., 202.

17. Cited in Charles E. Cuningham, *Timothy Dwight, 1752–1817: A Biography* (New York: Macmillan, 1942), 178–79.

18. *Christian Observer*, an English journal, is decrying the lack of respect among Anglicans for the Church of England clergy. Dwight contrasts that with the high regard of the New Englanders for their pastors.

19. By affiliation Dwight was actually a Congregationalist, rather than a Presbyterian, but as stated on pp. 75–76, any Calvinist could be called a Presbyterian in American parlance. In 1817 the denominational and polity distinctions between Congregationalists and Presbyterians were particularly muddied by the Plan of Union, a practical merger of ministries designed to cooperatively reach the frontier areas. Dwight was one of the framers of this plan in 1799, and it functioned until the New School-Old School Presbyterian schism of the 1830s.

20. This included Congregational churches. See n. 19.

### Chapter Seven *Revivalism and the Second Great Awakening*

1. Quoted in Frank G. Beardsley, *A History of American Revivals* (New York: American Tract Society, 1904), 80.

2. Most U.S. Presbyterians and the Congregationalists involved in Plan of Union churches (see chap. 6, n. 19) were governed by the General Assembly of the Presbyterian Church in the United States of America, usually called the Presbyterian Church in the U.S.A. The General Assembly was founded in 1789.

3. William M. Engles, ed., *Minutes of the General Assembly of the Presbyterian Church, 1789–1820* (Philadelphia: Presbyterian Board of Publication, 1847), 152–53.

4. Ibid., 177.

5. Ibid., 222.

6. Ibid., 260.

7. Ibid., 273–75.

8. Charles G. Finney, *Lectures on Revivals of Religion* (New York: Leavitt, Lord, 1835), 11.

9. Barton W. Stone, "A Short History of the Life of Barton W. Stone," in James R. Rogers, *The Cane Ridge Meeting-House* (Cincinnati: Standard, 1910), 165.

10. Whitney R. Cross, *The Burned-over District: The Social and Intellectual History of Enthusiastic Religion in Western New York, 1800–1850* (1950; repr., Los Angeles: Octagon, 1981), 155.

11. A fine survey of revivalism and reactions to it is found in Sydney E. Ahlstrom, *A Religious History of the American People* (New Haven, Conn.: Yale University Press, 1972), 472–77, 615–21.

### Chapter Eight *Redefining the Christian Message*

1. Sydney E. Ahlstrom, ed. *Theology in America: The Major Protestant Voices from Puritanism to Neo-Orthodoxy* (Indianapolis: Bobbs-Merrill, 1967), 45.

2. Ibid., 295.

3. It is reprinted in Ahlstrom, *Theology*, 296–316. For a full discussion of Emerson and the Transcendentalists see Perry Miller, ed. *The American Transcendentalists: Their Prose and Poetry* (Garden City, N.Y.: Doubleday, 1957).

4. Winthrop S. Hudson, *Religion in America: An Historical Account of the Development of American Religious Life* (New York: Scribner's, 1981), 177.

### Chapter Nine *The Rise of Cults and Deviant Movements*

1. Quoted in Alice F. Tyler, *Freedom's Ferment: Phases of American Social History to 1860* (Minneapolis: University of Minnesota Press, 1944), 73.

2. A number of good treatments of Mormon history are available; see the bibliography.

3. Carl Carmer, *Listen for a Lonesome Drum* (New York: McKay, 1950), 115.

4. George W. Noyes, ed., *Religious Experience of John Humphrey Noyes, Founder of the Oneida Community* (New York: Macmillan, 1923), 339.

### Chapter Ten *Reformers and New Rights*

1. Timothy L. Smith, *Revivalism and Social Reform: American Protestantism on the Eve of the Civil War* (New York: Abingdon, 1957), 78–79.

2. Ibid., 69, 70, 72.

3. J. Edwin Orr, *The Second Evangelical Awakening in America* (London: Marshall, Morgan and Scott, 1952), 31–33.

4. For information on the reform movement and the benevolent societies see Charles Cole, *The Social Ideas of the Northern Evangelists, 1826–1860* (New York: Columbia University Press, 1954); Oliver W. Elsbree, *The Rise of the Missionary Spirit in America* (1928; repr., Philadelphia: Porcupine, 1980); Charles Foster, *An Errand of Mercy: The Evangelical United Front, 1790–1830* (Chapel Hill, N.C.: University of North Carolina Press, 1960); Clifford Griffin, *Their Brothers' Keepers: Moral Stewardship in the United States, 1800–1865* (New Brunswick, N.J.: Rutgers University Press, 1960); Keith J. Hardman, *Charles Grandison Finney, 1792–1875* (Syracuse, N.Y.: Syracuse University Press, 1987).

5. George M. Marsden, *The Evangelical Mind and the New School Presbyterian Experience* (New Haven, Conn.: Yale University Press, 1970), 14ff.

6. The story of how Finney encouraged a large number of women to enter the women's rights movement is told in Nancy A. Hardesty, *Your Daughters Shall Prophesy: Revivalism and Feminism in the Age of Finney* (Brooklyn, N.Y.: Carlson, 1991).

### Chapter Eleven *The Growth of Roman Catholicism*

1. Quoted in H. Shelton Smith, Robert T. Handy, and Lefferts A. Loetscher, *American Christianity: An Historical Interpretation with Representative Documents*, 2 vols. (New York: Scribner's, 1960), 1:38.

### Chapter Twelve *The Agonizing Question of Slavery*

1. Gilbert H. Barnes, *The Antislavery Impulse, 1830–1844* (New York: Harcourt, Brace and World, 1964), 42. Barnes' book is one of the most probing analyses of the Northern abolitionists that discounts Garrison at a number of points. For a balance to this, see Anne C. Loveland, "Evangelism and 'Immediate Emancipation' in American Anti-slavery Thought," *Journal of Southern History*, 32 (1966): 172–88.

2. *Liberator*, 30 June 1837.

3. *The National Enquirer*, 3:33.

4. This entire episode is related in Barnes, *Antislavery Impulse*, 88ff.

5. Ibid., 231.

6. J. C. Furnas, *Goodbye to Uncle Tom* (New York: William Sloane, 1956), 4, 7.

### Chapter Fourteen *Liberalism and Christian Orthodoxy*

1. Quoted in C. Howard Hopkins, *The Rise of the Social Gospel in American Protestantism, 1865–1915* (1940; repr., New York: AMS, 1982), 85.

2. Henry Ward Beecher, *Statement before the Congregational Association of New York and Brooklyn, etc.* (New York: Lucas and Hill, 1882), 12–18.

3. Sydney E. Ahlstrom, *A Religious History of the American People* (New Haven, Conn.: Yale University Press, 1972), 740.

4. Ibid., 784.

5. H. Richard Niebuhr, *The Kingdom of God in America* (1937; repr., New York: Harper and Row, 1959), 192–93.

6. Benjamin B. Warfield, "The Essence of Christianity and the Cross of Christ," *Harvard Theological Review,* 7.4 (October 1914): 556–58.

## Chapter Fifteen *Concerns for the Poor and Downtrodden*

1. Conwell, Russell H. *Acres of Diamonds* (Old Tappan, N.J.: Fleming H. Revell, 1972), 19–20. The Revell edition of this lecture is one of the more recent reprintings, but it has often appeared in print, varying only in reference to the city in which Conwell happened to be speaking.

2. Among more recent works on the story of the black church and its challenges see Leon Litwack and August Meier, eds., *Black Leaders of the Nineteenth Century* (Urbana, Ill.: University of Illinois Press, 1988); Henry J. Young, *Major Black Religious Leaders, 1755–1940* (Nashville: Abingdon, 1977); Milton C. Sernett, *Black Religion and American Evangelicalism: White Protestants, Plantation Missions, and the Flowering of Negro Christianity, 1787–1865* (Metuchen, N.J.: Scarecrow, 1975); John Hope Franklin and Alfred Moss, *From Slavery to Freedom: A History of Negro Americans* (1969; repr., New York, Knopf, 1987).

3. Sydney E. Ahlstrom, *A Religious History of the American People* (New Haven, Conn.: Yale University Press, 1972), 786. Ahlstrom gives an excellent history of the Social Gospel movement, 785–804.

4. Charles H. Hopkins, *The Rise of the Social Gospel in American Protestantism, 1865–1915* (1940; repr., New York: AMS, 1982), 216.

5. Walter Rauschenbusch, *A Theology for the Social Gospel* (New York: Macmillan, 1917), 144–45.

## Chapter Sixteen *Pluralism and the American Catholics*

1. Robert D. Cross, *The Emergence of Liberal Catholicism in America* (Cambridge, Mass.: Harvard University Press, 1958), 98–99.

2. Ibid., 56.

3. Ibid., 72–90, passim.

4. Ibid., 95–98.

5. Josiah Strong, *Our Country: Its Possible Future and Its Present Crisis* (New York: Baker and Taylor, 1891), 222.

6. Ibid., 212.

7. An excellent summary of the intricate issues involving the Roman Catholic Church in America after the Civil War is found in Winthrop S. Hudson, *Religion in America: An Historical Account of the Development of American Religious Life* (New York: Scribner's, 1981), 239–61.

## Chapter Seventeen *The Fundamentalist-Modernist Controversy*

1. Shailer Mathews, "Theology as Group Belief," in Vergilius Ferm, ed., *Contemporary American Theology: Theological Autobiographies,* 2 vols.. (New York: Round Table, 1932–33), 1:173.

## Chapter Eighteen *Challenges of the New Millennium*

1. Sydney E. Ahlstrom, *A Religious History of the American People* (New Haven, Conn.: Yale University Press, 1972), 1079.

# Index